Kin of Another Kind

Kin of Another Kind

Transracial Adoption in American Literature

CYNTHIA CALLAHAN

The University of Michigan Press

Ann Arbor

For my family

Copyright © by the University of Michigan 2011
All rights reserved
Published in the United States of America by
The University of Michigan Press
Manufactured in the United States of America
⊗ Printed on acid-free paper

2014   2013   2012   2011   4   3   2   1

A CIP catalog record for this book is available from the British Library.

Library of Congress Cataloging-in-Publication Data

Callahan, Cynthia, 1972–
      Kin of another kind : transracial adoption in American literature
   / Cynthia Callahan.
         p.   cm.
      Includes bibliographical references and index.
      ISBN 978-0-472-11758-1 (cloth : alk. paper)
         1. American literature—20th century—History and criticism.
      2. Interracial adoption in literature.   3. Race in literature.   I. Title.
      PS228.I69C35   2011
      810.9'35254—dc22   2010033756

Acknowledgments

Many friends and colleagues made this book possible. I am grateful to Debra Moddelmog, James Phelan, and Margaret Homans for their generous, thoughtful readings of earlier drafts of the manuscript. Their comments and guidance helped to make this study stronger. My Columbus English Department colleagues—Beth Hewitt, Chadwick Allen, Steve Fink, and Valerie Lee—read drafts of chapters and offered comments and suggestions, for which I am very grateful; this book is better for their contributions, even when I was not able to act on all of their suggestions. Other readers have also been instrumental. Catherine Carter, a deliberate, careful reader and an incisive editor of prose, helped immeasurably, particularly at the end of this long process. Lori Askeland and Mark C. Jerng applied their considerable knowledge of the field of adoption studies to their readings of several chapters; in addition, Mark generously shared the manuscript version of his own book with me, allowing my scholarship to benefit from his important research. As scholars from outside the field, Susan Delagrange and Norman Jones also brought valuable perspectives to their reading of chapter drafts. I am also grateful for the guidance offered by my editor, LeAnn Fields, who has done so much to foster the study of adoption in the humanities.

I appreciate the institutional support of the Ohio State University at Mansfield, including the Professional Development Committee, which awarded me research leave time. I also extend special thanks to the campus's dean and director, Evelyn Freeman, who generously provided other research time that I needed to complete the manuscript, and to Barbara McGovern, who is an unfailing advocate for junior faculty. I am pleased to include a revised version of material that appeared originally in *Modern Fiction Studies*, under the title "'The Confounding Problem of Race': Passing and Adoption in Charles Chesnutt's *The Quarry*."

I know for certain that I would not have finished this book without the steadfast moral support of friends and colleagues, especially Catherine Carter, Brian Gastle, Debra Lubar, Paula J. Kelly, and Juliette Levy, all of whom have lived every triumph and negotiated every stumbling block along the way with me. My lively and generous colleagues at Ohio State–Mansfield create a stimulating environment and a sincere commitment to both scholarship and teaching that has helped to foster me and my work. Many thanks to Barbara McGovern, Hannibal Hamlin, Susan Delagrange, Norman Jones, Carolyn Skinner, Noah Comet, Elizabeth Kolkovich, and the late J. F. Buckley, who helped to hire me and who we lost far too soon. I am also grateful to other friends who have become like family: Dawn Kitchen, Jim Nicholson, Norman Jones, Heidi Jones, Steven Joyce, Mary Joyce, Terri Fisher, Paul Loeber, Laura Brackett, John Thrasher, Barbara Lehman, Dan Lehman, Guy Daly, Meg Zapata, and Mary Ruth Warner. Finally, and most important, I am grateful for the loving support of my family, to whom I dedicate this book. With each new addition and each new relationship forged, my understanding of the meaning of family continues to grow in wonderful ways.

Contents

Introduction: Reading Transracial Adoption in American Literature

Transracial adoption can be found nearly everywhere. Accounts in gossip columns of celebrity adoptions from Africa, online communities of international adopters, and life writing by adoptees have made the practice of transracial adoption so familiar that the marker "transracial" has become almost redundant. That transracial adoption is both widespread and familiar was made clear in a *New York Times* series about adoption called "Relative Choices: Adoption and the American Family," which omitted discussion of domestic inracial adoption altogether. In the latter decades of the twentieth century, transracial adoption was controversial, an accurate characterization even today as the public continues to debate the parameters of the American family; yet even before transracial adoption was legally practiced or considered cause for debate, it appeared in American literature. During the late nineteenth and early twentieth centuries, mixed-race adoptive families were relatively common in fiction, which suggests that this unique form of kinship—across both familial and racial "bloodlines"—resonated with authors and readers as strongly then as now.

Kin of Another Kind examines American literary representations of transracial adoption to expand the collective understanding of where and how the practice appeared in American literature from the turn of the twentieth century to the beginning of the twenty-first. Reading transracial adoption in fiction allows us to trace cultural attitudes toward this particular kinship practice as it evolved over time. In this endeavor, *Kin of Another Kind* joins an ongoing project in the humanities and social sciences of exploring how individual families created through adoption are shaped by larger cultural forces.[1] But fictional adoptions are not simply mimetic; as a literary trope, adoption allows authors to metaphorically speak to broader questions about identity and belonging. Even as adoption as a family-making practice changed dramatically over the time period covered in this study, its symbolic function in fiction has remained fairly consistent, enabling authors to respond to concerns about what constitutes authentic identity in a nation deeply conflicted about the significance of individual and collective origins.

The content of *Kin of Another Kind* can be divided into two parts, with World War II as a "watershed" moment in adoption practice, a turning point after which transracial placements became legally and socially acceptable (Carp and Leon-Guerrero). Before World War II, transracial adoption was legally forbidden but very much alive in literature and unsanctioned practice. Afterward, Americans began to look across the boundaries of nation and race to adopt in increasing numbers. These and other changes affecting adoption are an important meter of the nation's response to the challenges of modernity, something historian Ellen Herman argues in *Kinship by Design*. During the twentieth century, she explains, adoption became ruled by "ordering processes [that] aspired to alleviate the existential severity of chronic uncertainty" (14). One of the central challenges of modernity was reckoning with racial and ethnic difference in the nation as a whole. As Herman explains, adoption practices in the early part of the century focused on preventing the introduction of ethnic, racial, and religious differences into the family; after World War II, however, changing attitudes toward race eventually led to the purposeful incorporation of difference into adoptive families. Throughout the century, fictional representations of these families were important sites for exploring the implications of racial norms. Tracing the period from the mid-nineteenth century to the late twentieth, Mark Jerng identifies the important intersection between transracial adoption in literature and significant national conflicts: "Transracial adoption appears most prominently in literature, public discourse, and social practices during precisely some of these large-scale national traumas focused on the formation of its citizenry and the question of national and racial belonging: Native American removal; slavery and emancipation; the height of Jim Crow/segregation; and the Korean and Vietnam wars" (xii). Examining these crises through the lens of transracial adoption, as Jerng does, shows how kinship and race are mutually constitutive participants in the creation of citizens. *Kin of Another Kind* narrows its focus to the twentieth century—loosely defined to include the "turns" at each end—to examine the ways in which depictions of adoption across racial boundaries in literature allowed authors to explore the meaning of individual and group affiliations; as this study will show, transracial adoption as a literary trope accommodated the divergent concerns of a diverse group of American authors. Fictional adoptions enabled authors to imagine national crises over the substance of American belonging in alternative ways, sometimes replicating existing power hierarchies and sometimes configuring them in forms that significantly challenge the social order.

As a work of literary criticism, *Kin of Another Kind* explores literature's capacity to convey the changing meaning not only of transracial adoption but also of individual and collective identity at certain flashpoint moments. It thus illuminates both the mimetic and symbolic functions of adoption in literature. On one level, *Kin of Another Kind* treats fictional representations of adoption as important indicators of cultural attitudes toward the practice, an idea first advanced by literature scholar Marianne Novy in *Reading Adoption*. She identifies three "mythic" adoption stories: the disastrous adoption, which leads to a search for birth parents; the happy reunion, in which separated birth kin find one another; and the happy adoption. All three, explains Novy, presume that there can only ever be one set of "real" parents (7). Beyond shaping a collective understanding of adoption, these plots also establish narrative expectations for how conflicts over the practice might be reconciled. At the same time, they tend to represent, as Novy points out, a rather limited range of lived adoption experiences. Building on that idea, *Kin of Another Kind* expands fictional adoption's frame of reference to answer a related question: what other cultural work might these adoption plots do, beyond contributing to the culture's understanding of adoption at a given moment? To answer that question, this study explores the metaphorical potential that transracial adoption plots offer authors. In real-life adoption, families are formed by law and affinity rather than through biology, a situation that can cause a crisis of belonging, one often magnified by racial differences within adoptive families. In literature, both of these disruptions create a unique set of conditions through which authors explore problems that relate to racial, ethnic, and national affiliation. In this way, these texts perform "cultural work," in the sense that Jane Tompkins uses that term to refer to texts that "offer powerful examples of the way a culture thinks about itself, articulating and proposing solutions for the problems that shape a particular historical moment" (xi). As Novy has already persuasively argued, these fictional texts offer scripts that help to narrate the experience of adoption; *Kin of Another Kind* takes the significance of adoption's cultural work farther to demonstrate how these kinds of texts can also access issues of authenticity and belonging that resonate far beyond an individual family.

The fiction discussed here uses familial relationships to symbolize national issues. In this way, these texts function as what literature scholar Werner Sollors calls "kinship dramas" (*Beyond* 165). Focusing on marital relationships in early twentieth-century immigrant fiction, Sollors observes that the process of an ethnic immigrant becoming an American national citizen is metaphorically represented through the character's shift from a family of birth to a family of law (*Beyond* 149–68).[2] The family of birth is the immigrant's parents and grandparents and associated with his ethnic identity, while the family of law is represented by an American wife and connected to American citizenship (*Beyond* 151). The choice to marry an American symbolizes the ethnic immigrant's transition into national citizenship. Fictional adoption narratives operate similarly: through moving a child from a family of birth to one socially constructed through adoption, they dramatize different means of defining one's relationship to larger groups during the twentieth century. Is identity a matter of birth, an essential quality endowed through biology? Or is it environmental, constructed through social relationships and affinities? Or is it a combination of both? In pursuing answers to these questions, the texts in *Kin of Another Kind* help elucidate what Herman identifies as the paradox between the "official story" of adoption as liberal nationalist exemplar of affinity trumping ancestry and the "shadow stories" that reveal anxiety over authenticity when belonging is voluntary rather than endowed by birth (8). These authenticity crises are negotiated within and through fictional families, often in competing terms of biology and environment.

Beyond revealing how fictional adoptions shape the public understanding of the practice, as well as adoption's symbolic function as a trope, attending to adoption in literature adds important nuance to our interpretations of the texts themselves. As this study will show, consciousness of transracial adoption as a practice grew in the second half of the century, making readers and authors with otherwise no personal experience of such adoption aware of its logistics and attendant issues; as a consequence, the depiction of those specific details can very much inform the plot and affect interpretation. Likewise, to recognize the ways in which adoption shapes individual identity is to provide insight into the stakes of characters' choices and produce alternatives to conventional readings of these texts. In many cases, reading through the frame of adoption clarifies the otherwise inexplicable behavior of some characters. This phenomenon is evident, for example, in Toni Morrison's *Tar Baby* (1981). The protagonist, Jade, is frequently dismissed by critics as racially self-abnegating because she resists the essentialist view of ancestry as the defining quality of a healthy racial identity that others impose on her. By attending to her status as an adoptee, we recognize the inadequacy of that model to persuade her, someone raised more or less outside of a biological family line. Moreover, when we acknowledge that racial and familial identities are intimately entwined, adoption's presence in the text adds more dimensions to what, on the surface, appear to be strictly "racial" or "cultural" problems. In both early- and late-century texts, behaviors that are presumably the result of racial identity crises can, when paired with adoption, also be seen as significant "family problems": the consequence of orphancy, the absence of a definitive genealogy, or even death and divorce. Foregrounding adoption in these texts also provides new insight into important American literary genres, including passing, captivity, and immigrant narratives. For example, when paired with adoption, race passing, a phenomenon depicted in the fiction discussed in chapters 2 and 3, takes on added dimensions, as the familial disruptions of adoption reveal the degree to which racial category is "known" through the family. When that family ancestry is missing—as it often is for orphans and adoptees—the entire system for racial categorization becomes destabilized. While not all of the texts discussed here fit into these particular genre categories, those that do show how foregrounding adoption can highlight new facets of long-standing literary forms. Reading for adoption in literature elicits multiple insights on the level of both theme and plot.

The term *adoption* applies to a diverse set of family arrangements. The possibilities range from "kinship care" relationships within genetically related extended families to foster care to "second-parent" adoptions (undertaken by same-sex partners) to step-parent adoption; the breadth of this spectrum makes it difficult to generalize among lived experiences of adoption or, indeed, representations of them. Likewise, one can expect that each member of the adoption "triad"—birth parent, adoptive parent, and adoptee—might view adoption in very different terms, which affects its representation and interpretation in fiction. While I am attuned to the differences among these particular perspectives, I cannot claim to cover them all equally. As is regrettably the case in many studies of adoption, the perspective of the birth parent is not well-represented in this study. In addition, the discussions that follow are limited almost exclusively to "formal" adoptions, those legally conducted through the state or other social institutions and between biological strangers. Arrangements of these kind have always been quite rare, all the more so since the 1980s (Herman 5), yet because they occupy such a significant place in the cultural imagination, they are valuable subjects of study. Focusing on formal adoptions across racial lines, specifically, also draws attention to the role of social institutions and the legal system in shaping not only individual adoption experiences but also racial and national identities, a point made by Sandra Patton in regard to the lived experience of adoptees and, as this study will show, traceable in fiction as well. While these forces are at work on all people, the unique displacements of adoption draw special attention to them. Moreover, as Jerng argues, institutions mold us into particular kinds of citizens: "The parent-child bond and the specific regulation of kinship bonds used to guarantee transmission and filiation are crucial sites through which persons are both nationalized and naturalized" (xvii). In the age of secrecy in adoption, for instance, a social worker could, quite literally, turn an adoptee from "black" to "white" by choosing not to disclose key information about a child's ancestry (Patton 33–45). Laws and policies also implicitly define the relative value of families, as recognizable in today's sliding scale of adoption fees that means an African American infant costs much less than a white one (Quiroz) or in the general attitude that certain families are less capable of raising their own children, one routinely communicated by social services agencies in regard to American Indian families in the mid-twentieth century (Westermeyer; Blanchard). By focusing on formal adoptions, I foreground the power dynamics of legal and social institutions as authors engage them—explicitly or indirectly—in fictional form.

When adoptions join individuals of different races into families, they are usually called "transracial" placements, despite the sometimes problematic assumptions that lie behind that term. For instance, while "transracial" should mean any adoption by parents who do not share the child's racial origins, it generally connotes the adoption of African American or biracial children by white parents, unless otherwise indicated ("Transracial Adoption" 272). Furthermore, children of a different national origin than their adoptive parents are almost always considered "international" ("intercountry" or "transnational") adoptees, rather than transracial, even though white Americans in the late 2000s adopted most often from Russia, China, and Guatemala ("Total Adoptions"); the latter two nations' citizens are generally classified as nonwhite within the American racial order. In another seemingly arbitrary distinction, the adoption of American Indians by white Americans can be labeled "international" as easily as "domestic," by virtue of tribes' national autonomy, yet this practice is frequently grouped under the term *transracial*.[3] To acknowledge the specific dynamics of tribal sovereignty central to contemporary American Indian adoptions, I adopt Pauline Turner Strong's approach and generally use the terms *extra-tribal* or *out placement* in place of *transracial* when referring to the adoption of American Indian children by people who are not Native (Strong, "To Forget" 470). At the same time that I make that distinction—and remain conscious of the limitations of this approach—I choose to retain *transracial* in this study as the umbrella term that encompasses the adoption of African American, American Indian, and Korean and Chinese children across racial, national, and cultural lines. *Transracial* emphasizes the perception of enduring, inherent differences united within individual families, so often associated with these kinds of adoption. It calls attention to the complexity of American racial hierarchies, arrangements that are neither as polar nor as fixed as we often assume them to be. Even if not all groups are equally "racial," each group's experience with adoption has been defined within racialized frameworks. As I discuss in chapter 1, the rise in adoptions of American Indians and children from Korea and other nations in the middle of the century reflects, among other things, white adopters' aversion to taking in black children; they were more comfortable with children they perceived to be less "racial" (Herman 198). This study will demonstrate that even as these groups occupy very different places in American social and racial hierarchies, they are all deeply connected within the wider frame of twentieth-century adoption. In regard to international adoption, I limit my focus to children from Korea and China exclusively, since adoptions from those countries are so prominent in both literature and contemporary culture and because Asian international adoption's longer history provides a scholarly and historical critical mass from which to draw for these literary analyses.

This study unites a diverse group of authors, both white and of color, in a collective conversation about the meaning of familial and national belonging, even as they approach the topic from their own culturally determined perspectives. In doing so, I take my lead from scholars such as Werner Sollors, Eric Sundquist, and Henry B. Wonham, each of whom intentionally traverses the boundaries of literary canons and racial groups in their scholarship to better understand the collective—and often contentious—process of defining American national values. Speaking of literary scholars' tendency to separate African American and European American literatures in distinct canons, Wonham asks, "Must literary history . . . be organized according to the genetic transfer of biological traits, or do ideas, images, literary and rhetorical forms circulate in interesting ways across racial boundaries?" (5). Transracial adoption is, by definition, an act that crosses boundaries, eschewing biological lines as the foundation of family and race, which means that authors from a variety of subject positions have a stake in its representation. Considering these authors in subsets would neglect the full spectrum of possibilities created by transracial adoption as a literary trope. Without this comparative approach, we would not see how Barbara Kingsolver's representation of adoption in *The Bean Trees* (1988) and *Pigs in Heaven* (1993), two of the adoption narratives that are most familiar to readers, was vigorously challenged by Sherman Alexie and Leslie Marmon Silko, both of whom shared their own, much different perceptions of the practice. As this study will make clear, I, too, am skeptical of privileging the "genetic transfer of biological traits" over all else, whether in families or in literary criticism; at the same time, I also believe that it is necessary to acknowledge the pervasiveness of these genetic lines and to recognize how subjective experiences voiced in terms of essential identities or genetic connections can add important insight. My study extends Wonham's logic to a more complex intersection of ethnic and racial texts to examine the ways in which American identity is produced at the crossroads where differences meet.

The first half of this book begins with a chapter that establishes the historical and cultural context for adoption in twentieth-century American fiction, before moving into the literary analyses of the later chapters. Chapter 1 examines the nature/nurture binary, not to reinforce it as the defining paradigm of adoption, but to treat it as a means to the larger end of understanding how and why it becomes such an important part of controversies over transracial adoption. This chapter argues that people advance one or the other side of the polarity in order to secure the meaning of individual and collective identity that has been destabilized by the act of adoption or at other cultural moments when social categories are precarious. It traces the ways in which rhetorical appeals to nature (or nurture)—and their companion concepts, essential or constructed identities—reveal a fundamental anxiety about what, exactly, makes our identities "real." In its examination of some of transracial adoption's most controversial moments, this discussion illustrates how the rhetorics of nature and nurture function strategically as well as contextually, reflecting the specific concerns of the cultural groups involved and the historical moment. The controversies discussed in this chapter imply an enduring ambivalence over the meaning of authentic identity in American culture, ambivalence that can be traced in the literature discussed in subsequent chapters. While this ambivalence is not exclusive to adoption, it is certainly central to adoption's metaphorical function as a literary trope.

The next two chapters examine fictional representations of adoption before it was legally sanctioned practice. In the texts under discussion, the adoption of racially ambiguous children creates a crisis over authenticating racial purity, as their seemingly white bodies might nonetheless disguise the crucial "one drop" of black blood. Chapter 2 looks at the work of Charles W. Chesnutt, an author who consistently relied on the family to dramatize national fears about race mixing. This chapter reads Chesnutt's "Her Virginia Mammy" (1899) and *The Quarry* (1999, written ca. 1928) as variations on the dominant passing narratives of the time; these texts illustrate the role played by family reputation in categorizing individuals whose physical characteristics do not mark them racially. Light-skinned orphans and adoptees who are without confirmed ancestry occupy a precarious social position, but it is one that also enables them to move practically at will across the color line, able to fit equally well into white or black families. This mobility creates a crisis for both characters, particularly when combined with the kind of "passing" encouraged by secrecy in adoption; nevertheless, both of Chesnutt's adoptees resist prescribed categories and choose their racial identities, a situation that speaks to Chesnutt's desire to envision liberation from the otherwise rigid racial categories of the early twentieth century.

Chapter 3 focuses on Kate Chopin's short story "Désirée's Baby" (1893) and William Faulkner's *Light in August* (1932) as alternatives to Chesnutt's idea that resisting oppressive racial roles is possible. In both texts, adoption denies the possibility of knowable origins, leaving characters without firm racial categories, a situation with grave repercussions for individual and community alike. As in Chesnutt's fiction, both texts are passing narratives that emphasize the role of family stories and genealogies to uphold the racial status quo. Unlike Chesnutt, however, Chopin and Faulkner refuse to confirm the racial ancestries of the passers, which initially seems like a much more radical statement about the knowability of race, yet both authors treat racial ambiguity as a challenge to the status quo that must be punished. As a consequence, the characters' tragic fates ultimately imply the impossibility of subverting racial hierarchies. The texts in chapters 2 and 3 highlight the expansiveness of adoption's metaphorical potential, able to provide authors a potentially liberating means of avoiding rigid categories of identity while just as easily lending itself to a reassertion of strict racial hierarchies.

The texts discussed in chapters 4–6 illustrate the intersection of adoption's metaphorical potential in literature with changing practices of real-life adoption in the late twentieth century. Authors continued to speak through it to explore larger concerns about authentic identity, sometimes locating authenticity in essential qualities and sometimes treating it as a construct. This variability reveals deep ambivalence about what, exactly, constitutes "real" familial, racial, and national identities. At the same time, however, authors and readers also brought to texts an understanding of adoption's logistics that would grow with every decade after World War II. As a consequence of the increasing intersections between the mimetic and the real, adoption's literary role became more multifaceted in later-century texts.

The novels examined in chapter 4 use transracially adoptive relationships to articulate some of the factors shaping African American identity in the decades following integration. The chapter begins with Robert E. Boles's out-of-print experimental novel, *Curling* (1968), in which the protagonist's existential crisis as a black American is symbolized by his status as the adopted son of an elite white family. Although largely overlooked by scholars, Boles's text is revealing in its almost prescient depiction of adoptive identity, which anticipates the objections that opponents of transracial adoption would raise several years later. In his divided consciousness, Boles's Chelsea Burlingame resembles Toni Morrison's protagonist in *Tar Baby*, Jadine Childs, a light-skinned black woman adopted formally by her aunt and uncle and informally by the couple's white employers; the two couples represent the polarity within which Jade must navigate a sense of self as a black woman. Although the novel's reliance on natural images and emphasis on biocentric definitions of ancestry strongly imply that racial and gender identities are essential qualities, *Tar Baby*'s inclusion of adoption undermines the exclusive privileging of biology. This novel has sometimes been interpreted as an indictment of Jade as too white-identified, yet reading through adoption releases her from the accusations of racial self-loathing cast by critics and instead depicts a self-conscious process of establishing an identity within and against prevailing social pressures.

The fictional texts discussed in chapter 5 participate in an implicit and uniquely intertextual discussion about the adoption of children out of American Indian tribes. The chapter begins with a brief discussion of Sioux author Dallas Chief Eagle's *Winter Count* (1967), which highlights alternate definitions of extra-tribal adoption as both "rescue" and "captivity." It then traces a conversation initiated inadvertently by Barbara Kingsolver's *The Bean Trees*, which features a Cherokee child adopted by a white woman. Responding to criticism that this novel overlooked federal policies outlawing the extra-tribal adoption of American Indian children, Kingsolver wrote another, *Pigs in Heaven*. The second modifies her earlier representation with more culturally sensitive and historically accurate information. Both Leslie Marmon Silko (Laguna Pueblo), in *Gardens in the Dunes* (1999), and Sherman Alexie (Spokane/Coeur d'Alene), in *Indian Killer* (1996), also augment Kingsolver's original novel. Silko calls attention to the longer history of assimilationist policies at work on American Indians by linking the boarding school movement and adoption as culturally destructive forms of captivity, while Alexie imagines an American Indian adoptee as tragically schiz-ophrenic. All of these authors employ adoption as a metaphor to pursue broader concerns about American Indian and American national identities, but they also debate, implicitly and sometimes explicitly, the importance of accuracy in the representation of American Indians and of adoption itself.

Adoption as metaphor and adoption as real-life practice align most closely in chapter 6. The transnational adoptions in the texts discussed there reflect an awareness of the logistics of adoption on the part of both authors and readers, while still serving as a vehicle for accessing other forms of transnational migra-tion. The discussion begins with Sui Sin Far's short story "Pat and Pan" (1912), which lays the literary foundation for contemporary treatments of adoption and immigration in Anne Tyler's *Digging to America* (2006) and Gish Jen's *The Love Wife* (2004). Both contemporary texts join transracial adoption and im-migration through the concept of origins, exploring, from various perspectives, the degree to which origins—individual and cultural—should matter. The re-sponse of immigrants and second-generation Americans to gaps in their knowledge of or ability to access their origins parallels adoptees' own struggles with origins, yet the adopted characters are more prepared to deal with these crises. By virtue of their atypical kinship ties, they approach ambivalence as the solution to identity problems, rather than the problem. They confront the chal-lenges presented by their obscure origins directly, a strategy that other charac-ters—American-born and immigrant—then employ to redefine their sense of what makes them belong. Jen's novel, in particular, suggests that the acceptance of paradox and ambivalence might be an effective—indeed, even optimal—re-sponse to the problem of origins in adoption specifically and in contemporary American life more generally.

The conclusion explores the relative consistency demonstrated by these texts as they resist any definitive resolution of the nature/nurture tension. Even fiction that most explicitly depicts identity as an essential quality cannot fully endorse it as such, a situation revealed when individual characters defy that es-sentialism through acts of self-fashioning. On one level, these narratives could be interpreted as contradictory, which may explain why so many of them, even those written by canonical authors, receive less critical attention relative to the authors' other works. The ambivalences about nature and nurture are not nec-essarily the sign of incoherence they might seem, at first glance, to be. As the conclusion argues, these contradictions are actually the strength of these texts, not their weakness, embracing, as they do, the tensions that clearly underlie American culture's attitude toward belonging.

As with many who study adoption, my interest in it is not only professional.

I was adopted at birth (though not transracially) and often feel that I embody a paradox about origins—the consequence of possessing two families, each with legitimate claims to being the "real" one. Part of adoption's paradox comes from the prevailing cultural understanding of kinship as biogenetic, which renders families that are formed through volition "kin of another kind." Adoption challenges the idea that "real" kinship is grounded in "blood." Not only does it offer an alternative model for successful kinship, but it also disputes the myth of immutable blood ties. The prevailing metaphor for kinship, "blood" symbolizes the endurance of family connections; yet adoptive kinship, constructed to be "as if" biological, is, ironically, predicated on the belief that blood ties can be torn asunder to make way for a new family. Ironies like these are captured by sociologist and adoptee Sandra Patton, who describes learning in graduate school about the "insider-outsider" stance that ethnographers assume as they conduct their research; she found herself strangely comfortable in that role. As an adoptee, she is familiar with the norms of kinship yet slightly removed from them. Being a participant-observer in the world of biological kinship can result in a profound sense of ambivalence about what constitutes a "real" family.

Concerned not just with biogenetic kinship, Patton also traces the contradictions that surround adoptees' relationships with the past. For adoptees, she observes,

> Our identities are forged without genealogical patterns, without biological histories beyond our embodied selves. By their very absence, these mysteries of heritage construct our selves as much as our known families do, for the sense of being without a "true" family history and identity—in a society that demands familial "truth" through biology—shapes our vision of our selves and our place in our families and in society. . . . Our origins are somewhere else, but we have so thoroughly "adopted" the kin system and culture we are in that the lines of demarcation between our original and adopted cultures have been blurred. (6–7)

Our sense of self is constructed as much by what we do not know about our heritage or genealogies as by the families who raised us. Not knowing, a condition reinforced with every medical history we cannot fill out, becomes the only thing we know for sure. That point is perhaps no better illustrated than when we discover something new about our personal history, from the minimal "nonidentifying" information allowed adoptees in states with closed adoption records to the reunion with birth kin. While informative, neither can provide complete access to one's origins; even a reunion may raise more questions than it can answer.

The fictional representations of transracial adoption explored in the following pages are sites for negotiating the relative importance of origins, not just in kinship, but in matters of belonging on the level of race, culture, and nation as well. These texts span the last hundred years and demonstrate a consistent, enduring ambivalence about the real substance of belonging, even as the terms in which they convey it vary in response to historical moments and cultural concerns. In these texts, adoption serves as a check on tendencies to overprivilege either nature or nurture as identity's determining factor. This longer view on adoption, as conveyed through its fictional representations, encourages us both to be wary of the polarizing binary of nature and nurture that remains so stubbornly attached to adoption and to question and redefine the terms of the discussion. By seeing adoption as paradoxically defined by discourses of both nature and nurture and, further, by acknowledging how much those discourses serve other agendas in securing identity at moments of cultural instability, we may hopefully develop new strategies for understanding it that resist the pressure either to privilege origins or to eschew them altogether.

CHAPTER 1

Voluntary Belonging:
Historical and Cultural Contexts

Conversations about adoption in the twentieth century are frequently framed in terms of nature and nurture. Although scientists have generally concluded that all individuals, adopted or not, are shaped by a combination of genetic and environmental influences, adoption is often associated with the nature/nurture binary, and one side is often presumed to prevail over the other. This phenomenon can be seen, for instance, in discussions of adoptees' search for origins, as ancestry is frequently equated with the adoptee's "true" self. While adoption has been intimately linked with this paradigm since Sir Francis Galton coined the phrase *nature-nurture* in the nineteenth century as he conducted heritability studies on adoptees (Gossett 155; "Adoption Studies" 19), adoption is, in fact, defined by social and historical forces that extend beyond that binary. As Sandra Patton reminds us in regard to contemporary transracial adoption, "Little attention is accorded to the possibility that other social forces, such as public policy and social institutions, fundamentally shape the lives adoptees lead. . . . The nature-nurture polarity masks the power relations involved in the construction and maintenance of selves in contemporary society" (15). Indeed, the nature/nurture polarity has been overstated when it comes to adoption; it is often the end point to any discussion about the practice's individual or social meaning. But that does not mean that it should be put aside completely from critical explorations of adoption, since the paradigm serves as an important bridge between the larger social forces that Patton identifies and the evolving public perception of adoption in the twentieth century. This chapter explores the ways in which concepts of nature or nurture function discursively in the realm of literal, actual transracial adoption, arising at moments when some segment of the population feels that the meaning of family—and of other individual and collective identities—needs to be secured. This cultural and historical context provides a necessary framework for the essentially literary discussion of subsequent chapters, which will illuminate the ways in which fictional representations of transracial adoption undercut and interrogate that dichotomy and, as a consequence, suggest the constructed nature of all family and all identity.

Adoption, which creates family out of volition rather than biology, constitutes a crisis in the meaning of kinship, especially in a culture that defines family in terms of shared "blood." As I mentioned briefly in the introduction, Ellen Herman's historical study of adoption in the twentieth century explores the various ways that Americans have attempted to make adoption more authentic, positing that the implications of these attempts go beyond any one family: "To the extent that American culture has defined nature as a product of blood-based (now gene-based) identities that are fixed, unchosen, and beyond the scope of social arrangement, adoption illustrates the authenticity crises that plague many forms of voluntary belonging, including democratic citizenship itself" (8). Underlying adoption, in other words, is the anxiety that this particular family arrangement may not be "real" enough when compared to "blood-based" or "gene-based" kinship. Further, what makes adoption so trenchant at so many different times in the twentieth century is the degree to which this worry resembles the concerns we collectively share about other forms of voluntary belonging. Thus, while nature/nurture often seems to be a defining paradigm of adoption, it may not actually be its defining *problem*. Instead, what underlies invocations of nature (or nurture) in both fiction and public discourse about transracial adoption is a fundamental anxiety about authenticity. The nature/nurture binary operates as a powerful rhetorical means by which individuals attempt to secure identities that exist outside the norm, to make them seem more "real."

In the fiction and nonfiction discourses discussed in this study, the nature/nurture paradigm sometimes appears explicitly; at other times, it is expressed in the terms of blood, genes, biology, or essential or inherent traits, all of which exist in opposition to environment, culture, heritage, or learned qualities. By examining how these concepts characterize adoptive as well as racial and national identities, I respond to Patton's call to see adoption as larger than nature or nurture alone, and I show instead how these concepts are employed at flashpoint moments in ways that reveal the power relations working on adoptees. After all, the controversies surrounding adoption are about more than individual families; they are also attempts to redefine social relations and to address inequalities that have manifested in but are not limited to adoption practices. Those social relations intersect with adoption in the fictional texts I address in upcoming chapters, texts that grapple with the anxieties about individual and collective authenticity that adoption often produces. Sometimes they engage explicitly with the practice and perception of adoption as it changed over the course of the century, but even when adoption's significance is more covert, it still operates as an expansive metaphor through which authors attempt to define the parameters of authentic belonging on the level of family, race, and nation.

The power dynamics at work in literal transracial adoption inform the fictional representations discussed in this study. To some, transracial adoption represents progressive racial politics (Melosh, *Strangers* 159; Bartholet 103) or even evidence that Americans have achieved a "color-blind" society, able to see beyond racial differences (Quiroz 3–4); nevertheless, race and social power more generally both remain salient in all aspects of everyday American life and particularly in adoption practice. As Pamela Anne Quiroz argues persuasively, a "color-blind" approach to adoption over the last few decades has encouraged some to see transracial adoption as the epitome of advancement past racism in the United States, yet racial hierarchies and the preferences of affluent white adopters still influence many adoption practices (4). The movement toward color-blind placements seems to serve the interests of white adopters (who want access to the widest pool of available children) more than the needs of the children themselves.[1] Adopter preferences and the laws of supply and demand become particularly evident in the pricing system for adoption, a subject also explored by Quiroz. Adoptable children are currently placed into three tiers: "white," "honorary white" (which includes mixed-race, Latin American, and Asian children), and "collective black" (Quiroz 5). The fees charged by private agencies vary according to where the children fit, with white and internationally adopted children costing more than a domestically adopted African American child (Quiroz 74–75). Quiroz concludes,

> Adoption practices can be understood as part of what Omi and Winant . . . called "racial projects," the sociohistorical processes involved in explaining, organizing, and distributing resources according to racial categories. . . . Examining such practices illuminates the depth of globalization and the role of U.S. cit-

izens as "consumers" in a world marketplace that includes not just retail products and services but also human lives. (6–7)

Beyond race specifically, relative social power also dictates which people are permitted to adopt and which children become available for adoption. As Rickie Solinger has argued, the "choice" that Americans exercise when adopting from abroad is dependent on the relative lack of choice for women in developing nations to care for their children (*Beggars* 20–35). Furthermore, gays and lesbians looking to adopt domestically or abroad also face discrimination and are either prevented from adopting outright, must do so covertly or with extra effort,[2] or are expected to take "special needs" children with physical or psychological disabilities, a situation journalist and adoptive father Dan Savage irreverently characterizes as the "damaged-goods adoption option" (*The Kid* 55).

The implications of these inequalities in social power are further complicated by the act of adoption itself, a distinctly atypical form of kinship. To understand how adoption works metaphorically in literature, it also helps to recognize the multiple disruptions of cultural norms that occur when an actual adoption takes place. Because adoption makes family out of individuals not biologically related, it challenges the cultural assumption that kinship is based in "shared blood"; indeed, it undermines the very foundation of legal kinship in the United States. As anthropologist David Schneider asserts, American kinship is normatively biogenetic; although we may consider relatives through law (spouses, stepchildren and stepparents, adopted kin) to be "real" kin, the discourse surrounding kinship privileges biological ties over all else (23).[3] Upheld by the rhetorically weighty metaphor of "blood," these biogenetic norms signify the involuntary, inseverable connection that Americans associate with kinship. In the United States, "blood" suffices as an explanation for why family members look or act alike, how they are linked across generations, and why we still loan money to the cousin who never pays us back. "Blood" equates the abstract qualities of relatedness with a life-giving substance; it naturalizes kinship, locating it in the body and making it inherent. At the same time, it also obscures the fact that the substance of family connections derives less from shared genes and more from established codes of conduct—the fulfillment of our roles as siblings, children, and parents. Adoption embodies the exceptions to the rules of blood kinship. Traditional stranger adoptions, in which birth certificates and adoption decrees are sealed to prevent parties to the adoption from knowing one another's identities, belie the fundamental rule of blood kinship by demanding the irreversible dissolution of the blood tie between birth parents and child and the creation of a new relationship modeled as if it were blood (Modell 2). Adoption establishes parenthood through contract rather than physical conception, making blood paradoxical, a reminder of a tie to the birth family with the potential to undermine the integrity of the adoptive relationship. In the contradictions of adoptive kinship, the presumption of innate blood kinship bumps up against a strictly socially constructed familial relationship.

This paradox also has implications for racial identities. Adoption's disruption of "blood" as the binding substance of kinship results in a corresponding subversion of the social norms that presume race to be shared within families and, implicitly, in bloodlines. Historically, racial difference in America has been understood as inherent, with racial hierarchies sustained by a complex interplay of perceived biological differences, social impositions, and the metaphor of "blood." If, as Henry Louis Gates claims, "race" is a metaphor for difference, then "blood" helps "race" do its rhetorical work.[4] "Blood" creates a conceptual link between family and race that reveals the family's role in creating and sustaining not only racial identities but racial categories as well. The family helps to instill racial identity and then socializes its members into their culturally prescribed roles.[5] Transracial adoption undermines the shared naturalizing discourse of "blood." It forces important questions: What is the source of racial "traits"? How are our beliefs supported by the intertwined relationship between blood kinship and racial "blood"?

Adoption across national boundaries introduces yet another set of related issues: the ambiguous substance of national belonging. As a nation conceived through the collective rejection of bloodlines as a precondition to national membership, the United States has not always lived up to that ideal. Theory and practice remain at odds with the imposition of immigration quotas, broken treaties, and citizenship restrictions. Adoption foregrounds questions about how we "belong" on a national scale, revealing a collective ambivalence about the source of national membership. As Carol Singley observes, "Adoption narratives dramatize the struggle of individuals and families to draw and redraw the lines of bonds and affection; on a larger scale, they portray a nation wrestling in multiple ways with conflicting notions of citizenship in which belonging and entitlement are bestowed either by birthright or ideology" (79). She suggests that fictional adoptions serve as a measure of the evolving criteria for national belonging; in asking what makes a family, they engage with corresponding questions of what constitutes citizenship.

On the level of family, race, and nation, adoption thus demands alternative ways of articulating what it means to be authentic in the absence of biology. As Ellen Herman argues, much of twentieth-century adoption has revolved around ways of responding to its departures from biological kinship norms. Adoption professionals and participants alike have attempted to make it seem more real through purposeful acts of "design." Herman explains, "Enduring beliefs in the power of blood, and widespread doubts about whether families could thrive without it, fueled ardent efforts to subject adoption to regulation, interpretation, standardization, and naturalization. These combined operations accomplished two related goals. They identified adoption as an important social problem and designated kinship by design as its solution" (7). Even as the responses to biogenetic differences in the adoptive family have shifted over the century, the absence of "blood" connection has remained a problem stubbornly attached to adoption for many (Herman 297–98). The problem of the absence of metaphorical blood can be found in writings by and about adoptees and birth parents and in some of the debates that surrounded transracial adoption in the late twentieth century; nevertheless, some scholars have also begun to view adoption's detachment from biology not as a flaw but, rather, as an opportunity to redefine the terms with which we understand identity, to make it more expansive and self-directed.

Literature scholar Margaret Homans has argued persuasively on several occasions that the absence of origins experienced by many adoptees may not be the loss that people often make it out to be.[6] She observes that contemporary adoption culture is fixated around familial and cultural origins that are coded, in various ways, as biogenetic or innate; in turn, the absence of knowledge of those origins—a consequence of the adoption process—constitutes a loss or deprivation ("Origins, Searches" 61). But Homans suggests that we recognize some of the possibilities that unknown origins might afford, including a process of "self-making" ("Origins, Searches" 65) that can detach identities from an essentialized notion of roots. She says, "Adoption . . . has the potential not only to destabilize binaries such as nature and culture, blood and water, but also to put into practice 'another configuration of primary attachment' for which there is not yet a language" ("Origins, Searches" 63). Although the exact means by which these identities can be created remain yet undefined, adoption, as Homans suggests, represents an important alternative to essentialism. Other scholars have also viewed adoption in terms of its capacity to advance more social constructionist models for identity. For example, Vincent Cheng asserts that adoptions across racial and cultural lines "make a radical mockery of any notions of an authentic identity" because adoptees have no lived knowledge of their birth parents' culture, despite the efforts of adopters to preserve what they might call "cultural heritage" (70). Cheng argues that adoptive identity, like all identity, is hybrid and contingent, learned through life experience rather than innate. Approaching the issue of constructed identities from a somewhat different direction, Barbara Yngvesson and Maureen M. Mahoney examine how actual adoptees respond to their status by constructing new narratives to address the "gaps" in their life stories. Touching on the ways in which origin narratives are attempts to feel authentic despite the lack of biogenetic connection to their families, the authors point out that adoptees

> are caught in the pursuit of "realness".... Their very "in between-ness" and their (ultimately unresolvable) efforts to become *either* this or that, point to the vulnerability of all identity, its politically and historically contingent "nature." It is from these irresolvable contradictions in the experience of adoptees, contradictions from which no culturally consistent narrative can be told, that the potential is found for challenging "identity" and the fixed belongings this implies. (82–83)

Striking a more ambivalent tone than Homans or Cheng in their emphasis on an "ultimately unresolvable" liminality, Yngvesson and Mahoney suggest that the adoptees' position can nevertheless be an opportunity to construct new ways of defining the self, an approach that might be relevant outside of the experience of adoption.

Many of the literary texts discussed in the following chapters translate that potential for establishing new forms of self-definition into a fictional context, using adoption to elude restrictive identities defined in terms of blood. Even those written when both race and family were understood almost exclusively in terms of heredity employ adoptive scenarios to suggest that race is not biological at all. For instance, Charles W. Chesnutt's The Quarry places a racially ambiguous orphan first in a white family and then in an African American one to suggest that race is a matter of context, not inheritance. Moreover, the protagonist, Donald Glover, eventually gets to choose which racial category he prefers, an overt act of self-fashioning. Treating adoption as a source of potential liberation from narrowly defined identities, as Homans and Cheng and, to a lesser extent, Yngvesson and Mahoney do, can be appealing for a variety of reasons. Among other things, it repositions adoptees, moving them from anomalous, slightly suspect figures—perpetually damaged—to the advanced guard of hybrid identities. It creates space to redefine the meaning of kinship in more expansive ways as well as to understand other kinds of nonfamilial identity differently.

At the same time, however, some fictional representations of adoption included in this study provide a distinct counterweight to the potential for transformation. Many of the novels and short stories discussed here remain, in various ways, embedded in an understanding of identity as something inherent, revealing a tension between the image of adoption as yielding new, more self-defined identities and one that depicts it in terms of enduring essential identities that are difficult to relinquish. Both William Faulkner's *Light in August* and Kate Chopin's "Désirée's Baby," for instance, touch on adoption's capacity to remove adoptees from rigid categories by featuring orphans who cannot be racially defined, yet as a consequence of that amorphousness, both characters become a threat to the social order that must be destroyed. Their subsequent deaths are a grim antithesis to their potential for liberation. Sometimes transformation and rigid definitions for identity remain in unresolved tension, as in Toni Morrison's *Tar Baby*, which represents identity, very overtly, as innate, while at the same time undermining this depiction through adoption's disruptions of biological norms. Within this study—and sometimes within a single text—the possibilities adoption allows for forging new kinds of identity are balanced by the persistence of identity essentialism as the explanation for what makes an individual "real" within a family, a racial community, or the nation as a whole. In light of the scholarly move toward adoption's transformative potential, these tensions are also worth exploring, to identify the kinds of cultural work done when authors and activists depict identity as inherent. As the discussions that follow suggest, this impulse toward essentialism is not necessarily a retrograde discourse; it is more complex than it seems, a response not only to the unique configurations of adoption—which still remains distinctly outside the kinship norm in the collective consciousness—but to a larger national ambivalence about what, precisely, makes us real or legitimate members of our communities.

To that end, the rest of this chapter investigates the tension between adoption's potential for transformation through socially constructed identities and a tendency toward essentialism as it arises in the public discourses surrounding transracial adoption; these public discourses are part of the cultural and historical contexts that frame the fictional adoptions that are the focus of the chapters that follow. They also show that while, on the surface, this tension may seem to be yet another manifestation of the nature/nurture binary applied to adoption, biology (and environment) also function as authenticating mechanisms that help articulate the meaning of belonging. My purpose in exploring this particular line of thinking is not to downplay the significance of adoption's potential to lead us past rigid, biogenetic explanations for identity. Not only does that potential clearly exist in the fiction discussed here, but recent scholarship by Homans and others offers exciting possibilities to reimagine identity in new, more inclusive terms for literal adoptees as well. Nevertheless, it is important to explore some of the reasons for and the implications of treating identity as located in inherent qualities with regard to adoption, in order to better understand why such treatment persists despite the potentials that Homans and such fiction authors as Chesnutt have identified. Furthermore, the tension itself merits examination, as a means of understanding the strategies that individuals and communities employ to stabilize identities at moments of crisis.

Before discussing some of the historical and cultural contexts that frame the fictional adoptions examined in this study, I must pause briefly to consider the potential value of essentialist language in articulating adoptive identities. Autobiographical narratives such as Jane Jeong Trenka's *The Language of Blood* (2003) illustrate the difficulty of finding language to express the sense of alienation that some feel as a result of being adopted. This insight, in turn, can help to explain why essentialist discourses remain attached to adoption despite its seemingly obvious constructed status.

Trenka writes about her life as a Korean adoptee raised in Minnesota and her return to Korea to find her birth mother. Shortly after they reunite, Trenka's birth mother becomes ill with terminal cancer, and Trenka nurses her. After a lifetime of feeling physically different from her white adoptive parents and community, Trenka connects with her birth mother based on their bodily similarity. She remarks, "I saw for the first time what you as a mother already knew: that I am made in the image of you; I am a daughter after your body and after your heart. Even if I fail to create you again with words, I will carry you with me, in the language of blood" (*Language* 160). This passage highlights the problem of the body in adoption and in strict social constructionist approaches to it. Identities may be constructed, but bodies—with physical similarities, not just in skin color, but also in unique features shared within biological families—become a quite literal sign of origins that cannot be easily dismissed as a construct. In this passage, Trenka captures the degree to which that similarity can carry a narrative of its own, one verifiable if only in her experience of difference within her adoptive family and within her homogeneous hometown. Her difference—and her sense of the bodily sameness that she shares with her birth mother—has a personal truth-value that she communicates through the essentialist language of blood connectedness. As Linda Martín Alcoff puts it, "Categories of social identity are fundamental, even while they are contextual and relational. Whether or not they are essential to the self, they are certainly essential to the way the self experiences the world" (92). Trenka's experience of embodied difference defines how she expresses her relationship to the world and yields a perspective that may be uncomfortably essentialist for some readers, even as it remains meaningful to her—indeed, "essential," in Alcoff's sense of the word.

One might argue that Trenka is falling into the trap of reasserting blood kinship as the most authentic of all kinship arrangements, making it more entrenched, rather than less so. Yet other parts of her text suggest that "blood" is not as monolithic as her language in this section implies. Trenka later suggests that the truth of her experience as an adoptee may not necessarily be found in blood any more than it can be found in the documents that supposedly authenticate us as citizens and family members. Trenka notes the failure of official documents to offer the complete story of any individual experience, calling her own birth certificate a "partial truth." Closed adoption records mean that she has no documents to prove, for instance, that Korean infant Jeong Kyong-Ah indeed became American Jane Brauer. Even family photos become suspect: "Even if I had [documents], who could legally prove that the baby in the photo is the same one they sent to America?" Trenka concludes that "what remains through the rubble of the years is emotional truth, as fictional as it may seem" (*Language* 232–33). In this statement, Trenka approaches adoptive identity through paradox. Throughout her narrative, she embraces the possibility that her whole story may not be tellable, by fictionalizing it through the use of drama and fairy tales and by imagining events at which she was not present. At the same time, she authenticates her story by very explicitly locating her familial and cultural identity in "blood" and thus rendering it immutable. The contradiction in these two approaches is embodied in her description of the narrative she tells herself: "emotional truth, as fictional as it may seem." "Emotional truth" is an oxymoron, as emotions are generally understood as "subjective," while truth is presumed to be "objective." By qualifying her position as "as fictional as it may seem," Trenka undercuts the possibility that it might be dismissed because it is too subjective; her truth, in effect, lies in paradox.

For Trenka, as for many other actual adoptees, certain qualities seem innate and crucial to her identity, even as she acknowledges that the narrative on which she bases her self-conception may be fictional in the end. Her memoir encourages us to bear in mind that identities are constructed, yet they are also subjective, in the sense that they are shaped by lived experiences that may cause us to perceive of certain qualities as inherent. To see social identity as "fundamental," as Alcoff suggests, does not negate the importance of understanding the fictive qualities of the narratives created around adoption, but it does allow us to make room for articulations of identity that seem, at least on the surface, to be deeply invested in inherent qualities that might seem problematic in a strict social constructionist paradigm. Trenka's paradoxical approach to identity, as both a matter of blood and a fiction, adds another dimension to the phrase "the language of blood." By emphasizing the idea of "language" in the phrase, one can see Trenka's approach as strategic, a rhetorical move to capture the emotional truth of her experience. Deeming it rhetorical does not render it insincere but, instead, highlights the personal value in holding on to innate identities to communicate the ways in which "the self experiences the world," to use Alcoff's phrase.

The overall contradictions in Trenka's attempt to define her identity also provide a way to understand the rhetorical significance of nature and nurture in regard to adoption. Neither "nature" ("blood") nor "nurture" ("fictional truths") completely articulates Trenka's sense of self. The contradiction reflects ambivalence, an ambivalence that may actually be as crucial to how she identifies herself as "blood" or "fiction," capturing the truth of her experience in ways that one or the other side of the binary can only partially accommodate. Such a recognition enables us to see beyond the nature/nurture binary as such, to explore the kinds of work that employing one or the other side—or, indeed, both at the same time—might do for people. After all, if identity is both relational and fundamental, then, as Alcoff concludes, "the categories of intrinsic/non-intrinsic and essential/nonessential confuse more than they clarify in thinking about the nature of the self" (92). Rather than focusing on the nature/nurture paradigm as the problem of adoption, we may do better to examine the rationale behind advancing one category over the other. Doing so can shed light on what it means to be "real" or "authentic" at a given cultural moment and in a particular context.

Trenka's use of the "language of blood" to help express her sense of embodied difference, in combination with the contradictions that surround it, inform our understanding of the shifting adoption discourses of the twentieth century. As the historical and cultural discussions that follow illustrate, grounding personal and collective authenticity in nature or nurture can be a strategic act aimed at securing unstable identities, and they are very much informed by context. Even in the early twentieth century, when eugenic thinking privileged heredity over environment in defining the substance of belonging, many still believed that families and communities could be constructed by affinity; and even though transracial adoption as such did not yet factor into public conversations directly, it did appear regularly in the literary imagination as a consequence of failures to determine an orphan's racial ancestry before adopting. These scenarios allowed authors to explore the meaning of belonging on a wider scale, engaging anxieties about authentic whiteness (and blackness) through fictional adoptive families. In contrast, by the late twentieth century, transracial adoption was often a public issue, debated in conflicting terms that can be organized loosely within the frame of nature and nurture. Yet while that paradigm was a useful default, the controversies over the practice were also about securing identity, a concern that extended well beyond validating the adoptive family in contrast to the biological. African Americans and American Indians, for instance, protested in order to have their respective kinship patterns recognized; that is, among other concerns, they wanted their families to be respected, to be considered as "real" as the white, middle-class, heterosexual, nuclear ones after which so much child welfare practice was modeled. Participants in transnational adoptions from Asia are also interested in establishing authenticity by managing adoption's intersections with both global migration patterns and domestic racial hierarchies. The historical and cultural contexts discussed in the following pages are the literal frame for the discussions of adoption and identity through fiction that appear in the later chapters. They highlight how individual adoptions become a point of convergence for more general anxieties over defining racial and national identity. In fiction, when transracial adoption appears as a literary trope, it allows authors to address these issues in relation to a much broader sweep of concerns: multiracial identity, mixed-race families, social change following the civil rights movement, tribal autonomy, and immigrant identities.

Eugenics is a central contextual frame for adoption and its literary representation in the early twentieth century and, indeed, throughout the century. At its foundation, eugenics was a family matter, a theory that evolved through genealogical studies meant to prove that certain traits were hereditary and passed down to future generations; the only logical response to the inheritability of dysgenic traits, some believed, was sterilization or other reproductive restrictions to break that chain within individual families. Eugenic thinking also included the converse, that selective breeding could encourage the proliferation of "positive" traits. In her study of the effects of eugenics on literary modernism and the Harlem Renaissance, Daylanne English argues that eugenics developed "in a context of nascent superpower in tension with anxieties regarding widespread foreign immigration and domestic migration" (11), and its embrace by a broad and disparate swath of Americans suggests the power of biology to stabilize identity in a changing world. Eugenics affected nearly everyone in the early twentieth century, explaining differences in class, gender, sexuality, race, religion, and ethnicity.[7] It upheld white supremacy by providing scientific justification for discrimination against African Americans, Asian Americans, American Indians, immigrants, and virtually any other population that could not be categorized under the rather arbitrary heading of "Anglo-Saxon." In a time of uncertainty, eugenics defined the criteria that determined authentic belonging expressly in biological terms.

The family studies that supported eugenic policies of sterilization and the institutionalization of the "unfit" profoundly affected the way social workers and other specialists approached adoption. As historian Rickie Solinger observes, many scientists believed that "illegitimacy occurred at the intersection of negative sociological and biological conditions and was an expression of an inhering, unchanging, and unchangeable 'physical' defect" (*Wake Up* 16). The purported sexual deviance that led to pregnancies outside the confines of marriage could easily be passed down to illegitimate children. Once illegitimacy was linked to mental deficiency, adopted children—many conceived out of wedlock—were also implicated as potentially deficient (Carp, *Family* 18). Historian E. Wayne Carp explains the effects of hereditarian beliefs on adoption in the early decades of the twentieth century: "The supposed link between feebleminded unwed mothers and their illegitimate children cast a pall over all adoptions; even popular magazines warned adoptive parents against the risk of 'bad heredity.' Adopted children were thus burdened with a double stigma: they were assumed to be illegitimate and thus tainted medically *and* they were lacking the all-important blood link to their adoptive parents" (*Family* 18). The perception of genetic taint made adoption seem risky, at least to adoption specialists, yet prospective adopters were willing to discount or overlook the perceived threat of genetic deficiency in order to create a new family. As historian Barbara Melosh notes, adoptive parents worried less about heredity than did social workers (*Strangers* 42). When the abstractions of policy met the emotional immediacy of a family's desire to adopt a child, heredity became significantly less monolithic. This dynamic would continue over the century, as adoption participants looked, in various ways, to heredity to define their relationships to their families and communities. Dysgenic traits were a concern well into the 1960s— in terms of both adoptees' intelligence and their racial ancestry—yet fears of unpredictable biology were often met by individuals willing to take the risk.

The concerns about heredity and family circulating in society at the turn of the twentieth century extended into American literature in subtle ways as authors attempted to define the meaning of race. The "one-drop rule" employed the ambiguous metaphor of racial blood to quantify ancestry, stripping the privileges of whiteness from anyone with even a distant relative of African descent. In numerous narratives involving passing, switched babies, and the tragic mulatto, American authors attempted to test the one-drop rule's logic through representations of families that highlighted the arbitrariness of the racial system.[8] Although recent scholarship has approached these texts, especially passing narratives, as potential subversions of racial categories, rarely does the relevance of kinship come into the analysis, despite its centrality to categorizing individuals racially.[9] Often, however, it is the very absence of biological kinship ties that illustrates the family's importance as a racializing force. Exemplary texts such as Charles W. Chesnutt's *The Quarry* and "Her Virginia Mammy," Kate Chopin's "Désirée's Baby," and William Faulkner's *Light in August,* discussed in chapters 2 and 3, portray orphans of indeterminate racial heritage adopted by strangers, and they engage the same issues of the color line as traditional passing narratives; at the same time, they position passing directly within a familial setting, to make explicit the ways in which family relationships construct individual racial identities and sustain rigid categories.

Late twentieth-century adoption history illustrates the ways in which definitions of kinship and identity as inherent circulated alongside competing arguments about the importance of environment and the relevance of cultural integrity in shaping the self, adopted and otherwise. These discourses intermingled with one another and were sometimes used interchangeably, a reflection of a continuing negotiation of the meaning of "authentic" familial, racial, and national identities as more and more children were adopted across racial lines. Over the course of the twentieth century and especially in the period of social change that followed World War II, adoption regularly became a point of convergence for generalized anxieties over defining identity, yet these discourses also reflect the particular historical and cultural circumstances of the groups involved.

The recent history of African Americans and adoption illustrates in a particularly striking way how discourses of heredity and environment are deployed in response to social change, representing an ongoing process of defining (and redefining) African American identity, sometimes for radically divergent political purposes. In the post–World War II period, African American women who were pregnant and unmarried faced a very different social welfare landscape than did their white counterparts. While single white women were treated as neurotic but salvageable as long as they relinquished their children for adoption, black women were expected to be punished for their transgression by keeping their children.[10] Public officials explained black women's circumstances in deterministic terms—as the result of what Rickie Solinger calls "the biological stain" of promiscuity (*Wake Up* 9)—and then used their purportedly inherent flaws to justify the lack of social services available to them. Perceived as flawed for not relinquishing, African American women rarely had adoption services extended to them, and, further, many black families preferred to keep their families intact (Solinger, *Wake Up* 201). When families did need help caring for children in need, they arranged it informally, making use of extended family and community contacts and largely eschewing white-run official services (Herman 231). When considered against a wider backdrop than any individual family, conversations about "black illegitimacy" can be understood as part of a larger project of shoring up white power. Biological determinism justified discriminatory practices. When legislation aimed at single black mothers was packaged with bills that resisted desegregation initiatives (Solinger, *Wake Up* 47), biology, "illegitimacy," and civil rights were implicitly linked as a means of social control. Some black activists challenged this deterministic language, arguing that racist and impoverished environments caused single pregnancy; identifying the lack of adoption services available to black women as a problem, they advocated for more formal, agency-supported adoption opportunities for black families. This approach also had wider implications: integrating social welfare agencies became one battle in the larger war against segregation (Solinger, *Wake Up* 195–99).

To encourage black families to adopt, the National Urban League initiated a national campaign in 1953. Although this project had little effect in diminishing the overall number of black children needing adoption or in increasing the numbers of black adopters, it had the unintended consequence of calling white adopters' attention to African American children available for adoption and implicitly encouraging them to cross racial lines to create their families ("African-American Adoptions"). This shift toward transracial adoption coincided with white Americans' acknowledgment of racial disparities that the civil rights activists were protesting, which in turn caused some whites to see adoption as an opportunity to form a color-blind society (Ladner 51). Moreover, it also corresponded to disparities in supply and demand for adoption; as fewer white infants became available for adoption (a result of more widely available birth control and diminishing social stigma for single motherhood), prospective adopters looked elsewhere for children. At their height, in 1971, transracial placements of African American children reached 2,574 (Carp, *Family* 168), compared to roughly 90,000 adoptions of children by nonrelated adults in 1970 ("Private Domestic").[11] As the numbers suggest, these adoptions were more significant symbolically than statistically; nevertheless, in 1972, the National Association of Black Social Workers (NABSW) protested the increasing numbers of transracial adoptions out of concern for African American adoptees who might fail to develop a strong sense of racial identity or the survival skills necessary for navigating a racist culture. This objection reflects a black nationalist position that African American communities can and should take care of their own, derived from a long history of white state interventions in black homes (Satz and Askeland 54). The organization's advocacy of "race matching"—that is, keeping black children with black adopters—resulted in a dramatic decrease in transracial adoptions to 831 by 1975 (Carp, *Family* 169). In the early 1990s, debates over the transracial adoption of African Americans resurfaced. Those opposed to transracial placements still worried about racial identity, and they were confronted with a strong counterargument against "race matching" and for more "color-blind" placements (Patton 3). The 1990s debates rehashed arguments from earlier in the century by implicitly linking transgressive black sexuality to welfare reform and, in the process, further stigmatizing black single mothers; they departed from that history by implying that white families were representative of good family values and thus more capable of parenting black children than were black families (Patton 5).

In the 1970s and again in the 1990s, the legitimacy of transracial adoption was articulated in conflicting definitions of race as either biological or socially constructed (Patton 25). Those who felt that white people should not parent black children opposed it in largely essentialist terms. The NABSW statement, for instance, argued, "Only a black family can transmit the emotional and sensitive subtleties of perception and reaction essential for a black child's survival in a racist society" ("NABSW" 133). Although one could argue that this statement suggests that children need to be in a racially aware environment created by black parents, it also strongly implies that black parents are inherently equipped with this knowledge, particularly in the context of the statement's overall point that such awareness cannot or will not be learned by white adopters. It is no surprise that the NABSW statement, drafted in the early 1970s, would rely on racial essentialism, since it came out of a larger movement of black nationalism; it expressed the frustration that some felt when the civil rights movement did not yield the equality that many had expected. As Barbara Melosh explains, objections to transracial adoption reflected national divisions that undermined the "postwar consensus, exposing the class and racial privilege underlying its affirmations of upward mobility and assimilation" (*Strangers* 176). Rather than a symbol of progress, transracial adoption represented a threat to the integrity of black families, which, in turn, destabilized the black community as a whole. In this way, transracial adoption served as just one manifestation of broader erosions of government support for at-risk families and concerns about the most effective ways to enact reform to ensure racial equality. Those in favor of transracial placements often supported their position by appealing to the power of environment, arguing that the most important factor in a child's life is a safe and loving home; they point to statistics that say that transracial adoptees have positive adjustment rates compared to other adoptees (Bartholet 102; Simon and Altstein), evidence, in their view, that children of color can develop a healthy sense of identity—including a racial one—in a white home.

In each position on transracial adoption, essential or environmental explanations for difference operate rhetorically to support a particular point of view, but both also mask a more fundamental concern about the legitimacy of particular families arranged through adoption. For some, the position taken by those who oppose transracial placements seemed unnecessarily "political," a distraction from the needs of individual children. Elizabeth Bartholet assesses opposition to transracial placement and concludes that race matching advocates unite "powerful and related ideologies—old-fashioned white racism, modern-day black nationalism, and what I will call 'biologism,' the idea that what is 'natural' in the context of the biologic family is what is normal and desirable in the context of adoption" (93). Indeed, essentialist arguments for race and family are invoked in opposition to transracial placements, a rhetorical move that turns earlier stereotypes aimed at black single mothers into a powerful argument in favor of black autonomy, in an attempt to address the long history of neglect experienced by black families in regard to child welfare. Of course, stances in favor of transracial adoption, such as Bartholet's own, are equally ideological, employed to serve the end of a "color-blind" approach to adoption and, as some have suggested, to serve the needs of white adopters seeking a shrinking pool of available children ("NABSW" 133).[12] Margaret Homans takes up the issue of essentialist discourses surrounding transracial adoption, and she observes that even pro-transracial adoption arguments that privilege environment can "sound essentialist," employing the terms *race, heritage,* and *culture* as synonyms ("Essentialism" 260). The blurring of language suggests that the stakes may be "ideological" but not, perhaps, in the ways that

Bartholet implies. These debates are also about asserting the authenticity of particular kinds of family at a time when the image of the American family was changing. They reflect fears that the legitimacy of black families was not respected, as well as a desire to protect them from the intervention of social services agencies that had not served them well previously and, perhaps more important, to assert their value, one comparable to a mythical white, middle-class nuclear family standard by which they continued to be judged. For proponents of transracial placements, at stake was the legitimacy of a different kind of family: the mixed-race one created through adoption, which resembled the families of the growing number of children from legally, socially sanctioned mixed-race relationships. The concerns that some voiced about whether or not a black child raised in a white home could ever "really" be black (Ladner 81) also had implications for children raised by biological parents of a different race. These issues of authenticity fit into the larger cultural moment: as the civil rights movement turned more nationalist, it also prompted a collective, if implicit, conversation about what would make African Americans equal members of American society—that is, what would grant them the legitimacy of citizenship that had long been withheld. The fictional transracial adoptions of African American children discussed in this study are framed by these debates even when they do not engage with them directly. In their novels, Robert E. Boles and Toni Morrison incorporate a black character into a white family to explore the meaning of authentic racial identity in the immediate postintegration period, and both characters suffer from identity crises that stem from the sense that they do not belong in their families or, sometimes, within their racial communities. These novels are explored in chapter 4.

The NABSW statement prompted policy changes but yielded no statutory limitations on the transracial adoption of African American children; in contrast, objections raised at roughly the same time by Indian tribes and their supporters, who were concerned about large numbers of American Indian children placed for adoption with white families, resulted in the Indian Child Welfare Act of 1978 (ICWA), a federal law that prohibits the adoption of Native children outside of the tribe. There are many surface commonalities between African American transracial and American Indian extra-tribal adoption in the 1960s and 1970s, including white parents' interest in adopting children from both groups (a consequence of changing adoption patterns) and subsequent protests against these adoptions that arose out of the larger nationalist movements within each group. At the same time, however, the adoption of American Indian children occupies a much different historical and cultural context. Placing the two groups together under the larger frame of adoption calls attention both to the different ways each group articulated its desire to protect the integrity of families and to how those discourses circulated alongside one another. The unique relationship between American Indian tribes and the U.S. government accounts for the specific language with which tribes and their supporters responded to extra-tribal adoptions. Unlike the biological arguments opposing the transracial adoption of African American children, tribes generally emphasized the preservation and maintenance of culture as the reason to limit extra-tribal adoptions of children, rather than using the language of inherent differences or racial integrity. Not only did that language reflect the issues of tribal autonomy underlying protests against the practice, but it also articulated the connection between Native cultural traditions and individual families, implicitly arguing for the authenticity and, indeed, the merit of Indian families, which were often judged inadequate when viewed through the frame of the white nuclear family.

Before discussing adoption specifically, it makes sense to briefly outline a few of the significant cultural and historical contexts for American Indian adoption. Adoption, as such, was not always the threat to tribes that it became in the mid-twentieth century and had long been practiced in ways that enriched tribal communities and differed starkly from European/American kinship practices. During first contact between tribes and colonists, prisoners of war were often incorporated into tribal communities, and captives replaced lost members of the tribe (Askeland, "Informal" 4–7). Adoption sometimes involved people with living parents who joined another family either in a ceremony or simply as a matter of fact (Holt 23). Just as tribal adoption practices have differed from European/American ones, so do kinship patterns, which, for tribes, often extend beyond the nuclear family to include extended families and sometimes members of the community. As historian Marilyn Holt explains, the traditional extended family in tribal communities raised children collectively, which means that the untimely death of parents did not result in orphancy in the same way that it did in American society; rather, other family or tribal members would care for children without parents. These extended family relationships also served an important socializing function, instructing all children in their cultural practices and ensuring the vibrancy of the tribe (Holt 20). Because of the centrality of the extended family to tribal life, any initiatives that weakened the family also undermined the community. One of the most significant of these initiatives, a precursor to the mass adoptions of the mid-twentieth century, was the boarding school movement, established by the federal government in the late nineteenth century with the goal of mainstreaming American Indian children by sending them to boarding schools far from their reservations. The boarding schools were part of a larger assimilationist strategy that included, in particular, the division of collectively held tribal lands into individual allotments on reservations. While in boarding schools, children were forbidden from using their native languages or practicing their customs. Intended to "civilize" Indians (Stark and Stark 127), the boarding school movement had far-reaching consequences—not only for the children, who returned to their reservations unable to speak to their families and unfamiliar with traditional practices, but for the communities that relied on each individual's active participation in the culture (Holt 15–16).

Within this longer history of family disruption, the outplacement of Indian children for fostering and adoption remains particularly problematic, the consequence of U.S.-tribal relations and shifting attitudes toward adoption in the nation as a whole. The Indian Adoption Project (1958–67), initiated by the Bureau of Indian Affairs and the Child Welfare League of America, was held up by its administrators as a success (Herman 240), yet the placement rates tell a different story of the damage done by this and other policies that privileged foster care and adoption over solutions that kept children with their tribes. As many as 25 to 35 percent of children were removed from their tribes and placed in non-Indian homes by the early 1970s (Herman 241). Individual placement rates were sometimes much higher, as in Wisconsin, where "Indian children ran the risk of being separated from their parents at a rate nearly 1600 percent greater than non-Indian children" (Stark and Stark 131). Social services agents who viewed Indian families through the lens of white, middle-class nuclear family models often encouraged adoptions and deemed Indian childcare practices inadequate (Unger; Byler).

Beyond the cultural disconnect between social workers and tribal families and the general disregard for the integrity of tribal communities, the adoption of American Indian children in the middle of the twentieth century was driven by the changing culture of American adoption. Native adoptions out of the tribe were remarkable because they departed from the "matching" policies of the midcentury, which placed children with families on the basis of similar physical characteristics, intellect, religion, and race. As adoption demand grew, those who could not adopt "blue-ribbon" white infants because of eligibility limitations—age or already having biological children—turned to Native children as a viable alternative. Adopters did not necessarily prefer American Indians as such, though some did profess an affinity for tribal culture (Fanshel 82).

Instead, the practice reflected the relativity of American racial hierarchies, with difference measured within and against the poles of black and white. As Ellen Herman puts it, "White adopters of Native American children in the 1950s and 1960s were far less willing to consider adopting African American mixed-race children (even in cases where the child's appearance did not testify to his or her racial background) than 'Oriental' children, children older than eight, children with mental retardation, or even children with serious, uncorrectable physical disabilities" (198). American Indians were more desirable candidates for adoption because they were deemed less racially "other" in the view of some whites.

The federal Indian Child Welfare Act of 1978 addressed objections—voiced in congressional hearings, tribal resolutions, and the media—to the large number of adoption and fostering placements in white homes. It prohibits the adoption of American Indian children outside of the reservation without the permission of the tribe and lays out a series of priorities to help govern child placement ("Indian"). In the public discussion preceding the ICWA, tribal leaders and their supporters framed their concerns in terms of cultural impact. Critics of the practice often cited cultural loss and damage to the tribes, linking adoption to larger projects of assimilation and encroachments on tribal sovereignty. For instance, William Byler, executive director of the Association on American Indian Affairs, testified before the Senate Subcommittee on Indian Affairs in 1974, "I think it's a copout when people say it's poverty that's causing family breakdown. I think perhaps the chief thing is the detribalization and the deculturalization, Federal and State and local efforts to make Indians white. It hasn't worked and it will never work and one of the most vicious forms of trying to do this is to take their children. Those are the great emotional risks to Indian families" (Byler). Eschewing much of the language of race common in the African American debate, Byler articulates these practices in terms of culture and identifies them as an attack on tribal cultures, which are comprised of and sustained by Indian families and their children. Like Byler, tribal chief Calvin Isaac, of the Mississippi Band of Choctaw Indians, focuses on adoption's long-term consequences, and he uses similar language. Isaac testified,

> Culturally, the chances of Indian survival are significantly reduced if our children, the only real means for the transmission of the tribal heritage, are to be raised in non-Indian homes and denied exposure to the ways of their People. Furthermore, these practices seriously undercut the tribes' ability to continue as self-governing communities. Probably in no area is it more important that tribal sovereignty be respected than in an area as socially and culturally determinative as family relationships. (Quoted in "History")

Isaac establishes the interconnection of issues, designating children as a crucial component of ensuring tribal heritage: adoption outside of the tribe does a disservice to the children by denying them their culture; further, it undermines the community itself; and finally, but not least, it violates tribal self-government.

The issue of tribal sovereignty raised by Chief Isaac helps to explain why opposition to the adoption of American Indian children was often voiced in terms of culture and tribal environment rather than race or other concepts that signal innate differences, language that appeared frequently in debates over the adoption of African American children and would arise again, in more muted form, around the adoption of children from Asian countries. Not only were tribes that lost significant numbers of children potentially unable to maintain communities and at risk of eradication, but the intervention of social workers from outside meant that tribes themselves were not granted the right to determine the well-being of their own members in accordance with their own values. Thus, despite the fact that American Indian extra-tribal adoptions most frequently get grouped under the category of "transracial" placements, the primary concern for tribes was not racial integrity as such but national sovereignty, an issue that went hand in hand with the cultural health of a vibrant, populous tribe. This observation is not to say that advocacy for the ICWA was articulated exclusively in terms of culture or tribal sovereignty.[13] In fact, as Stark and Stark point out, these implicit appeals to tribal sovereignty may not have been as persuasive to many legislators as another central theme in the hearings, the effects of adoption on the psychological development of individual children (134). With the debates over African American transracial adoption fresh in the public consciousness, the argument based on psychological impact would have been familiar and persuasive; moreover, it fits with the "best interest" mandate of American child welfare, which privileges the individual child over other, more holistic concerns. Responding to the welfare of individual children and their psychological needs is much less "political" than explicitly affirming the rights of American Indian tribes as distinct cultural entities and, furthermore, as sovereign nations. These concerns intersect in the adoption novels of Dallas Chief Eagle, Barbara Kingsolver, Leslie Marmon Silko, and Sherman Alexie, discussed in chapter 5. They attempt to navigate the competing concerns about individual and cultural identities raised by extra-tribal adoption, at the same time that the authors speak through adoption to address tribal sovereignty, cross-racial relations, and individual self-definition.

The international adoption of children from Asia differs from domestic transracial adoptions in its administration and its public perception, for the adoption of Asian children from abroad is less controversial than domestic transracial placements, and the rhetoric surrounding it is generally less inflammatory. Nevertheless, this practice also gets articulated in ways that reveal anxiety over the substance of belonging. The discourses of international transracial adoption often conflate essential and constructed identities, a response to the complex global and national contexts that frame it, as well as the recent, often contentious history of domestic transracial adoption. These adoptions are often approached in terms of cultural difference and adoptees' heritage, but because they are also inseparable from domestic racial hierarchies, they reveal, through their paradoxical treatment of culture as both learned and inherent, deep uncertainty about what will make adoptive families and individual adoptees' identities "real" in these atypical arrangements.

The rise of international transracial adoption in the late twentieth century is connected to domestic adoption practices in several subtle ways. International transracial adoption rates increased at precisely the moment that domestic transracial adoptions became controversial. Ellen Herman observes that the admittance of "immigrant orphans" to the United States had increased 350 percent between 1968 and 1975 and continued to rise through the end of the century. International adoption appealed to some prospective parents for reasons similar to the preference some had for American Indian children over African American ones: "Most of these [international] adoptions did not involve the specific kind of racial difference that had bothered Americans and had tortured their history most. Children adopted from overseas were not black" (Herman 252). Moreover, the racial difference of children from abroad, perceived as "orphans" regardless of their actual family status, has historically been defined by narratives of need. Speaking of China adoption specifically, Sara Dorow postulates that some adopters perceive African American children as available for adoption because of circumstances of their parents' own making, which suggests character flaws, whereas Chinese children are innocent victims of politics and thus deserving of a chance at a new life in the United States (52–56). This attitude plays into a broader historical trend of depicting certain adoptions as a form of rescue. That discourse has a great deal of currency today, not only in regard to the consequences of China's restrictions on families that have led to child abandonment and infanticide, but in other nations in which poverty has left children considerably more disadvantaged than their American counterparts. The rescue narrative is magnified by the current prominence of transnational adoption among celebrities, as the move from abject "orphan" to privileged child of celebrity parents enacts a kind of rags-to-riches narrative of salvation that obscures the more complex politics of adoption.

The rise in international transracial adoption was also motivated, in part, by other developments in domestic adoption practice. Adopters looked overseas in greater numbers after the adoption rights movement in the 1970s began to call attention to the negative consequences of secrecy in adoption in ways that made it seem impermanent. Activists advocated for reform in adoption practices, both formally, through legislative changes that allow individuals access to birth certificates, and informally, through independent searches for and reunions with kin separated by the adoption process. Autobiographical search narratives, along with narratives published in the news media and reunions facilitated on television talk shows, called attention to and actively encouraged the desires of some participants in adoption to know their birth kin.[14] This movement coincided with a series of highly publicized disrupted adoptions in the 1980s. The heart-wrenching sight of a toddler removed from the home he or she had been raised in and returned to biological kin made domestic adoption seem precarious, at best, and prohibitively traumatic, at worst. International adoption seemed more inviolable to those who feared such disruptions. Anthropologist Christine Ward Gaily notes the desire for "unambiguous" rights to parenthood and quotes one of her subjects as saying, "Once the child is out of the country, you can relax—no custody fights years later" (50).

Especially prominent in the last fifteen years (with the rise of adoptions from China), international adoptions have occurred since the end of World War II. Adopters responded to the plight of war orphans and the children of U.S. servicemen left behind in Germany, England, and Japan. Ellen Herman remarks that while Americans were moved by sympathy for abandoned children, adoption also became "infused . . . with the particular patriotism of the cold war era" (217). International adoption in the United States has certainly not been limited to Asia, but American adopters have had a particularly close relationship with Asian countries. In 1949, Pearl S. Buck established Welcome House to help place children of Japanese women and American servicemen after World War II (Herman 210). Holt International, established in 1956, focused on matching Korean children, many displaced by war, with American families (Melosh, *Strangers* 192). Later, in 1975, Operation Babylift evacuated children, not all of whom were actually orphans, from Vietnamese orphanages, for adoption in the United States and other countries (Herman 252). From 1971 to 2001, roughly 150,000 children were adopted from Asia into American families, and from 1958 to 2001, 100,000 of those were from Korea alone ("International Adoption Facts").

As with other forms of adoption, international transracial adoption from

Asia exists in a wider historical and cultural context. It cannot be separated from war and poverty on an international scale, nor can it be viewed as distinct from the immigration patterns of Asians to the United States in the late nineteenth and twentieth centuries. Americans of Asian descent have historically been subjected to virulent racism, from the immigration of Chinese laborers in the late nineteenth century and the subsequent restrictions on the entry of Chinese as well as other Asian immigrants to the internment of Americans of Japanese descent during World War II. Until 1965, immigration to the United States from Asian countries was severely restricted (Chan 145). This history of racism and discrimination shapes the American culture in which adoptees from Asia grow up. David L. Eng asserts that transnational adoption from Asia is a privileged form of migration, categorizable with war brides, and "marks not only a striking gendered reversal of this history of racialized exclusion but also an emergent form of Asian American subjectivity of considerable consequence to Asian American politics, history, and community" (11). Despite this consequential development with repercussions for American race relations, international adoptees from Asia are generally considered products of their original national culture, rather than shaped by a domestic American racial system.

Adoptions from Korea and China at the turn of the twentieth century are far less inflammatory than were those of African American and American Indian children adopted by white parents in earlier decades. This relative lack of controversy may actually obscure the complexity of the practice, which embodies cultural and racial differences that shift as children move across borders. Contemporary adoption practices encourage international adopters to attend to their children's "heritage" as a way of helping them to develop a healthy identity (Cheng 75) and to offset the kinds of adjustment problems that earlier generations of adoptees from Asia—people like Jane Jeong Trenka—experienced. Those adopting from China and other nations are encouraged to expose their children to the cultures of the nations they were adopted from, through language lessons and culture camps, as well as by observing holidays and celebrations. Vincent Cheng documents some of the ways in which these well-meaning attempts to help international adoptees also understand the culture of the child's original nation as inherent. For instance, he considers the case of an adoptive parent who says that her child "may be growing up American, [but] her soul is Chinese"; in another instance, a group of adoptive parents organized a screening of the film *Mulan* as part of a strategy to preserve cultural heritage (Cheng 76). Culture, something learned, becomes an element of the "soul," a presumably inherent quality, while authentic culture is located in a Disney adaptation of a traditional Chinese story. These examples may not be representative of every adoptive parent's response to the difficult task of addressing the differences within their families, yet as incidents reported in the media, they still help to define the broader cultural perception of what international adoption means. They suggest that culture is, paradoxically, something both innate and learned. Margaret Homans asserts that, despite its own unique cultural, national, and, indeed, racial issues, international adoption replicates the logic of the debate over African American transracial adoption, resulting in convoluted language that suggests that internationally adopted children possess a national "culture" that functions as a "racial essence that even the youngest abandoned baby carries with her from the moment of her birth" and that "for her own sake she needs to have it reinforced as she grows" ("Essentialism" 262). In the discourses around international adoption, culture—usually understood as learned behaviors and practices—operates as an essential part of adoptees' identities, yet, paradoxically, it is also something that adoptive parents are encouraged to learn and impart to their children.

While ostensibly about cultural authenticity, this convoluted language actually reveals an underlying concern with domestic racial identity. As Vincent Cheng suggests, the adoption world's strong preference for cultivating a sense of connection between adoptees and their original countries is actually an indirect response to the complexities of racial differences within the family. After all, the imperative to immerse transnational adoptees who seem "white" (those from Russia, for instance) into their "birth culture" is not nearly as intense as that surrounding children from Asia or Latin America, who are also physically marked in ways that make them "racial" in a U.S. context. Cheng puts it well when he says, "The real parental guilt at stake here is not over cultural or national difference, but over that old bugaboo of a reified difference that can't even be defined (and really doesn't even exist), that tragic accident we have learned to call 'race' (or really, here, skin color)" (80). As white parents respond to the differences in their own family, Cheng explains, they employ "the essentialisms of absolute difference" rather than the more complicated reality of hybrid identities that so many, adopted and nonadopted, share (80–81). "Culture" becomes almost interchangeable with "race," upheld by essential differences in order to respond to differences in the family. Moreover, the attention to heritage may be doing transnational adopters a disservice by distracting them from the impact of the racial hierarchies in the United States. The fact that children from Asia may seem less "racial" than African American children does not mean that Asians are not racialized in very specific ways, as the model minority or, in gendered terms, according to stereotypes of Asian girls and women as "hard-working, agreeable, and passive . . . , ever eager to please" (Eng 12). An awareness of Chinese heritage may not prepare adoptees and their families for navigating the racial minefield of the United States. As Margaret Homans cautions, "Transracially adopted children, including many transnationally adopted children, need to be equipped for a lifetime of being interpellated—often in racist ways—as belonging to the race of their birth parents, but this need is not necessarily being met by the assertion that roots or cultural heritage are the same as genetic inheritance" ("Origins, Searches" 62).

Ultimately, the focus on culture and heritage may have as much to do with the task of creating a "real" family by atypical means as it does with race or culture or nation. Acknowledging something external, like culture, is a way of addressing internal family differences, of establishing kinship through something other than biology and, in addition, in response to the physical differences among family members that make adoption so noticeable. This attention to culture may also be a way of creating "authenticity through difference"—a difference more manageable because it seems to be "cultural" rather than "racial," that is, different but not too different. Ellen Herman observes that as adoption practice moved from racial matching in the early part of the twentieth century to a greater acceptance of adoption across racial lines, a fundamental shift occurred, from familial authenticity achieved through "similarity" to establishing "authenticity through difference" (247). Those who focus heavily on culture and heritage in their adoptions are not only trying to address the psychic needs of their adoptees—as encouraged by adoption specialists; they are also responding to their status as atypical families, authenticating themselves by asserting and then incorporating their differences. As the discussion in chapter 6 demonstrates, authenticity in international adoption can become the route to—and sometimes the obstacle preventing—the creation of adoptive kinship ties.

As is demonstrated by the examples in this chapter, the presence of competing discourses of nature and nurture in transracial adoption reflects fundamental concerns about establishing and maintaining a sense of authenticity in the absence of biogenetic foundations. Appeals to biology and/or environment work to secure the meaning of identity, sometimes highlighting, by their very essentialism, the degree to which it is contextual and relational. The continued reemergence of the problem of defining authentic identities in new and different guises reflects a collective ambivalence over what constitutes truly authentic belonging. As Herman and other scholars have noted, the opportunity to define new affiliations apart from biology, which is characteristic of adoption, is also central to the American myth of reinvention. Herman says, "To claim, as liberal nationalism did, that Americanness was forged by willing participants whose common creed and experiences were more powerful than their disparate ancestral ties was to imagine the nation as a metaphorical adoption narrative in which all citizens were adoptees. American national belonging was deliberately made" (8).

Herman goes on to say, however, that "voluntary belonging" has proven to be more precarious than the mythos suggests, and this is one of the many implications of the fictional representations of adoption addressed by the body of this study. Whether one's primary interest lies with adoption as experience or (as in the case of this study) with the many ways in which literary authors represent a kind of national identity crisis through the experience of adoption, the dichotomy between nature and nurture, genetic essentialism and utter self-fashioning, is only the beginning of all that these texts imply about identity and authenticity at levels ranging from the family to the nation. The fictional texts analyzed in the following chapters explicate and illuminate a more profound uncertainty at the heart of the American myth, in ways that help to redefine the characteristics of voluntary belonging; moreover, tracing these uncertainties through fiction illustrates the degree to which ambivalence may itself be one of the defining qualities of American literature. The sense of ambivalence arises when the attempt to define the qualities that make us "real" as members of our families, of our ethnic or racial groups, or of our nations may actually prove to be more "real" than the explanations (to which we so often return) that locate belonging in inherent or environmental qualities.

CHAPTER 2

Passing for Kin in Charles W. Chesnutt's "Her Virginia Mammy" and *The Quarry*

This chapter and the following one take up adoption's unique point of entry into the crisis of categorization caused by the person of unknown origins who may—or may not—possess the all-important one drop of black blood. At a time when the authenticity of racial ancestry was paramount, light-skinned individuals posed a particular dilemma, one that could be compounded when orphancy and/or adoption deprived individuals of biological kinship, genealogy, or family history to guarantee their racial purity. Charles W. Chesnutt, Kate Chopin, and William Faulkner all explore the instability of racial categories when these authenticating mechanisms are absent. Unlike most of the fiction discussed in the second half of this book, transracial adoption, legally and socially prohibited at the time, functions in these texts almost exclusively as metaphor; while these texts offer insight into the growing institutionalization of adoption as a practice in the early twentieth century, they feature adoption as a trope through which the authors explore the contradictions that underlie racial categories. For Chesnutt, adoption facilitates a certain amount of self-fashioning that resists prescribed identities; for Chopin and Faulkner, however, the social instabilities created by orphancy and adoption prompt swift restoration of the racial hierarchy, permitting adopted characters very little opportunity to assert individual identity outside of existing norms. The first half of this study is weighted toward relationships between African Americans and whites, in acknowledgment of the dominance of the one-drop rule and the color line in Americans' understanding of race, even as, then and now, the black-white racial system masks a much more complex interrelationship among various groups; this project, as a whole, investigates those interconnections. At the same time, transracial adoption seemed to be a particularly compelling means of interrogating race to a variety of authors, who extend beyond Chesnutt, Chopin, and Faulkner to include Mark Twain, Jessie Redmon Fauset, and Pauline Hopkins; for this reason, literature by and about African American transracial adoption warrants extended discussion.

In Charles W. Chesnutt's novel of passing, *The House Behind the Cedars*, John Walden leaves his hometown and his family to pass for white in another state. After ten years, he misses his family and returns for a visit, hoping to encourage his younger sister to join him in passing so that he might share his life with a member of his family. The opening scene of the novel depicts him on the way to his mother's house. He finds himself admiring the figure of a young, seemingly white woman walking down the street in front of him. Only after he reaches his mother's house "behind the cedars" does he realize that the woman is actually his own sister. He has been away so long that he does not recognize her. This confusion encapsulates the complexity of family life in narratives of passing. Successful passing requires distance, a literal "passing" from the location where one is known to one where anonymity permits the assumption of a new racial identity. Because race is presumed to be shared among family members, successful passing also often requires a rupture from family connections. For these reasons, Walden must leave the physical location where he grew up and distance himself from his darker-skinned mother, whose relationship to him marks him as black.

John Walden's clear physical attraction to his sister further illustrates how being estranged from the family may free one to pass yet can obscure crucial information. The incestuous impulse in the first chapter is somewhat defused when Walden recognizes that Rena is actually his sister, yet the initial attraction signals the risk that comes from alienating oneself from one's family. At its extreme, such distance may result in committing one of the greatest of societal taboos: incest. The allusion to incest lingers into the first half of the novel, as Rena Walden agrees to pass for white, live with her widowed brother, and help raise his son. Their arrangement resembles a marriage and blurs the boundary between sibling and marital companionship. This threat of violating the incest taboo is an extreme but not uncommon manifestation of risky family relationships in passing novels. James Weldon Johnson also introduces incest as a possible repercussion of passing when the unnamed protagonist of his novel, *The Autobiography of an Ex-Colored Man* (1912), finds himself attracted to a young woman at the theater only to realize that she is his white half-sister. Pauline

Hopkins's novella *Of One Blood* (1903) actually follows through on the incest motif by featuring the sexual entanglement of three siblings with one another, facilitated by passing. Anxiety over incest served a variety of divergent ideological purposes. For those who wanted African Americans to remain second-class citizens, these incest tales were a warning against the repercussions of miscegenation. For those who advanced black equality, they reminded readers of white culpability in the sexual exploitation of blacks.[1] Alienation from family and community allows characters to pass successfully, yet their alienation results in unexpected consequences.

Passing narratives often convey ambivalence about family. On one hand, passers experience a sense of emotional loss because they have no connection with their families. In addition, not knowing one's family can cause potentially dangerous missteps, such as sleeping with one's sister. On the other hand, families are dangerous to passers. Light-skinned passers' association with their black families will mark them racially, limiting their mobility. In order to pass successfully, one must leave family behind. Some narratives sidestep these family issues by featuring characters already alienated from the family through orphancy, as in Nella Larsen's *Passing* (1929), or through circumstances beyond their control, as with Johnson's ex-colored man, whose mother dies and whose father does not acknowledge him.

Despite this strong underlying tension about the importance of families, passing narratives and the critics who study them rarely pause to examine familial dynamics directly.[2] The role played by the family in establishing individual racial identity and larger racial categories remains subsumed under the politics of passing. Textual and critical treatments of passing focus on the performance of race and its ethical implications rather than on the family as a source of racial meaning. Ironically, the very absence of biological kinship ties in certain passing narratives calls the most attention to the family's importance. These texts, which portray orphans of indeterminate racial heritage adopted by strangers, engage the same issues of the color line as traditional passing narratives. Like prototypical passing narratives, they provide opportunities to interrogate essentialism and challenge rigid racial categories. Unlike traditional passing narratives, however, they position passing directly within a familial setting, to make explicit the ways that family relationships help to construct individual racial identities and sustain rigid racial categories. The narratives discussed in this chapter, Charles Chesnutt's short story "Her Virginia Mammy" (1899) and *The Quarry* (1999, written ca. 1928), feature orphans with undocumented family history and very light skin. Because the protagonists look white yet live on both sides of the color line throughout their lives, these texts qualify as passing narratives. Even so, both are better understood in the mutually informative contexts of passing and adoption; the act of passing, especially when undertaken by orphaned adoptees, creates crises of both kinship and racial categories.

Kinship and race share a foundation in biological essentialism, yet adoption and passing disrupt biology as a determinant of certain traits or relationships. Critics generally agree that passing undermines strict racial categories by demonstrating that race is a performance rather than a preordained fact. As many have noted, that performative quality helps to subvert the power of the color line by detaching racial difference from biology.[3] Adoption creates a similar crisis of category on the level of family relationships. Adoption introduces a biological stranger into a family unit, requiring the family to create a relationship based on something other than shared biology; the various kin roles remain the same, but their substance derives from the effort required to create relationships rather than from an assumed bond based on biology. In an adoptive context, the very performance of family roles makes kinship "real." Reading kinship through the lens of adoptive relationships calls attention to the ways in which all kinship can be understood as constructed, not necessarily preordained by biology. The performance of kin roles in adoption manifests when family members behave "as if" they are biological kin;[4] seen this way, adoption itself constitutes a form of passing. The model for American adoption for most of the twentieth century assumes that adoptees will live as if biological members of the family, yet that model has often failed to acknowledge that they also possess prior identities distinct from the group with which they are associated. When it comes to their families, adoptees are—much like race passers—not always what they appear to be.

Passing and adoption are thus mutually informative concepts, but adoption adds something more to our thinking about passing: the possibility to interrogate racial categories at the same time as we examine the ways in which the family itself functions as a source of racial knowledge. Disrupting assumptions about family allows us to see not only how race is performed but also one of the forces that helps to shape that performance: family relationships. Cultural theorist Richard Dyer has established that racial categories are prescribed by both physical characteristics and family lines: "We may distinguish between two broad ways of categorising race: one genealogical, concerned with origins and lineages of reproduction, the other more statically biological, concerned with identifying and securing difference on and/or in the body itself" (20). In U.S. culture, the body is typically the primary source of racial categorization, yet as passing narratives suggest, physical appearance alone cannot completely guarantee racial purity for light-skinned people. Genealogical evidence often comes in the form of scrupulously maintained family histories, which provide verification of racial purity described euphemistically as "good blood." This reliance on family history during and after slavery implicitly acknowledges the fact that even a body that looks white can still contain the crucial one drop of black blood and threaten purported white purity. When the body is rendered unreliable, family origins become the sole determiner of racial category. A light-skinned orphan with no documentable family history violates both of these ways of "knowing" race and creates a crisis of categorization.

This categorization problem defies the expectations of both characters and readers; what seems to be real—race and kinship—may not be. This play with expectation and reality has always been central to passing narratives, both to the anxiety they produced for those who feared racial contamination and to their potentially subversive circumvention of racial codes. When passing is combined with orphancy and adoption, the disjuncture between expectation and reality becomes more disconcerting. Orphancy—particularly in the case of the foundling—can make family history unknowable, and adoption, by encouraging an "as if" model of family, makes it a construct. If what is visually certain on the body and genealogically guaranteed can, in fact, be wrong, then the whole foundation of race and family is no longer reliable. Both "Her Virginia Mammy" and *The Quarry* reveal the implications of uncertain family lineage when it comes to racial categories; in both cases, genealogical ambiguity exacerbates racial ambiguity, throwing into sharp relief the various signifiers by which race is known, signifiers usually veiled by invocations of essential biological differences. As these signifiers, such as reputation and appearance, become less reliable, so does the integrity of racial categories. Chesnutt demonstrates that these signs, when reconfigured, can expose how whiteness is upheld and manipulated by those able to exercise its privilege.

Charles W. Chesnutt's fiction depicts a number of families divided by the color line. The idea of American families as multiracial was not unusual for Chesnutt, whose own family crisscrossed the color line for several generations (Keller 173–204). It made him sensitive to the fact that white racial purity was a myth belied by the reality of individual family experiences. Many of his mixed-race characters are the children of prominent white men in the community, men who do not make arrangements for the future of their illegitimate mixed-race children (*The House Behind the Cedars*) or whose arrangements are disregarded by greedy white relatives (*The Marrow of Tradition*). In these families' communities, the official genealogies of upstanding white families collide with the unofficial but often widely known history of kinship across the color line. Chesnutt knew that the official family stories of the white elite disguised a pattern of ignoring financial responsibilities and denying social recognition to black relatives. His fictional mixed-race families confronted the collective lore of the white plantation aristocracy, which purportedly traced its families' heritages back to the Scottish cavaliers and undercut it with an alternative history of illegitimacy and social and financial disinheritance.

The Southern plantocracy's investment in genealogy served a variety of purposes, including the creation of an elite class in the supposedly classless United States and the verification of "bloodlines," a broad euphemism that applied to a variety of qualities, including legitimacy and, of course, racial purity. "Good blood" is an essential quality; one either has it or does not. Once established by genealogy, it was considered foolproof. But as Chesnutt's fiction points out, the use of genealogy and family lore as proof of racial purity was selective at best. Chesnutt recognized that family history functioned as what legal scholar Eva Saks calls a "title" to white privilege, the verification that would allow an individual to access the resources deprived by law to those of mixed-racial ancestry (Saks 70). He also knew, however, that those titles were not nearly as indisputable as many believed. They could be appropriated or falsified, an act that could undermine the integrity of an entire system constructed on the idea of white privilege. In Chesnutt's short story "Her Virginia Mammy," orphancy and adoption complicate the smooth function of family history as verification for white purity, showing the importance of genealogy as well as its potential for subverting the color line.

The main source of conflict in "Her Virginia Mammy" is Clara's recent discovery that she was adopted as a young child; the family history she always knew turns out to be an illusion, yet her biological ancestry remains frustratingly out of reach. Until she knows her family history and can guarantee her good breeding, she refuses to marry her boyfriend, John. John professes to care little about her background and hopes she will give up her obsession with the past so they can get married. Clara's adoption amplifies the importance of family history for both individual identity and social standing. Although Clara is not otherwise the voice of reason in this story—Chesnutt makes her seem naive and rather lacking in self-awareness—she poignantly conveys the links between family history and personal identity, connections seen most clearly when that family history is absent. Clara's language anticipates the adoption search movement and contemporary adoption narratives that equate self-knowledge with family knowledge. Her loyalty and affection for the people who raised her is offset by a sense of alienation. News of her adoption gives her insight into differences she previously perceived: "I knew they were fair and I was dark; they were stout and I was slender; they were slow and I was quick" ("HVM" 217). But that news also leaves her with a sense that she does not know who she is. In a culture preoccupied by bloodlines and concerns over bad heredity, this socially paralyzing news makes it impossible for her to move forward, for fear that her lack of family—or some information that might come out later—will affect her husband's career.

The solution to adoption's family history problem has frequently been a form of passing, passing for birth kin. Adoption changes the rules of family history; what is ordinarily considered irrefutable evidence of one's status becomes, under the circumstances of adoption, something that can simply be approximated. Adoption makes family history flexible. John's solution to their problem is for her to continue to represent her adoptive family's history as her own. They have "an ancestry that one surely need not be ashamed of" ("HVM" 212). He tells her, "You are known by a worthy [name], which was freely given you, and is legally yours" ("HVM" 211). His reasoning anticipates the approach to adoption that would become common for most of the twentieth century. During the period of official "matching" policies (roughly the 1920s to the 1970s), adoptees were placed in families with whom they shared a physical resemblance, and they were encouraged to take on the history of their adoptive family as if it were their own. Early matching efforts centered on physical features, race, ethnicity, intelligence, and religion. Specialists felt this strategy would encourage bonding among all family members. Though socially acceptable, the practice, in Clara's mind, is a pretense. Her adoptive family's name, to her, "seems like a garment—something external, accessory, and not a part of myself. It does not mean what one's own name would signify" ("HVM" 211). Clara rightly points out that a "good name," a metonym for "good blood" (itself a metaphor for essential connectedness and racial purity), no longer means the same thing if she does not actually share that blood. With orphancy and adoption, an individual is removed from the substantiating power of a family history; under these circumstances, the truth of family history becomes a collectively agreed-on fiction.

The integrity of family history as verification of pure bloodlines disintegrates with the introduction of orphancy and adoption. The situation seems untenable, a failure of adoption as a model of birth kinship, yet Chesnutt does not leave Clara in limbo. He introduces a mysterious stranger who knows

Clara's story and can validate her family history. While this story provides the answers Clara looks for, the reader recognizes that her "true" family history, as presented by the stranger, remains just as fictional as the adoptive family history she will not claim. As Mrs. Harper, the stranger, tells the story of Clara's birth parents and her orphancy, Clara jumps to the conclusion that Mrs. Harper was Clara's "Virginia mammy," rather than to the more obvious explanation that the woman, a light-skinned African American and former slave, is actually Clara's mother. Every piece of information revealed about her family can be read either as evidence that Clara is the legitimate white offspring of one of Virginia's first families or that she descends from a relationship between a slaveholder and his slave. Clara seizes on details about the couple's history as proof of her white ancestry. The woman remarks, "Your father was a Virginia gentleman, and belonged to one of the first families, the Staffords, of Melton County." Clara responds with satisfaction, saying, "I have often felt it. Blood will always tell." About her mother, she is told, "Your mother—also belonged to one of the first families of Virginia, and in her veins flowed some of the best blood of the Old Dominion" ("HVM" 220–21). The dash represents a slight hesitation, which recurs each time Mrs. Harper describes Clara's mother, and it suggests that she is withholding information. Her statement subtly indicates an important distinction between the two families; both parents "belonged" to first families, but one was a legitimate member, while the other was the human property of one of those families. That Clara's mother had "some of the best blood of the Old Dominion" flowing in her is no doubt true, reflecting the long history of masters exploiting their female slaves. Like the perceptive reader, John hears this story and understands the truth, that the woman Clara encounters is actually her birth mother, not her "mammy." The woman offers a silent plea to John to keep her secret, and he willingly complies, proving his earlier claim that ancestry really does not matter to him. The story ends with Clara satisfied that she has learned the truth of her past and playfully gloating about her family's prominence as the couple prepares to marry.

One of the many ironies of this story's conclusion lies in the "first family" status of Clara's birth family. Clara, who had no family history, suddenly finds herself part of an elite family. The Freudian family romance is borne out for Clara, who discovers that she is actually the equivalent of American royalty.[5] Although John immediately picks up on the evidence that Mrs. Harper is her birth mother, Clara seizes on the version of the story that most appeals to her, one that allows her access to social—and, implicitly, racial—superiority. Clara's haste suggests that she subconsciously senses the truth that her fiancé and Mrs.

Harper agree to conceal, so she does not ask a lot of questions, concerned only about what this information will mean for her future. That she may recognize the subtext in Mrs. Harper's account has already been foreshadowed by apprehension that she expresses earlier in the story: "I feel that even if I had but simply to turn my hand to learn who I am and whence I came, I should shrink from taking the step, for fear that what I might learn would leave me forever unhappy" ("HVM" 212). Indeed, she merely needs to look around to see the resemblance between her and Mrs. Harper that the narrator observes ("HVM" 219). Beyond her love for John, her precarious financial situation helps to clarify the stakes in her choice to embrace the story that most readily allows her to get married. A dance instructor, Clara recently took on a class of African American students in an attempt to make ends meet. At first apprehensive, she comes to find that she "hardly think[s] of them as any different from other people. I feel perfectly at home among them" ("HVM" 215). The irony, of course, is that she actually is "at home" with them, sharing, as she does, many of the commonalities of skin color and achievement that this group of the "talented tenth"[6] possesses. Choosing to believe the narrative that makes her white, however, allows her to get married and ensures a financial security that has been lacking in her life previously.

While Clara believes that she knows the truth of her family background, the reader understands that family history is not absolute, that it can be fictionalized when necessary. In her enthusiasm about belonging to one of Virginia's first families, Clara embraces the highly sanitized mythology of well-documented "bloodlines," yet readers recognize a more complicated view. While some of the best blood of the commonwealth indeed flows in Clara—as in her mother—she could probably not legally claim her status as a member of one of Virginia's "first families" if the true story were to come out. The adoption story allows Chesnutt to challenge the prevailing mythology of elite white families by introducing the obvious, though often unacknowledged, history of race mixing that underlies it. Only certain people qualify as members of Virginia's first families. Clara's pride in her newly discovered origins suggests that she, this newest representative, will declare her family's elite heritage, all the while unwittingly possessing the crucial one drop of blood. This irony reminds us that family history—no matter how well documented—can be faked. While it remains the source of the first families' sense of superiority, it is ultimately an unreliable signifier, a myth used to uphold the status quo.

Clara's adoption facilitates an act of inadvertent passing, as she claims white ancestry to which she is not legally entitled. Family history is meant to prevent passing or other attempts to achieve white racial privilege, and the fact that the passer Clara can be considered white suggests the vulnerability of the plantocracy elite. Family history is only as reliable as those who validate it, and even they may be willing to alter the truth for their own purposes, as John's intervention demonstrates. Recognizing, as he does, that Clara only understands part of what Mrs. Harper tells her, John has the power to clarify the story, reveal Clara's ancestry, and even call off the engagement, but he does not. Instead, he wordlessly conspires with Mrs. Harper to keep the secret, throwing his weight behind a whitewashed version of events for the sake of his fiancée's—and his own—happiness. Family history thus becomes more complicated with John's intervention. Clara's perception of events is not only a fiction but one that advances John's own interests. All along, the reader is meant to approve of John's progressive thinking when it comes to ancestry. For instance, earlier in the narrative, when Clara cites his impressive genealogy, he replies that none of it matters: "For the past we can claim no credit, for those who made it died with it. Our destiny lies in the future" ("HVM" 212). His attitude does not change, as reflected by his willingness to disregard information that many white men might have used as grounds to end the relationship. Nevertheless, it offers an important lesson in white privilege, as he bends the rules of the color line because it suits his purposes, romantic as they are. Concerning the choice between exposing his girlfriend's mixed racial background and keeping it a secret so that she can unwittingly pass for white, the story clearly privileges his decision to ignore the one-drop rule. Even so, his actions illustrate the arbitrariness of the mechanisms upholding white power, which derives, the story reveals, from its selective and sometimes benign application. Beyond that, Chesnutt sends a subtle but clear message that passing happens and should be tolerated. After all, why should a perfectly good love story be ruined by the one-drop rule?

Hidden beneath this seemingly happy ending, however, is another message about white privilege, in the degree to which John and Clara's future depends on Mrs. Harper's willingness to sacrifice her own claim to her daughter in order to ensure the couple's happiness. The circumstances of her life are tragic. As she and her fiancé ran away together to escape U.S. racial codes, they were in a steamboat accident. She lost her fiancé and assumed that her daughter also died; furthermore, without free papers, she was sold back into slavery. All of these trials would make the reunion with her daughter that much more desirable, compensation for all that she has lost. Instead, she puts aside her own needs for the sake of her daughter and her fiancé. John's choice, as well as Mrs. Harper's decision to hide her identity and let Clara believe what she wants, undermines the power of family history to establish racial categories. The well-documented family histories that uphold white power can be fictionalized, and white and black family members sometimes collude to uphold the fiction of racial purity to serve their own ends. Moreover, the collusion does not serve all members of the family equally, as Mrs. Harper's sacrifice indicates. Perhaps the greatest irony—and Chesnutt's little joke—is that the proudest representatives of white superiority, those deeply invested in the mythology of the Old South plantocracy, pass through life oblivious of their own mixed-race background, but the bitter pill underneath that joke is that such subversions of the color caste system still have adverse consequences for those who get left behind.

The portrayal of orphancy and adoption in "Her Virginia Mammy" shows how family history, an important source of racial verification, can be a fiction. The unreliability of family history and of the documents that supposedly validate it returns in Chesnutt's final novel, *The Quarry*, written in 1928, shortly before his death, and published in 1999. When Chesnutt began writing again at the height of the Harlem Renaissance, after having abandoned the craft when his sales were not strong enough to support his family, he felt that African Americans had turned a new corner. *The Quarry* reflects optimism about the ways in which restrictive racial roles could be sidestepped to yield greater personal agency for African Americans.[7] In this novel, written thirty years after "Her Virginia Mammy," Chesnutt revisits the ways in which family is the source of racial meaning, in terms of both individual identity and social category. In this text, adoption and orphancy detach the individual from the family, allowing its absence to call attention to the work it usually does to construct racial meaning. Donald Glover, the orphaned protagonist, moves from white adoptive family to black and functions as a blank signifier whose racial category is literally determined by his family context. Donald's unique status shows the signs that work together to make race meaningful—particularly reputation, phenotype, and heredity—and the way those signs can be reconfigured to undermine the racial status quo.

The Quarry is the story of Donald Glover, a young man who, as a baby, is adopted by a white couple, the Seatons. At the time of the adoption, the Seatons decline the opportunity to view Donald's records. Mrs. Seaton says, "I don't attach a great deal of importance to heredity. This is a good and beautiful baby and I'm willing to take him on faith. I don't see how he could have anything but a good heredity" (Q 10). Later, when he is about two, their friends start to whisper that Donald looks like a "little coon." His parents finally examine his file and come to find that Donald's father is reputed to be a "light mulatto," though they never actually locate him. They contemplate the idea of ignoring the one drop and raising Donald as white, but the Seatons eventually decide to relinquish him to an African American couple, the Glovers, to raise. The Glovers rear Donald to be a "race man"—well educated and a leader of his people. During Donald's adolescence, Mr. Seaton returns, offering to readopt him, but Donald refuses to leave his parents. Donald's very light complexion introduces the possibility of passing, an option that he considers several times but rejects. Roughly twenty years later, Mr. Seaton is notified by the hospital from which he adopted Donald that the young man's records had been mixed up with someone else's and that, in fact, his parents were both Americans descended from elite European families with absolutely no documented African blood. Mr. Seaton informs Donald, offering again to take him under his wing and give him all the opportunities that a rich white man can have, but Donald refuses, preferring to remain a member of the community that fostered him. Emphasizing his commitment to the African American community, the novel ends with Donald's marriage to his college sweetheart, a black woman.

Even this brief synopsis of the novel reveals the degree to which family is the primary determinant of Donald Glover's race. As an orphan with no family history, he is a blank signifier, implicitly taking on the racial identity of the family that has custody of him. Because of his age when the initial adoption is disrupted, Donald has no capacity to express a racial identity of his own. He is simply at the whim of the family, which provides the context for learning the roles associated with his racial group. When he is with the Seatons, he is reared to be white, until speculation about his racial background disrupts the adoption. His relocation from one family into another alters only his context—nothing else changes. Glover's fate as an adoptee reveals the extent to which perceived racial "traits" are a result of environmental influences rather than heredity—so much so, in fact, that only his family's racial status can determine his place on the color line. In this novel, characters draw on conventional notions of heredity, phenotype, and reputation to make sense of Donald's race. The novel encourages us to examine how these racial markers define perceptions of whiteness and blackness and work to uphold white supremacy in particular. It also demonstrates, however, the ways in which these racial signs can just as easily be reconfigured to undermine it.

One of the root causes of the Seatons' problem is their desire to keep the adoption of young Donald a secret; by not telling anyone that they adopted him, they have him pass for birth kin. The motivation is not difficult to understand. For one thing, they may not want their fertility issues to become public knowledge. Likewise, they are enamored with Donald's beauty and charm, attributes that reflect well on them when people assume him to be their biological offspring. Furthermore, in the early twentieth century, notions of inheritable traits widely influenced the public, affecting not only how they thought about race but also how they approached adoption. A broad range of conditions and circumstances—including physical and mental deformities, poverty, addiction, prostitution, and illegitimacy—were attributed to heredity. Adoption could be seen as a risky undertaking, something better kept quiet. Mrs. Seaton's declaration that she does not hold with the "doctrine of heredity," implying that she does not believe that an orphan of unknown background will automatically inherit his or her birth parents' bad habits, most likely refers to the taint of illegitimacy, something with which the adopted in particular were associated. Mrs. Seaton's professed unconcern reads initially as a sign of progressive thinking. It also signals a rejection of the developing institution of adoption in the early twentieth century that turned to the science of heredity to help manage the risks of adoption. As Mark Jerng observes,

> The modern twentieth-century institution of adoption was constructed in the context of Progressive reform, changing conceptions of motherhood and children, and the developing social science with regard to families and children. Social work agencies armed themselves with the expertise of social science on issues of heredity, the impact of the environment, and child care in order to justify their work in deciding which babies fit with which families and in ensuring that the parents were fit and proper. (91–92)

Jerng goes on to argue that the portrayal of adoption in this novel introduces the "problem of reference" that accompanies the absence of origin (113). This problem includes the reference to racial origin but rests as well on the lack of familial reference.

At first passing for birth kin, which secrecy encourages, works well for the Seatons and their new baby, but eventually it exacerbates the issues of racial difference that the family confronts. Donald's ambiguous heritage lies dormant in the family. It lurks below the surface and returns to become an issue when a visitor suggests that Donald looks like a "little coon." One woman remarks, "Perhaps he is. . . . The darky blood is very persistent, and some of the best families of the South are likely to be embarrassed by an occasional throwback to some ancestor of whose very existence they were ignorant. I think her grandmother came from Virginia, or was it Louisiana?" (Q 17). The very suggestion that Donald may have African ancestry comes solely through a visible marker of race that one woman believes she sees in his features, and that suspicion alone becomes a dire threat to the family's reputation. Ironically, Mrs. Seaton's friends leap to the conclusion of miscegenation, never considering the presumably more benign reason for any lack of family resemblance: adoption.

The crisis created by this supposition reenacts in a microcosm the anxiety over miscegenation in the United States. The perceived dangers of race passing include the possibility that a white person might accidentally marry and have children with someone of mixed ancestry, thus tainting white racial purity. The idea that Donald may not be white introduces the implications of miscegenation into the intimacy of this family. His biological uncertainty leaves his identity with no anchor, allowing the racial signs surrounding him to be read in a variety of conflicting ways. Heredity, once no big thing, becomes very important. Clearly, Mrs. Seaton's earlier disdain of the politics of heredity does not extend to the one-drop rule. The novel's narrator comments,

> No matter how liberal one might be in the matter of birth, however one might decry heredity and rely upon environment for the development of mind and character, it would be unreasonable to expect, in the United States, that the suggestion that the adopted son of white foster parents might have some Negro blood should prove anything but disquieting, so the pedigree of little Donald became, instead of a negligible thing, a matter of very great importance to the Seatons. (Q 18)

The most disquieting aspect of the situation is that the Seatons have allowed people to assume that Donald is their birth child; thus, the taint of the purported one drop extends to his adoptive parents as well. As the women's comments about Donald's race reveal, Mrs. Seaton's Southern ancestry and her own racial status become implicated, placing the entire family's social status at risk as a result of Donald's perceived racial difference.

The family's racial purity rests on reputation, something suddenly precarious, and the signs that might initially have signaled the family's whiteness can just as easily be read as racially suspect. The family is threatened by a combination of suspicion and innuendo, substantiated by observers with the racial logic of phenotype, biology, and family. The only suggestion of Donald's blackness is his skin color, described elsewhere in the novel as "Mediterranean" and "olive." The guest reads it to signify "coon," and then the group creates a narrative to justify the suspicion, linking Donald's olive skin to Mrs. Seaton's maternal ancestry in the South. What begins as an aspersion on Donald becomes a taint borne by and located within the entire family. Because the Seatons are reputed to be white, Donald, too, is assumed to be white; likewise, when Donald is thought to be black, not only is his reputation impugned, but so is his family's. The meanings associated with this "discovery" help to complete the narrative that undoes this family. Donald's blackness is connected to his mother, not his father, an allusion to the antebellum practice that makes the race of the child follow the mother's; such a reading endows the guest's speculation with a kind of specious historical credibility. The taint is also located in quasi-biological theories of the "throwback," a manifestation of the one-drop rule that suggests that a distant African ancestor's coloring can resurface many generations later.[8] The one drop will inevitably show itself. This logic of the color line allows Donald's "Mediterranean" complexion to be labeled "coon." Without genealogical evidence to substantiate his whiteness, Donald becomes a threat to the family's white status, and, furthermore, race is revealed as a system of signs that can be manipulated until they yield the desired outcome.

The very implication of blackness threatens the integrity of this adoptive family, demonstrating the pervasiveness of the one-drop rule and emphasizing the tenuousness of whiteness. The white family's racial reputation is not strong enough to hold off the mere speculation that one member might be black. This point is clarified by the unique nature of Donald's racial ambiguity, detached from genealogy and phenotype, the consequence of which is that the mechanics of racial signs are exposed. Through Donald and his situation with the Seatons, Chesnutt attends to the constructedness of whiteness, emphasizing the fragility of the racial codes that uphold white supremacy. In contrast, blackness and black identity, which Donald learns with the Glover family, is presented as hardier than whiteness, not because it somehow escapes being implicated by unreliable racial codes, but because it is also located in other sources, specifically a set of shared values that bond the family much more strongly than phenotype and reputation can.

In his second adoptive family, his mother, Mrs. Glover, takes charge of Donald's rearing, intent on making him a "race man," committed to the race despite—or perhaps because of—his light skin. Like Mrs. Seaton, she, too, eschews the "doctrine of heredity," but unlike Mrs. Seaton, Mrs. Glover's attitude is more historically informed. The narrator notes, "She anticipated the scientists of our day in maintaining that there is no essential intellectual difference in races, any apparent variation being merely a matter of development; that the backwardness of the Negro was due to his historical environment and to the restrictions with which he had always been surrounded and the repressions and inhibitions to which he was still subject" (Q 63). Beyond acknowledging the role that environmental influences play in the diminished progress of some members of the African American community, the passage underscores the fact that Mrs. Glover is committed to racial uplift as a way of improving the condition of African Americans who are less fortunate. She envisions Donald as a leader even greater than "the Crusader," a fictionalized W. E. B. Du Bois: "She saw [Donald] as one who would take hold of this inchoate, mixed mass of people, held together loosely by the dark blood which they shared in varying degree and which, had they been permitted, many of them would willingly have forgotten, but because of which they were forced back upon one another" (Q 64). Her language alludes to Du Bois's "talented tenth," through which the most educated (and often the lightest-skinned) African Americans would lead the masses to a more equitable social position. Like Du Bois—and perhaps Chesnutt—she has a somewhat elitist and messianic vision; nevertheless, she instills a strong sense of community consciousness in her son, who, later in life, commits himself to research aimed at eradicating the race problem.

The Glover family equates racial identity with social activism and a strong sense of values. This attitude creates an alternative narrative to neutralize the virulent racism of the time. For members of the novel's black community, racial identity is attached to commitment, service, and uplift. The family thus serves as the venue for learning about the value of community and, in another sense, makes racial identity something of value, worth cultivating. This alternative to the prevailing narrative of black inferiority is important for understanding Donald Glover's unwillingness to pass for white despite the numerous opportunities offered to him. It also explains why, even after his white "pedigree" is confirmed, he decides to remain with the black community. In this novel, while blackness is associated with community and valuable in its own right, whiteness is defined by a kind of self-serving materialism.

The contrast between these two families demonstrates the degree to which the family is vested with power to define the meaning of race for individuals. That point remains subtle in the early part of the novel, as Donald's move between families and races happens without his input. When he is older, he gets to choose which side of the color line to live on, an option that amplifies the relationship between race and family. Donald's first opportunity to pass comes with the return of Mr. Seaton when Donald is a teenager; Mr. Seaton realizes that perhaps he made a mistake in relinquishing Donald and offers the teenager the opportunity to live with him and be raised as a white boy. As I argued earlier, baby Donald's position in his respective adoptive families determined whether he was white or black. Now, for the first time, he has agency over his racial identity. Both sets of parents make a case for themselves. Mr. Seaton says, "I would send him to a good college and give him all the advantages which money could provide. He is worthy of the best" (Q 86–87). Unlike before, when he represented a potential racial alien in the family, Donald now becomes worthy of Seaton's investment; nevertheless, Donald's one drop would still need to be concealed. The Glovers acknowledge the material benefits that Mr. Seaton can provide and articulate them as "education, luxury, travel, society. . . . The freedom and opportunity that is open to a white man will all be yours." They declare that they "love him as a son," but they leave the decision up to him (Q 90).

This division between two families highlights yet again the unique situation Donald is in as a result of his orphancy. On one level, the expectation that this young man can move from family to family indefinitely diminishes the significance of his attachment to any one of them. This scenario says little for the integrity of adoptive families, but, of course, Chesnutt is not concerned with adoptive families as such in this novel. Instead, the potential to change families introduces Donald's own agency into the mix, allowing him to choose which racial group he wants to claim. His autonomy complicates the racializing power of the family unit: his capacity to decide for himself undercuts some of the influence of family in determining his racial identity, yet the situation is a reminder that family remains a primary context for how one knows race and for how one's race is known publicly. His choice is not solely about one racial group over another but about which family he will live with; should he choose Mr. Seaton, he must cut his ties with the Glover family, since a white man cannot be raised by a black family. Detached from the categorizing power of phenotype and genealogy, Donald has an unusual degree of autonomy to define himself as he wishes. That he chooses to remain with the Glovers and claim black identity privileges the value of being black. Chesnutt's novel juxtaposes the materialism of living in the white world with the personal and social value in being a member of the black community and determines that blackness is preferable.

Chesnutt's depictions of this and other opportunities Donald has to pass offer an extended meditation on the constructedness of whiteness. The novel represents whiteness as learned and sustained by a complex interplay of racial signs and deployed by other whites to suit their purposes. Each of Donald's opportunities to pass is offered by white people who will benefit from having Donald on their side of the color line. Passing narratives often focus on the advantages of whiteness for African Americans, but few point out that passing might benefit whites, too, and that white people might be willing to ignore the strictures of the one-drop rule if it suits their purposes. The unacknowledged secret of passing is that white people sometimes want and need light-skinned African Americans to pass. For example, Mr. Seaton wants Donald back because he is smart and handsome and presents a striking contrast to Seaton's own scrawny, sickly, unsuccessful children. Having Donald as a protégé would bring Seaton pleasure and would also reflect well on him with his peers. At the bottom of it, Seaton wants to be associated with Donald and willingly offers him the prize of whiteness in exchange. The other opportunities to pass depicted in the novel also show how passing actually benefits white people; these individuals might offer Donald something he wants, but just as important, he will provide them with something that they want, too. One of Donald's girlfriends, a white woman, suggests that they marry, and when he refuses, citing social disapproval for mixed marriages, she says, "Why be a Negro?" and encourages him to "forget it and come with me" (*Q* 133–34). His passing would benefit her by removing the only impediment to their marriage. Another white girlfriend offers Donald an opportunity to star in a film alongside her, but he must obscure his black identity, so he declines. This woman would earn a starring role if she could convince Donald to pass. The brother of yet another white girlfriend asks Donald to pass so that the couple may marry and Donald can join their elite European family, and once again, he refuses. Each case demonstrates how the color line can be selectively ignored according to white interests.

In each instance when passing is offered to Donald Glover, he refuses it, until the end of the novel, when he is informed that the records that supposedly verified his black blood were actually wrong and that he has a meticulously documented all-white genealogy. At that point, he decides to keep his white ancestry secret, choosing instead to pass for black, to show his commitment to the black community that nurtured him and, more personally, to allow him to marry the woman he loves. Both Mr. Seaton—who investigates the story told in the records—and Glover accept that the records documenting his white genealogy are accurate, yet we, as readers, should be more skeptical, since they, like the earlier ones, may not be Donald's at all. The novel has already demonstrated that records can get lost or mislabeled, and as "Her Virginia Mammy" points out, family history can be fictionalized. So how much can we trust these records to be true? Moreover, why does Chesnutt, who has built such a fruitful narrative on the confusion that comes from genealogical ambiguity, choose to restore Donald to an irrefutably documented family history?

Like everyone, Chesnutt is a product of his time and culture. As an author, he used passing to implicitly argue for the arbitrary nature of the racial order. Passing narratives of his time almost always juxtaposed racial passing with the passer's prior, more authentic identity.[9] Passing, in these texts, usually enacts an identity that the passer cannot legitimately claim. The gap between the prior, prepassing identity and the new identity claimed through the act of passing helps to prove that race is a performance, not an essential reality. If one can perform a role he or she is not entitled to, the role itself loses any semblance of authenticity. Passing narratives need a prior identity to make the case that race is a performance, and Chesnutt needed Donald Glover to have an authenticated identity to make what he probably felt was a more radical point about racial constructedness: that a man who has every right to a white identity would prefer to remain black. Chesnutt inverts the tropes of the passing narrative to show not only that race is a performance but that blackness can be more personally and socially valuable than whiteness.

Although the coupling of passing and adoption in *The Quarry* and "Her Virginia Mammy" introduces the possibility that all race is unknowable without the pretense of a family history—something itself unreliable—Chesnutt backs away from this rather radical argument in order to examine the power of whiteness more closely. His depiction of white characters manipulating the color line and all of its associated signs for their own purposes highlights the privilege that accompanies whiteness. An author who had sympathized with passing in earlier texts, Chesnutt distances himself from the attractions of whiteness, to expose it as somewhat pedestrian at the same time that it remains a powerful asset. Characters who bend the rules of the color line are motivated by rather mundane concerns, even as their actions tacitly acknowledge the inequalities that restrict the lives of the nonwhite. Underneath this arbitrariness is shallow materialism, as the rules get altered for profit; the power in whiteness comes from what it can buy or from the access it allows, not from some kind of intimate, personal value. When we contrast this image to that of blackness, which gains a sense of personal importance through kin ties and social activism, Chesnutt's decision to have Donald pass for black rather than acknowledge his white ancestry turns the value system of race on its head. But this reading is impossible without the unique perspective provided by orphancy and adoption, which extract Donald from the norms of kinship to expose how race is constructed on the level of the family. While fraught with complications, the disruptions of biological norms that accompany orphancy and adoption become, at least for Chesnutt, an important opportunity to step outside the bio-logically based racial system that dominated his era. Chesnutt's choice, in the end, to locate his adoptees in definitive racial categories raises important questions taken up in the next chapter: What are the implications when circumstances (or authors) refuse to confirm a character's racial category? What does that mean for characters and for the racial system itself? Finally, what does it tell us about adoption's potential for moving beyond rigid biogenetic categories?

CHAPTER 3

Unknowable Origins in Kate Chopin's "Désirée's Baby" and William Faulkner's *Light in August*

If the sins of the past, most of all the original sins of miscegenation, exist as silent mechanisms that govern behavior for generations to come, identity itself becomes a social construct of the most brittle, coincidental kind. Under the taboo of miscegenation which had become ingrained into the highest law of segregation, in fact, identity itself, either in an act of self-recognition or in the attribution of identity to another, had become a radical act of imagination. Despite the flood of racial theory that posited incontrovertible biological proof of racial differences, race remained, for all to see, a tormenting philosophical abstraction. (Sundquist 398)

This chapter explores an issue raised by Charles W. Chesnutt's fiction: the importance of family in defining racial categories in the Jim Crow era. Unlike Chesnutt's protagonists, whose obscure familial origins are eventually clarified with some sort of documentation that also locates them in a purportedly definitive racial category, Désirée in Kate Chopin's short story "Désirée's Baby" (1893) and Joe Christmas in William Faulkner's *Light in August* (1932) never learn anything certain about their ancestry. Orphancy detaches them from an identifying family lineage, and adoption, while providing a family, does not ensure their "bloodlines." Moreover, as a result of the one-drop rule, their light skin cannot guarantee their whiteness, so their race remains unconfirmed. Although they look white, their social standing is precarious, open to reevaluation if their race comes into question. Through orphancy and adoption, Chopin and Faulkner imagine transgressive figures who defy rigid racial codes, and these characters serve as a means of exploring the degree of constraint that works on individuals in a racially divided society. Unlike Chesnutt's protagonists, racial and familial ambiguity do not afford the characters in these texts the opportunity for liberatory self-fashioning; instead, racial uncertainty prompts individuals and communities to turn to biogenetic explanations for difference, with tragic consequences for the orphan-adoptees.

Unverifiable origins present a particular problem in late nineteenth-century and early twentieth-century American culture generally and specifically in the region of the South, the setting for these texts. Southern identity of this time period was embedded in narratives that connected individuals with the region through the retelling of family stories across generations (Stephens 3). Robert O. Stephens examines the specific ways that Southern families—fictional and real—socialize their members in response to the Civil War and the depression and poverty that followed it.

> The southern family has had to function as the individual's link with the past, as the place where cultural values are learned at the mother's knee, as an extension of church and school, as a model for manners, and as a matrix for models of citizenship and leadership. Indeed, the southern family has functioned primarily as families do in ethnic groups, by serving as a source for identification of the group, by allowing the family member to confine his social relationships to his own ethnic group during all stages of his life, and by adapting national patterns of behavior and values to its own cultural system. (2–3)

The family thus instills a sense of identity in individuals by mediating their relationships with various groups and communities. To put it another way, personal identity is created within the family context and relative (so to speak) to the community.

The family plays another crucial role, socializing individuals into their racial place. As Stephanie Coontz explains, "A family is the unit that determines the rights and obligations of its members in terms of inheritance, use of the prevailing set of resources, and initial 'social placement' . . . into the social configuration of labor and rewards" (11). One aspect of social placement involves the development of a sense of racial identity with which to navigate society. Personal racial identity cultivated within a family collaborates with the family narratives that provide individuals with a historical consciousness grounded in the South. These narratives also collaborate with the elusive measure of racial "blood" to distinguish black from white, for social and, more

significantly, legal purposes. As Eva Saks documents, legal inheritance rights after the Civil War were based on the unquantifiable—indeed, metaphorical—
concept of "black blood." Without measurable substance yet legally foolproof,
racial blood required other mechanisms to make it "real." Saks says, "On a substantive level, genealogy was made the determinant of race, thereby marking
former slaves permanently black and, within the values of miscegenation, as a
genetic underclass" (67). Family reputation, guaranteed through genealogy and
family history, helped to uphold the racial order. Family and racial identity
were mutually dependent, resting on biological kinship as well as a definition of
race as biological.

In this way, Southern family narratives carried a great deal of weight, but
they did not necessarily have to be "true" to function as a socializing mechanism. In fact, they required enough flexibility to respond to the current reality
of the family and region. Stephens notes,

> Central to all stories is the tendency to make them serve the family's needs: to
> provide a sense of social placement, to suggest paradigms for survival, to ex-
> plain the present, to establish a sense of unity, and to supply clues to tacit un-
> derstandings within the family. If the facts of history disagree, family stories
> imaginatively reshape the past to fit the family's vision of itself. Each generation
> has to reinvent the family past according to its own needs. (8)

Reinvention is a necessary facet of family stories, allowing the family to adjust
its sense of itself in a changing world by reframing the narrative. A family may
reinvent the past to preserve its reputation in response to new information or
to adapt to changing social norms. Much as family reputation authenticates a
family's whiteness, it also facilitates the adaptation of these family narratives,
providing "cover" for any variation. Even with their fictive qualities, these family narratives help to serve the status quo.

Collective origin stories shared within families—the kind Stephens addresses—become complicated when they try to accommodate orphans and
adoptees, who lack definitive personal histories to account for familial and
racial belonging. Orphans, particularly those who lose their families as infants,
may have no access to family information, while adoptees have a slightly different problem. Those who "pass" for biological kin, like Chesnutt's Donald
Glover, might adopt their families' genealogies and thus be shielded by their
confirmed history, but even the awareness of the adoptee's biological otherness
within the family means that his or her uncertain origins remain in play, liable

to become an issue at any moment. In response to the absence of reliable origin stories, transracial adoptees create flexible narratives that, much like the Southern narratives discussed by Stephens, help adoptees position themselves socially; at the same time, adoptees' fictive origin stories are oriented specifically toward compensating for what they do not know, a practice ethnographer Sandra Patton documents in her study of adult transracial adoptees born in the mid-twentieth century (6–7). Adoptees' origin stories must be adaptable to new information revealed over the course of a lifetime, after accessing birth records, meeting birth families, or learning new information from adoptive parents. Of contemporary adoptees, Patton observes, "our origin stories are told and retold, constructed and reconstructed as we come into being" (33).

Literature scholar Margaret Homans also argues that adoption's origin stories are fictive, but she focuses on both fictional and autobiographical narratives rather than ethnography. She asserts that contemporary adoption narratives are more about the present than about a past that cannot ever be accessed ("Adoption Narratives" 2), and she goes on to say that adoption "compels the creation of plausible if not verifiable narratives" to respond to adoptees' "absence at the origins" and to provide a personal narrative that can serve their present needs ("Adoption Narratives" 7). The studies by Patton and Homans are based on adoption practices vastly different from those of the early twentieth century, a time when racial difference in the adoptive family was most likely accidental and intolerable to society; nevertheless, the problem of adoption's uncertain origins and the turn to "plausible" narratives in response both add new insight to "Désirée's Baby" and *Light in August*. Orphancy and adoption illustrate the ways in which the racially ambiguous disrupt the social order, as well as the mechanism—flexible, if not necessarily "logical," narratives—that help to restore it again. Homans's contemporary frame of reference privileges the autonomy of individuals and their families to define themselves, an autonomy less available to the characters in "Désirée's Baby" and *Light in August*. Patton, while covering ground similar to Homans, emphasizes the degree to which fictive responses to adoption's absences come from a much broader set of sources beyond the individual or family; they include social institutions such as adoption agencies, social welfare offices, and the legal system, all of which work on adoptees in the service of sustaining racial, class, and gender narratives that extend beyond any one person.

This chapter combines these approaches to fictive narrative and ambiguous origins to read transracial adoption in "Désirée's Baby" and *Light in August*. Attending to the creation of plausible but fictive origins exposes how characters, authors, and readers respond to the absence of racializing characteristics. As floating signifiers, both Désirée and Joe Christmas are constructed into being by familial, social, and institutional forces. Their ambiguity leaves them open to the application of new and different narratives that attempt to locate them in a definitive racial category. They have very little power to resist the narratives imposed on them, a situation that illustrates the negative consequences of being without the qualities that otherwise anchor identity. Through these characters, the authors depict the racial system as socially contingent and imagine individuals to be almost powerless against it. Désirée is perhaps the most powerless, in the sense that Chopin grants her no agency to resist racializing narratives; even in her passivity, however, her racial ambiguity still threatens the social system until it is definitively contained. In contrast, Joe Christmas is more an agent of his own identity than he might appear at first glance. Constructed into an alienating sense of uncertainty about his family history, he still resists the imposition of a firm racial category. In both texts, attending to adoption reveals the stakes in their sometimes inexplicable decisions—namely, Désirée's suicide and Christmas's apparent capitulation to the lynch mob who seeks him—because it emphasizes the degree to which their problems with racial categories can also be understood as family problems resulting from unstable genealogies. Both narratives suggest the impossibility of remaining outside of the binarized racial system, a position that renders racial and familial ambiguity quite literally fatal. Through these nonnormative characters, Chopin and Faulkner express significant pessimism about the possibility that the racial order can be subverted or resisted in any meaningful way.

Kate Chopin's short story "Désirée's Baby" depicts the writing and rewriting of origin stories to serve the interests of those around the adoptee and in preservation of the racial status quo. As a child, Désirée was found asleep in the shadow of a pillar on the Valmondé estate, presumed to have been left by a group of Texans passing by, but once Madame Valmondé sees the baby, she concludes that "Désirée had been sent to her by a beneficent Providence to be the child of her affection, seeing that she was without child of the flesh" ("DB" 240). Désirée is a blank slate. Although her pale skin suggests that she is white, the cultural convictions that race is located in "blood" and, moreover, that white skin could mask "invisible blackness" mean that her race can only be confirmed through genealogy. Initially, however, Désirée's ambiguity allows her newly adoptive mother to think of her as a child of God, which supersedes any concern about her earthly origins. As the child of affection, Désirée does not necessarily need to possess a "good name" to be worthy of her adoptive mother's love. If anything, in a sentimental story such as this one, it may actually lend to the initial bond, as Désirée's lack of a sheltering family makes her sympathetic and in need of a mother's care, and the fact that she looks white seems enough, at least initially, to let them believe that she actually is white.

When Désirée grows up and falls in love with Armand Aubigny, a local plantation owner, the problem of origins easily dismissed in her infancy becomes more important. As the couple prepares to marry, Désirée's father wonders if they should investigate her "obscure origin," but Armand "looked into her eyes and did not care. He was reminded that she was nameless. What did it matter about a name when he could give her one of the oldest and proudest in Louisiana?" ("DB" 241). As in "Her Virginia Mammy," a good name is synonymous with good ancestry, a quality further meant to ensure racial purity. Also as in Chesnutt's fiction, the importance of a good name is at the discretion of the white ruling class. Armand loves Désirée, so her origins do not initially matter, because he sees her as he wants her to be, "beautiful and gentle, affectionate and sincere" ("DB" 240). Ellen Peel notes that Désirée serves as a blank slate not just for her mother but for her fiancé as well. Both her ambiguous origins and her passivity allow them to "project their desires," as her name suggests, for an ideal daughter or wife on her (Peel 225). Overlaying both characters' affection for Désirée is the degree to which her beauty and purity epitomize ideal white womanhood, an image that upheld the racial order in the Jim Crow period.

The title "Désirée's Baby" indicates the story's central conflict. Désirée and Armand's firstborn son has some undisclosed physical characteristic that suggests that he might be black, and everyone else notices before Désirée. When she finally sees something herself and asks her husband, he says, "It means . . . that the child is not white; it means that you are not white" ("DB" 243). Désirée informs her mother, who encourages her to come back to her childhood home with the baby, but when she leaves, she does not follow the road back to the plantation and instead walks off into the bayou, never to be heard from again. As the blank slate on which her family projected their ideals, Désirée can easily be redefined as the source of her child's coloring; blamed for possessing invisible blackness, she has no documentable ancestry to disprove the allegation. The lack of family name that was previously no problem suddenly becomes imperative in the context of marriage and reproduction, because she has failed to produce a white heir. After Désirée's suicide, Armand burns everything that belongs to her or to the baby and then throws into the fire a "remnant of one back in the drawer from which he took [Désirée's letters]," a letter from his own mother to his father, which says that she hopes he will never find out that his mother "belongs to the race that is cursed with the brand of slavery" ("DB" 244–45). More than just a shocking ironic twist, this revelation undermines virtually every conclusion drawn by the reader previously, creating a narrative disruption that mirrors the personal disruption that occurs in the absence of defined racial categories. This new information demands a revision of those previous conclusions and the reinvention of a plausible narrative in response.

One major narrative problem is how to interpret Armand's behavior in light of the story's last line. Did he find the letter after Désirée left, or had he known about it previously and secreted it away? If he found the letter only after the fact, then the irony derives from the implication that she died for a "sin" of which she is not actually guilty, the innocent victim of her husband's racial transgression. Leaving aside the assumptions about race conveyed through this interpretation, that irony intensifies with many readers' conclusion, not necessarily true, that Désirée must actually be white, a point I will return to after exploring the second possibility: that Armand had seen the letter before and knew about his own ancestry all along. Such a scenario is not without precedent in passing fiction. For instance, in Langston Hughes's "Passing" (1934), the narrator, a light-skinned man passing for white, claims that if his white wife has a dark-skinned baby, he will accuse her of adultery to protect his racial status. Although "Désirée's Baby" precedes Hughes's story, Werner Sollors documents the numerous cases in antiquity of genealogy actually vindicating white women who had borne dark children and were thus accused of adultery with a black man; by the end of the nineteenth century, however, genealogy could implicate as "black" a woman who gave birth to a dark child, without adultery even being mentioned. Sollors observes that "Désirée's Baby" bears a striking resemblance to earlier stories involving adultery and declares it "noteworthy" that the very idea of adultery does not even arise in the story (*Neither* 68). The fact that Armand fails to propose adultery as a cause of the baby's mysterious racial flaw is, perhaps, a sign of the relative transgressiveness of possessing black ancestry, a point that further informs a reading of Armand as conspiring to blame Désirée in order to protect his own status as a white man. Armand's unwillingness to investigate her family before their marriage supports the possibility that he already knows about his mother; had he confirmed Désirée's ancestry, he could not blame her later for any dark children they might have. Moreover, his "cold" response to her despair, answering her questions "lightly" ("DB" 243), might also suggest that he is not all that surprised about their son's coloring. Finally, his haste to get rid of her could, perhaps, be his attempt to deflect suspicion from himself by resolving the situation as quickly as possible. While there are certainly less nefarious explanations for why Armand responds with cold-ness—for instance, his horror at having accidentally committed miscegena-tion—the text leaves open the distinct possibility that he knew all along. More important, it shows one of the many ways in which Désirée's ambiguity causes an interpretive ripple effect, demanding a reassessment and potential reinven-tion of previous conclusions about Armand, too.

Armand's confirmed identity raises more questions than it answers and re-quires a return to Désirée and her identity in light of this new information. The story's ironic ending implies that, unintentionally or willfully, Armand was wrong: Désirée is not black at all. Readers tend to refer to her as if she were white all along, although there is no more information about her ancestry at the end of the story than there is at the beginning.[1] Perhaps they bring some subconscious assumption that if both parents had black ancestry, then the child would be darker than he is. More likely, however, it comes from the conventions of irony, on which the story's ending relies so heavily. When, at the end, the nar-rative reveals Armand's black ancestry, then Désirée must be the opposite of what readers previously believed her to be, even if there is no textual evidence to support reading her as white. Ellen Peel notes that her unmarkedness also leaves open another possibility: that Désirée also has African ancestry. Peel goes on to say, "Whether or not Désirée is black, the impossibility of knowing her race reveals the fragility of meaning more than Armand's knowable race does" (233). While Peel is right, she does not take the implications of this idea far enough. Désirée's ambiguous origins have repercussions beyond herself and her child, undermining the very notion of "knowable" race altogether by ex-posing, indirectly, the unreliability of purportedly pure ancestral lines, such as Armand's. Désirée's ambiguous origins threaten to expose the potential fictive-ness of even the confirmed origin stories, which, in turn, undermines the sta-bility of a social order dependent on genealogy to guarantee racial purity.

Désirée's suicide remains another of the story's unanswered questions, par-ticularly in regard to what it signals about Chopin's vision of race. On the sur-face, it appears that Désirée walks off into the bayou because of her horror over discovering she might have black blood. Having lost her husband and her sta-tus as a white woman, she makes her social death literal. In light of her am-biguous ancestry, however, another reading is also possible: that she commits suicide because she has no recourse to resist the implication that she might be black. Désirée's suicide is in keeping with her passivity throughout the story. Unwilling or unable to fight Armand's accusation or the social ostracization that she would suffer for being perceived as racially mixed, she chooses death, a fate, presumably, better than being black. There may be a subtle gender dynamic at work here, too. If, as Laura Wexler suggests, Kate Chopin's writing can be understood to express ambivalence about the white supremacist goals of the period, especially since those goals were sometimes advanced in conjunction with domestic violence against white women (Wexler 278), then Désirée, again, has no recourse. Her suicide is a gesture of futility in response to the threat of violence clearly embodied by Armand. Désirée was once the privileged white wife, but now her diminished status means that Armand's violence toward the slaves—frequently referenced in the text—is now transferable to her. The speed with which such a thing can happen, as evidenced by Désirée's rapid fall from grace, speaks to a dark alternative to the cult of "true white womanhood"; just because white women were put on a societal pedestal did not mean that they were protected from violence in their own homes. Désirée's shift in racial status parallels the precarious gender status not only of black women but of white women, too. Whether or not Chopin meant to challenge the racial status quo—Chopin scholars remain at odds about the degree to which her social critique extended to overt antiracist sentiment—she depicts in "Désirée's Baby" a system in which individuals, especially women and those marginalized as a result of their familial ancestry, are powerless against racializing narratives.

Désirée's inability to resist offers a distinct contrast to Joe Christmas, who is, like Désirée, a blank slate as a result of his orphancy and adoption. Christmas becomes the object of elaborate narratives that attempt to place him in a firm category, narratives that are "plausible" only insofar as they meet the needs of those around him. He struggles against these attempts to define him for much of his life, refusing to succumb to the social pressure to pick a single racial category; at the same time, however, he does not attempt to assert a mixed-race identity, either. In choosing to remain outside the racial order, Joe Christmas presents a profound threat to his Southern community, a threat that eventually leads to his death. Faulkner describes Joe Christmas's death in language of martyrdom that offers one final, redemptive identifying narrative, one that serves as Faulkner's commentary on the destructiveness of the South's rigid racial codes.

Light in August interweaves the stories of several characters who exist at the social margins of a rural Mississippi town. The main thread of the story involves Joe Christmas, whose father's ethnic and racial background is largely unknown; although Christmas's maternal grandfather, Doc Hines, calls the father a Mexican, he also maintains that the man was actually black, but neither point can be confirmed. The result is an utterly ambiguous family history, with Christmas's "parchmentcolored skin" (120) unable to categorize him definitively. The grandfather murders Christmas's father and refuses to get medical attention for his own daughter, who dies after giving birth. Doc Hines leaves baby Joe at the door of a white orphanage on Christmas Eve, an act that earns him the surname *Christmas*. Then Hines stays around the orphanage to insinuate to people there that Christmas is a "nigger"; the implication that he might be black results in his hasty adoption placement with the white McEacherns, who are not apprised of his possible mixed blood. With the McEacherns, he is raised in an environment of rigid Presbyterian asceticism. Although he lives as a white boy, Christmas remains conscious of his uncertain racial heritage and eventually runs away from his adoptive home to live on "the street," first as a black man, then as a white man, but in neither case committing himself to any racial category or laying down any roots. He eventually ends up in Jefferson, where he becomes involved in an affair with a white woman, Joanna Burden, who is murdered, presumably by Christmas. A manhunt ensues, fueled by the allegation that Christmas is a black man who has killed a white woman. Eventually caught and jailed, Christmas then escapes from police custody and is finally shot and castrated by a group of vigilantes.

The conditions surrounding Joe Christmas's birth highlight the uncertainty that will haunt him for the rest of his life. Nothing in the text confirms for certain that the circus worker who is identified as his father had "black blood,"[2] and there is every reason to disbelieve the allegation, since it comes from the unbalanced Doc Hines, who, in addition to his insanity, undermines his own account by blurring the distinction between black and Mexican in his description of the man he kills. The murder of his parents also leaves Christmas with virtually no conscious connection to the all-important family history that would help socialize him into the South and convey the rules of race. Like many adoptees, Christmas possesses an origin story that he cannot access and for which he must compensate by creating fictive ones. At the same time, Joe Christmas is not a typical orphan or adoptee; unbeknownst to him, his birth grandfather oversees his early years and, in effect, blurs the boundary between birth family and adoptive family by covertly assuming responsibility for the child. While he has no interest in claiming Christmas as his own kin and exhibits no familial nurturance in any traditional sense, Hines constructs a family narrative for Christmas that replaces the one lost in orphancy, making him, at least temporarily, a kind of adoptive parent.

Doc Hines provides Joe Christmas with an origin narrative, one Christmas himself never fully knows and one that readers learn only at the end of the novel. But rather than defining Christmas racially, Hines merely instills an enduring sense of doubt. To Doc Hines, his grandson represents the consequences of the double "abomination" of miscegenation and promiscuity. In accordance with his belief that Joe Christmas is the embodiment of invisible blackness, Hines initially creates the conditions that make Christmas seem white and then insinuates a purported mixed-race ancestry that subsequently casts doubt on that whiteness. It begins with Christmas's abandonment at the white orphanage, which establishes the child as white even though Hines already believes that he possesses the "one drop" of black blood. Had Hines left him at a black orphanage, Christmas would have been raised as a black child in conformity with the racial rules of the South. In that context, the outrage over miscegenation that Hines associates with Christmas's birth would become largely irrelevant, absorbed into the contradictions of Southern racial norms that recognize someone with one drop of blood as legally black and view race mixing as less problematic when the offspring are confined to the black community. Instead, Hines sets the child up to pass for white, only to impugn his racial purity later, thus enacting the threat that he believes Christmas represents: a purportedly mixed-race person attempting to gain the privileges of whiteness, not the least of which might include sexual relations with a white woman. In Doc Hines's mind, Joe Christmas is not only the potential threat of but also the consequence of miscegenation. All of these developments occur before Christmas is old enough to have any consciousness of it.

Doc Hines is not the only source of the racializing narratives at work on Joe Christmas. The members of the orphanage staff also collaborate to prescribe the child's identity. As one of the first adult influences on Christmas, aside from his grandfather, the dietician helps disseminate the idea that the child might have black ancestry, as revenge for him having "caught" her in a sexual tryst with one of her coworkers. Upon noticing him, she calls him "little nigger bastard" (*LiA* 122), continuing the process of labeling begun by Doc Hines, a process that leads to her having him removed from the orphanage in order to protect her reputation. As the narrator bluntly puts it, "She was . . . stupid enough to believe that a child of five not only could deduce the truth from what he had heard, but that he would want to tell it as an adult would" (*LiA* 123). To complicate this assessment, the dietician can also be seen, as Laura Doyle suggests, as the "corollary" of a "nigger bastard," "something like 'white woman subject to sexual policing'" (345). Like Joe Christmas, she is someone susceptible to identifying narratives that could have negative consequences for her. The "bastard" who lacks racializing markers becomes subject to the projection of the dietician's guilt and fear.

The dietician does not act alone, and the orphanage matron, while a minor character, possesses significant power to define Joe Christmas's identity and his future. Learning from the dietician that the child is actually black, the matron acts quickly to find a family for placement. Her actions mirror those of Doc Hines. Although she believes the child to be African American, she does not do what would be appropriate by the racial rules of the time—that is, send him to a black orphanage or perhaps find a black couple to adopt him. Instead, she passes him off as white by placing him with the McEacherns and not informing them of what she "knows." Even after Mr. McEachern inquires about "parentage," the matron says "immediately, almost a little too immediately: 'We make no effort to ascertain their parentage. . . . If the child's parentage is important to you, you had better not adopt one at all'" (*LiA* 142). Mark Jerng reads the exchange between McEachern and the matron as conveying the values of nineteenth-century religious adoption (102) that treated adoptees as at once property and "children of sin needing to be reformed" (89). While McEachern certainly remains consistent with this mindset, the matron has another motive to deliberately eschew origins: to cover her inability to regulate her own orphanage. In this way, the matron fits Sandra Patton's characterization of contemporary adoption social workers as "omniscient creators," those with institutional power to write adoptees into racial being with whatever information they choose to disclose. In her study, Patton notes several examples of adoptees who learned as adults that agency employees selectively disclosed information that changed the adoptee's racial or ethnic categorization, in essence whitening them up so as not to discourage potential white adopters.[3] As they matured, some had to reconcile the physical markers of racial difference with a narrative that claimed they were just as white as their adoptive families. Patton concludes, "The most striking commonalities in the origin narratives I have discussed center on the role of social institutions in the construction of identity and family. Social welfare agencies and the judicial system implement and enforce ideological definitions of identity, race, ethnicity, gender, (dis)ability, class, and family" (61). While Patton's assessment applies to adoption practices and racial and familial dynamics that are specific to the late twentieth century, her core point sheds light onto how Joe Christmas's identity comes into being, racialized into uncertainty as a result of individuals who, with institutional backing, act in their own self-interest.

The matron has the power to decide if Joe Christmas will be white or black, the only racial categories available to him as he matures and categories that he does not really understand. The orphanage's black gardener spells out the implications of these racializing narratives in a way that articulates the novel's central problem of familial ambiguity. The child, aware that the others call him a "nigger," follows around the only other person in the vicinity who is so called, finally asking him, "How come you are a nigger?" (*LiA* 383). This peculiar question asks not, "Are you one?" but, rather, "What makes you one?" or, perhaps, "What did you do to become one?" The gardener, for whom the term has an unmistakably clear significance, retorts by introducing the polarity that circumscribes Christmas's life. He says to the child, "Who told you I am a nigger, you little white trash bastard? . . . I aint a nigger . . . You are worse than that. You dont know what you are. And more than that, you wont never know. You'll live and you'll die and you wont never know. . . dont nobody but God know what you is" (*LiA* 384). Which is better, Joe Christmas asks, to be a "nigger" or a "white trash bastard"? For the gardener, the answer is clear. While the term may be pejorative, demeaning, and indicative of the lowest social standing, at least a "nigger" knows what he is, knows his family story and his relatives, and he also knows, for better or for worse, his place in the social order. A "white trash bastard" may start out "white trash," but he can still become a "nigger." Being a "bastard" with no known parents might, perhaps, be the most crucial category. It deprives him of a familial reputation to secure his racial status and renders him a blank slate on which the identities of "nigger" and "white trash" become virtually interchangeable, subject to the whims of others.

For most of the novel, identifying narratives are imposed on Joe Christmas by family and institutions, but as Christmas becomes an adult, he has a certain degree of power to identify himself. Initially he experiments with both whiteness and blackness, what Owen Robinson calls a "gradually developing process of self-realisation and experimentation with the series of strict frameworks he is forced to work in" (125). To fully embody the role of whiteness, Christmas "tricked or teased white men into calling him a negro in order to fight them, to beat them or be beaten." Just as completely, he plays the opposite role, that of a black man: "now he fought the negro who called him white." In the north, "he lived with negroes, shunning white people. He ate with them, slept with them, belligerent, unpredictable, uncommunicative. He now lived as man and wife with a woman who resembled an ebony carving" (*LiA* 225). This approximate marital relationship suggests the depth of his exploration. Not a dalliance with a prostitute like many of his other sexual experiences, his relationship with this unnamed woman is an attempt at permanency, emotional and perhaps racial as well. During this time of experimentation, "he thought that it was loneliness which he was trying to escape and not himself" (*LiA* 226). Yet the loneliness is a central part of himself; it accompanies the uncertainty as he holds himself off from other people, as if a "foreigner," or because whenever he discloses his fears about his ancestry, he expects punishment as a result.

In the face of this uncertainty, Christmas could seize the opportunity to pick the category that he prefers. Light enough to pass, he could live the rest of his life as a white man, or he could invoke the one-drop rule for himself, assert a physically undetectable African ancestry, and live as a black man. He does not choose the latter, for reasons that stem from his status as an orphan and an adoptee. As a child and young adult, the retribution he suffers for his purported black ancestry encourages Christmas to view blackness as loathsome, an attitude largely indistinguishable from that of most of the whites in his community. Furthermore, raised by and around whites, he has been socialized into whiteness, which further accounts for his resistance to living as a black man. He has little experience in or comfort with black communities. At the same time, the insinuations of his childhood and subsequent lingering doubt about his identity keep him slightly detached from whites, as if he does not believe he fully deserves to be white. Under these conditions, Christmas declines to pick a racial category, because neither reflects what he knows, which is virtually nothing. To commit to one would, in a sense, be a lie, a rejection of the only thing he knows about himself, which is that he does not know. Robinson recognizes that Christmas defines himself expressly in terms of this uncertainty when he embraces the name given to him at the orphanage. McEachern, his adoptive father, says that Joe will take their family name, and Christmas thinks to himself, "*My name aint McEachern. My name is Christmas*" (*LiA* 145). Acknowledging that some see the name *Christmas* as representing his rootlessness, Robinson goes on to say, "Joe takes the negative implied by his name and claims it for himself. True, it is a name arbitrarily given by strangers, but in identifying himself with it he embraces all that this emptiness allows. His name may signify a lack of identity, or a nebulous identity imposed by others, but his adherence to it and the connotations it has turns this formlessness into a defining characteristic" (126). Christmas, stubbornly honest about his origins, only claims what he knows for certain, but in the polarized racial system of the South, choosing "not sure" as a racial category cannot stand.

Changes in early manuscripts of *Light in August* show that Faulkner altered the text in order to make racial uncertainty the specific problem confronting Christmas. As Regina K. Fadiman explains in her study of Faulkner's revisions of *Light in August,* the author purposely removed "most of the narrator's explicit statements on the subject and revised the manuscript to stress the fact that Joe himself did not know but was haunted all his life by the fear that he was a Negro. In the final version, neither Joe, the narrator, nor the reader can ever know if in fact Christmas had Negro blood" (165). Faulkner's own statements about the novel further suggest that Christmas's inability to fit himself into a racial category is central to the plot. Asked about Christmas's undefined racial composition, he once said, "I think that was his tragedy—he didn't know what he was, so he was nothing. He deliberately evicted himself from the human race because he didn't know which he was. That was his tragedy, that to me was the tragic, central idea of the story—that he didn't know what he was, and there was no way possible in life for him to find out" ("Session Nine" 72). At another time, Faulkner said, "He knew that he would never know what he was, and his only salvation in order to live with himself was to repudiate mankind, to live outside the human race. And he tried to do that but nobody would let him, the human race itself wouldn't let him" ("Session Fourteen" 118). Faulkner was clearly interested in the implications of lacking racial identity, circumstances that could be achieved through a unique configuration of familial detachment and physically indeterminate features. In his comments about the "human race's" intolerance of that ambiguity, he draws attention to the ways in which Christmas's ambiguity implicates both himself and the community, all of whom must fit him into their system of racial signification.

Christmas's relationship with the community, especially in the last weeks of his life, illustrates the extent to which "plausible" narratives that establish racial classification do not actually need to make rational sense, as long as they conform to a community's accepted logic. Up until Joanna Burden's murder, Joe Christmas is accepted by the community as a "foreigner" and a white man. A potential coconspirator, Lucas Burch, attempts to deflect attention from himself by revealing that Christmas is black. Manipulating the community to his own ends, Burch redirects its suspicions by invoking the stereotype of the predatory black man. At the suggestion that the murderer is black, the community immediately shifts its thinking and determines that "it was an anonymous negro crime committed not by a negro but by Negro" (LiA 288). This narrative of presumptive guilt has framed all of Christmas's life and becomes instrumental in his death, yet it also presents a problem for the community, who must retroactively reconcile what they previously "believed" to be true, that Christmas was a white man, with what they now "know" to be true, that he is a "nigger." Christmas's affront is not simply that he might possess the one drop of black blood (although for them there is no "might" about it—the mere allegation makes it fact) but that he has also confused their sense of what makes someone black or white. "Believing" and "knowing" are proved equally unreliable, because the specious logic that grounds racial knowledge has become untenable.

Faulkner offers a Greek chorus of anonymous voices who attempt to make sense of the newly discovered information about Christmas's reputed black blood. The public reaction to Christmas's racial indeterminacy demonstrates the pervasive yet arbitrary nature of their system of racial signification. They try to interpret his behavior, coming up with a contradictory set of evidence to prove that they knew all along that Christmas was black. A shopkeeper says, "I said all the time that he wasn't right. Wasn't a white man. That there was something funny about him. But you cant tell folks nothing until—" (*LiA* 308–9). If the anonymous shopkeeper's intuition is not enough evidence, he also reads Christmas's choice not to flee the area after he escapes as a sign that he "never had no better sense . . . show he is a nigger" (*LiA* 309). Despite the fact that Christmas does not "look any more like a nigger than I do," as another anonymous townsperson says (*LiA* 349), his "nigger blood" can still account for his getting caught. These anonymous characters exposit the racial rules, weaving conflicting signs into foolproof evidence of what the townspeople desire to believe about Christmas. All of the characteristics they draw on—intellect, social behaviors, and phenotype—are attributed to the biological differences between the races, and when confronted with practical evidence that their criteria for judging racial difference is flawed, they simply reconfigure the signs, adding narrative elements that strain to support their conviction that Joe Christmas is black. The community's central problem with Joe Christmas is clearly articulated by yet another anonymous character, who points out candidly, "He never acted like either a nigger or a white man. That was it. That was what made the folks so mad" (*LiA* 350). All attempts to label Christmas according to the accepted rules of the community are frustrated by his unwillingness to act like or claim to be either a white man or a "nigger." He disrupts their racial assumptions and, as a result, threatens the social system.

In a society in which the category actually means more than the "truth" and in which "truth" rests on elaborate fictions about racial purity, Joe Christmas is a rather radical figure. Through him, Faulkner reflects on the absurdity of the racial order, first by depicting various efforts to racialize him and finally by providing Christmas with one last origin story, a counternarrative that links him to redemption through analogies to Jesus Christ, offsetting the dominant narrative of guilt that circumscribes him. Shortly before Christmas's death, his grandparents provide more information about his infancy, particularly the moment when Doc Hines leaves him outside the orphanage. The orphanage employees who find the abandoned infant note the resemblance of the situation of a child in need of shelter to the situation of the Holy Family in the Nativity story and declare, "We'll name him Christmas" (*LiA* 384). When Doc Hines, who has lingered nearby to watch their reaction to the baby, intervenes to tell them that his name is Joseph, they "christen" him in language reminiscent of the Old Testament: "It is so in the Book: Christmas, the son of Joe. Joe, the son of Joe. Joe Christmas" (*LiA* 384–85). The name *Joe* emphasizes the child's anonymity—he is an "average Joe"—while also creating an allusion to Christ in the shared initials *J.C.* Designating the baby "Joe, son of Joe" indicates Christmas's fatherlessness. The phrase also suggests that he is *both* father and son, which references Jesus's relationship to God in the Holy Trinity. Furthermore, it references Jesus's adoptive father, Joseph, as the child's namesake and, at the same time, acknowledges how Christmas has been deprived of a father; he is father to himself.

Joe Christmas's origin story also foregrounds the adoptive elements of the Holy Family's construction. In traditional "stranger" adoptions, adoptees enter their new families not through biological conception but through social volition; likewise, the virgin birth of Jesus and Jesus's status as "begotten, not made," resembles the volitional, nontraditional family contract in adoption. Furthermore, in the biblical story, Joseph raises Jesus, a child he does not physically conceive, as his own. These allusions to the Holy Family elevate Christmas beyond the abject position of "bastard" and reconfigure the untenable condition of being outside the racial order by making it analogous to divinity. Like Joe Christmas, Jesus and the Holy Family are—in theory, if not in practice—beyond race. Also like Joe Christmas, Jesus was "an ordinary bastard abandoned by his true father, God." While Jesus is also the "miracle child, born to the extraordinarily virginal Mary" (Shell 139), the similarities between Jesus and Christmas are clearly meant to be redemptive for Christmas. The analogy suggests that Christmas's suffering occurs to save humankind from its sins (in this case, the commitment to a cruel and arbitrary racial system), which casts his life and death in more sympathetic terms.

Faulkner extends the analogy between Joe Christmas and Jesus in his depiction of Christmas's death by lynching. Faulkner depicts his death twice, which suggests that the two accounts communicate different ideas or are, perhaps, not equal in value. The first, relayed by Gavin Stevens, a minor character in this novel, is a completely speculative account steeped in racist theories about human behavior; the second, provided by the omniscient narrator, casts Christmas's horrific castration and murder in redemptive terms that associate it with Jesus's crucifixion. Much of the end of Christmas's life is spent eluding the authorities who seek his arrest for Joanna Burden's murder, and though it appears that he easily could have left town—due to the ineptitude of those who pursue him—he chooses not to escape. He acknowledges the irony in his situation: "They all want me to be captured, and then when I come up ready to say Here I am *Yes I would say Here I am I am tired I am tired of running of having to carry my life like it was a basket of eggs* they all run away" (*LiA* 337). Perhaps the burden of maintaining a sense of self-conscious identity in the face of others' attempts to define him finally exhausts him, so he allows himself to be taken in, only to escape from custody for reasons never really clarified. He is pursued by a local vigilante who catches, castrates, and kills him, declaring, "Now you'll let white women alone, even in hell" (*LiA* 464). The narrator describes Christmas's spilled blood as a "black blast" on which "the man seemed to rise soaring into their memories forever and ever. They were not to lose it, in whatever peaceful valleys, beside whatever placid and reassuring streams of old age, in the mirroring faces of whatever children they will contemplate old disasters and newer hopes. It will be there, musing, quiet, steadfast, not fading and not particularly threatful, but of itself alone serene, of itself alone triumphant" (*LiA* 465). Not only does he lose the substance that sustains his life, but gone, too, is the metaphorical "black blood" that supposedly marked him racially. Only now is he truly beyond race. At the same time, however, he is killed precisely because he tried to be without race. Lynched ostensibly for the crime of raping and murdering a white woman, his true sin is his refusal to abide by the racial logic of his community. Lynching restores him to the racial order ex post facto, providing him with a racial narrative—"black rapist of white woman"—that almost everyone in the community recognizes and agrees on. In ensuring their serenity through his death, he becomes a martyr, dying so that the townspeople's assumptions about race remain intact. However, the serenity that they achieve, the calm after lynching's storm of violence, comes at a cost. His memory will endure, haunting them not in vengeance as much as in one of many vague memories of violence perpetrated in the name of racial purity or regional pride. As punishments go, this one does not seem like a very high price to pay, though if read in conjunction with other characters in the novel—Reverend Hightower and Joanna Burden, who are haunted by their families' histories of racial violence—the repercussions may linger for generations.

Reading through the frame of adoption's creation of fictive narratives helps to make sense of the conflicting stories surrounding Joe Christmas, his otherwise inexplicable choices, and the commentary that Faulkner makes about the

South. Christmas is a radical figure, and consequently his fate makes a firm statement about the rigidity of racial categories, yet it does not go so far as to challenge the system directly. While the omniscient narrator clearly critiques the lengths to which individuals will go to preserve their racist assumptions, his authoritative voice communicates its own racist assumptions—about how Negroes smell or think—that undercut any overall sense of sympathy for the plight of the black citizens who live in Faulkner's fictional world. Moreover, in depicting the consequences of racial uncertainty as utterly dire, Faulkner offers an image of a society unable to change. In contrast, Chesnutt treats fluid identities as the means to challenge the racial order by demonstrating its failure to contain the embodied exceptions to the racial rules and, additionally, the power of some individuals to disengage from racial ideology and think beyond socially devised polarities. Perhaps Chesnutt's optimism derived from conditions available to people like him, who physically could pass for white and who might not mind embedding themselves in a racial category if it helped to subvert the whole system. Or perhaps it was wisdom that developed from the personal experience of racial oppression, something that allowed Chesnutt to recognize that the absurdity of the color line could be the source of its eventual downfall. In the worlds imagined by Chopin and Faulkner, however, the racial order is insurmountable. Whether one absorbs the ideology without question, as Désirée appears to, or resists, as Joe Christmas does, the system cannot change, and a rebel will die for the misfortune of having been born outside of typical racial categories and, even worse, for having presumed to define himself apart from the black/white binary. So while Faulkner reveals the mechanisms of the racial order and the thinking of those who police it, he, like Chopin, offers little that suggests the possibility of subversion. Maybe, as with Chesnutt, their view is also a reflection of their subject position. No matter how sympathetic each may be—critics have devoted many pages attempting to define the attitudes Chopin and Faulkner held toward race—they did not, perhaps, have the tremendous incentive to imagine change in the way that Chesnutt did.

While reading through adoption helps us to understand Joe Christmas better, Joe Christmas also adds insight to the theory of fictive origins in adoption and in the family narratives that upheld the social order of the South. The experiences of both Désirée and Christmas illustrate that the range of fictive origin stories available to adoptees can be limited by existing social norms. Both Désirée and Joe Christmas live in a society fixated on authentic, essentialized origins. While there was no stricture against defining themselves as black in order to accommodate doubts about their racial purity, they were not permitted the "fiction" of passing for white, not under the conditions in which they lived (a restriction in opposition to Chesnutt's characters, whose passing was accommodated by the whites whom it served). Nor, in the case of Joe Christmas, could he choose to live without category if his community could not tolerate it. In this way, these texts illustrate the degree to which successful fictive origin narratives are collaborations among the adoptee, his or her family, and the community, and they depend, to a certain extent, on the consent of the adoptee himself or herself. In the case of Joe Christmas, for instance, his grandfather circulates the narrative that Joe is a "nigger," and while that narrative causes life-long doubt for him, he never fully accepts it as his own; more important, perhaps, he refuses to live his life according to that particular fiction, and, as a result, he is killed. Conversely, an adoptee can willingly embrace a fictive origin story, as Désirée does when she conducts her life as a white woman, only to find her belief challenged by an externally imposed narrative. When her origins—specifically her whiteness—come into question, the fictive narrative that served her well previously cannot stand up against the one assigned to her by her husband, whose social authority gives him the power to invent a narrative that trumps her own.

Margaret Homans's theory of irrecoverable origins suggests that Joe Christmas's problem, in particular, is that he is fixated on the truth of his identity, a truth that can never be obtained. This interpretation would hold up, since Christmas is, indeed, defined by an irrecoverable past. What Christmas also reveals, however, is that fictive origin stories come in many shapes and sizes and serve a variety of diverging projects. In the early twentieth-century South, the option of embracing fictive origin stories was not equally available to everyone. Certain fictions carried more social weight, especially those advanced by and consented to by the ruling white elite. Armand Aubigny, in "Désirée's Baby," is a good example of that phenomenon, as he has power, money, and the apparatus to destroy any evidence that he is not white—indeed, he has his slaves build the fire into which he casts that evidence. Those without social power—the bastards and foundlings, for instance—might find their fictional creations of identity to be precarious. Read through the frame of adoption's fictive narratives, Joe Christmas and Désirée, as well as Clara and Donald Glover (discussed in the previous chapter), highlight the arbitrary and contingent nature of fictive origin stories. On one level, all origin stories are fictive, as illustrated by Armand and Clara, both of racially mixed ancestry but passing for white. White privilege allows certain fictions to stand. At other times, such fictions are completely unacceptable, transgressions so disruptive that they must be remedied, by violence if necessary.

CHAPTER 4

Integrated Families: Robert Boles's
Curling and Toni Morrison's *Tar Baby*

The fictional adoptees discussed in the first half of this study all look white even though they purportedly possess the one drop of blood that would categorize them as black in the early twentieth century, a time when scientific racism, strict segregation policies, and social codes all reinforced the boundaries of the color line. This social rigidity in combination with the mobility of adoptees whose light skin permits them to move across the color line allow transracial adoption to function as a means of critiquing a social order rooted in the mutual dependence of biological kinship and genetic racial differences. The adoptees discussed in the second half of this book, however, are almost all visibly different from their families, a reflection of the growth of adoption across racial and ethnic lines that occurred in the second half of the twentieth century. The problem of racial difference in the adoptive family sparked periodic controversies, and, in turn, those controversies had repercussions for how adoption appeared in literature. While it still functions metaphorically (as a vehicle authors employ for exploring the meaning of familial, racial, and national belonging), fictional representations of adoption have become more complicated, as readers and authors grapple with the expectation for veracity in representation that has grown out of the practice's public prominence.

The metaphorical and mimetic significances of adoption intersect—and sometimes clash—in the texts discussed in this and the following chapters. Robert Boles and Toni Morrison are not explicitly concerned with depicting adoption accurately in their novels discussed in this chapter, but by the end of the century, veracity became very important, dictating how readers responded to texts, as in the case of Barbara Kingsolver and Anne Tyler, both of whom seem to have overlooked historical realities in their depictions. Even with authors and texts that were not necessarily controversial, the logistics of adoption practice, along with its historical contexts and cultural consequences, became a regular part of adoption fiction, as can be seen in various manifestations in the fiction of Sherman Alexie, Leslie Marmon Silko, and Gish Jen. Adoption creates the conditions that detach individuals from biogenetic kinship norms; these authors engage with the potential for self-definition afforded by that situation, sometimes by embracing that potential and at other times by reasserting essential qualities—racial, gender, and national—as the foundation for a strong identity. These varying strategies highlight the problem of securing authentic identities, a problem that originates in the family but that applies to cross-racial and cross-ethnic relationships in the late twentieth century.

The African American transracially adopted characters of the mid-twentieth century discussed in this chapter depart from their predecessors in both characterization and historical context, and they foreshadow the changes in how Americans understood adoption that inform the late twentieth-century adoption literature examined throughout the second half of this study; in this way, they serve as an important pivot between transracial adoption as almost strictly a literary trope and the concerns about the accurate representation of adoption practices that would become explicit in later texts. Both Chelsea Burlingame of Robert E. Boles's long-overlooked novel *Curling* (1968) and Jadine Childs of Toni Morrison's *Tar Baby* (1981) are adoptees whose dark skin creates a visible marker of their difference from their families and from white America, which sets them apart from the adopted characters in the fiction of Chesnutt, Chopin, and Faulkner. Moreover, the novels are set during and shortly after the civil rights movement, a period in which the racial hierarchies of the early century were slowly dismantled, permitting many African Americans greater access to the opportunities previously exclusive to white Americans. These transracial adoption narratives are products of their times. Adoption across racial lines allows Boles and Morrison to explore the meaning of racial, gender, and national identity for African Americans who cannot blend physically with white America but who find themselves equally at home—and equally alienated—in both white and black worlds.

Transracial adoption in these texts highlights the implications of integration for African American identity and provides a venue for renegotiating the expectations for what constitutes a healthy identity under changing social conditions. Set in the middle of the civil rights movement, as the earlier integrationist goals splintered into conflicting strategies for attaining equality, *Curling* uses a transracial adoptee to illustrate the psychic division that comes not only from the alienation of being a black man in a white world but from the pressures of deciding how best to act to resolve the race problem. The result, the novel suggests, is a stagnating state of double consciousness. In *Tar Baby*, Morrison elaborates on and modifies this notion of divided consciousness by depicting the multiple factors—gender, class, and nationality—that shape identity. By the early 1980s, the novel's setting, the overt civil rights clashes of the previous decades had diminished, yet ideological disagreements about how to define identity and how to continue advancing toward equality still remained. *Tar Baby* intervenes into those disagreements about what, exactly, constitutes authentic racial and gender identity, by using movement between and among adoptive families to undermine rigid essentialism and to offer self-fashioning as a viable alternative. Reading through the frame of adoption also offers important insights into subtle aspects of each narrative's plot. *Curling*, a novel clearly about racial identity, is also about family identity and the degree to which racial and familial alienation can become mutually constitutive. Foregrounding adoption also allows for a new understanding of Jade, the protagonist in *Tar Baby*. Often derided by critics as self-loathing and white-identified, Jade behaves in a manner consistent with her identity as an orphan and an adoptee. What some scholars see as a rejection of her black ancestry is, in fact, a response to the pressure to ascribe to racial categories that cannot accommodate the racial and familial influences in her life.

As the following discussions will show, these adoptees occupy a liminal space betwixt and between racial categories constructed and maintained through normative biological kinship. The texts themselves also reside in a liminal space between early-century depictions of transracial adoption in fiction that imagine an otherwise unsanctioned practice and late twentieth-century representations informed by a growing public consciousness of the practice itself. Written during and shortly after the increase in the adoption of African American children by white parents that began in the mid-1950s and peaked in the early 1970s, these novels show how transracial adoption as a thematic device was slowly influenced by the public discourses surrounding its real-life practice. Those public discourses incorporated some of the same issues of racial identity and cultural tradition that these texts negotiate metaphorically through adoption. Questions about the racial identity of transracial adoptees and the loss of culture that they might experience through the adoption process parallel the concerns in both *Curling* and *Tar Baby* about maintaining a healthy racial identity in an integrating but still racist society. Thus, while adoption served as a useful metaphor for Boles and Morrison, adoption practice itself—in the "real" world—was implicated by the same issues more directly. These concerns boiled over in 1972, when the National Association of Black Social Workers issued its statement objecting to transracial adoption, a position that yielded fierce debates over the practice that have informed the public's understanding of it ever since. Ironically, while Boles's *Curling* anticipated the NABSW's position before it was publicly taken, Toni Morrison's *Tar Baby,* published long after the initial debate, does not actually address it directly, using adoption almost exclusively as a metaphor for racial and gender belonging. This disparity reminds us that adoption in fiction can still operate largely on a metaphorical level, despite and sometimes because of the adoption discourses surrounding it. Nevertheless, the questions *Tar Baby* raises about where identity comes from, what constitutes "authenticity," and how much independence one has to resist ascribed identities all mirror those raised by the transracial adoption debates.

Robert E. Boles's novel *Curling* has long been out of print and overlooked by critics, perhaps because its protagonist's deep ambivalence about race might have seemed out of step with the activist literature of the Black Arts Movement of the late 1960s and early 1970s. The Black Arts Movement advanced a nationalist stance through art that was "functional, committed, and collective" (Karenga 175) and that resisted ambiguity—in politics or style. *Curling*'s stream-of-consciousness prose and clear existentialist influences likely did not fit with the period's activism.[1] Although the few reviews that exist were fairly positive,[2] *Curling* and Boles's earlier novel, *The People One Knows* (1964), appear to have gone out of print shortly after publication, and there is no record that he published any other novels.[3] *Curling* is nevertheless valuable not only for providing a fuller understanding of African American literature in the middle of the century but also for the study of adoption in literature. It depicts a transracial adoptee, Chelsea Burlingame, whose extreme sense of alienation results from his adoption and his inability to fit into either the black or the white world. A first-person account of one weekend in Burlingame's life, the novel uses transracial adoption to imagine integration in the most intimate context, the family, and speaks to its psychological effects. Equally interesting is the novel's portrayal of transracial adoption's negative psychic impact, an issue that would arise in highly public debates only a few years after its publication. To come to any firm conclusions about what, if any, interest Boles had in the practice of adoption itself, both *Curling* and Boles require more extensive biographical research than fits the scope of this project. *The People One Knows* deals with similar issues of divided racial consciousness but does not mention adoption at all, and reviews of *Curling* do not suggest that Boles had any personal connection with adoption. At the risk of raising more questions about Boles than I can reasonably answer, I begin with the novel because its characterization of Chelsea's adoptive identity is so intriguing in the way it captures the gravest concerns of opponents to transracial adoption. Anticipating, as it does, the identity conflicts that anti-transracial adoption activists warned would be faced by the rising numbers of transracial adoptees, it illustrates the growing overlap between fictional representations of transracial adoption and a heightened public consciousness of the practice itself. Hopefully, this short introduction to the novel will prompt more scholarly attention to it and to Boles's other writing.

Chelsea Burlingame, an African American engineer in his late twenties, is *Curling*'s narrator. He feels disconnected from both black and white communities, a condition that derives from his adoption into an upper-class white family that also socializes him into the white world. His adoption as an infant took place under circumstances he never fully understands, and Chelsea wonders what his life would have been like had he been raised in a black family. Largely character-driven, the novel is an extended flashback made up of odd and disjointed events that occurred over a weekend in the mid-1960s. He begins by reminiscing about a Friday afternoon when he leaves work to wander Boston for hours in the snow, on his way to meet his best friend and that man's girlfriend for dinner. Chelsea is deeply ambivalent, preoccupied variously with his status as the only black man in his workplace and social group and with his love for Anne, his best friend's girlfriend, who has sex with Chelsea once but does not consider getting romantically involved with him. His stilted mourning for his adoptive brother, who died unexpectedly the previous summer, underlies all these other concerns. The rest of the novel traces Chelsea's experiences over that one weekend, interspersed with flashbacks and fantasies that are often indistinguishable. On his walk, he encounters a homeless black man living in a half-constructed building that Burlingame helped design and imagines a spiritual connection to him. He returns later to discover that the man has died from exposure to the cold, but he does not call the authorities and instead leaves him there to be discovered by construction workers. The weekend also involves a visit to Chelsea's vacation home on Cape Cod; a party with his elite, white social group; and more wandering the city in the snow. Intermingled with these scenes are long ruminations about his relationship with his family and his feelings of ambivalence about race generally and his identity. The novel culminates with a trip to New Bedford, Massachusetts, where he gets pickpocketed. After following the thief down an isolated street, Chelsea beats him to death. Because of his prominent family, he does not face the criminal charges that he probably deserves, and the novel ends with his return to Boston, with little change in his life or psyche. Even his act of violence fails to dislodge his sense of ennui. *Curling* employs adoption to explore the depth of Chelsea's alienation, using his incorporation into a white family to speculate about the psychic effect that the national push toward integration could have on individual African Americans.

Chelsea's adoption creates the conditions of his lifelong alienation from both white and black communities. As a child, his difference is pointed out to him by his mother, who asks that he call her "m'am instead of Mother," and he is "supposed to call his father Uncle especially when in public" (*C* 156). By recasting him as a nephew rather than a son, Chelsea's adoptive mother denies him a secure place in the family. Although he has a warm relationship with his siblings and father, his race continually draws attention to his difference within the family, which also undermines his sense of belonging. That alienation is exaggerated by his father's choice to keep the details of Chelsea's adoption secret from him. Chelsea shares a middle name, *Meredith*, with his adoptive father's oldest son, who was banished from the house and family after doing something hateful—no one will say precisely what—that involved Chelsea. Typical of the novel's narrative structure, the story of Chelsea's origins is disclosed indirectly and uncertainly. He hears as rumor that he was born of a "hysterical" mother who died shortly after his birth, and he never discovers anything about his birth father. Chelsea suspects that Meredith was a doctor or someone with the power to fill out his birth certificate. Out of anger toward his father for remarrying, Meredith gives the infant Chelsea the Burlingame name and then includes on the birth certificate various genetic flaws, perhaps to suggest that the elder Burlingame had fathered a child with a mentally ill black woman. While it could be that Chelsea is actually the birth son of his adoptive father, the narrative never suggests that possibility when accounting for Chelsea's obscure origins (*C* 196–97). This story links adoption with racism and spite (over the father's decision to remarry), yet Chelsea's adoptive father seems to have followed through on the parental responsibility indicated on the birth certificate, even if the document was a fake. However, by naming Chelsea after the banished brother and keeping the circumstances a secret, he also permanently ties Chelsea to that racist act. The mystery of Meredith's disappearance preoccupies Chelsea as a child, and, ironically, he identifies with Meredith more strongly than with his other family members, because Meredith is a fellow outsider and, perhaps more subtly, because Meredith has the power of a creator, responsible for Chelsea's incorporation into the Burlingame family. Although Chelsea essentially replaces the other son, the secrecy surrounding the situation creates a sense of disjuncture that leaves him profoundly uncertain of his place in the family and of his own origins.

In his larger community, made up almost entirely of whites, Chelsea also occupies a liminal position. On one hand, he fits. Raised into an upper-class white society, his closest friends are affluent and white, yet they also seem to understand his pervasive sense of discomfort. They share an exacting set of social codes and manners—from wearing formal evening wear at parties to enjoying classical music and European art to being conscious of the appropriate time of day to drink certain beverages. On the other hand, Chelsea's difference is constantly noticed. To acquaintances, he represents "his people," in whose goals liberal whites profess their allegiance: "I took on a battery of apologies. I felt myself to be an unappointed ambassador. I sympathized, frowned when frowning was appropriate, battled a point or two and found that I won too easily—no one was willing to really fight" (C 128–29). As a representative rather than an individual, Chelsea constantly questions the motives of the white people around him, never sure if they react to him or to "a Negro." These experiences, in conjunction with the everyday acts of racial intolerance he experiences with strangers, make him constantly self-aware.

Despite his self-consciousness as a black man in an otherwise white society, Chelsea has little affinity with or understanding of African Americans, because he has had minimal contact with them. On his few trips into black neighborhoods in Boston, he feels like a trespasser, and "being black didn't help," despite the "clubbishness" he notices as people on the street nod to him. He complains that it "will always offend me, I suppose. Strangers nod and exchange greetings for no other reason than being members of the same race" (C 88). Living completely outside of this system, Chelsea cannot interpret the social codes of the black community, and he rejects these gestures of inclusion, acknowledgments of commonality, as "clubbishness" that implicitly exclude him. The form of his complaint suggests, however, the ambivalence underlying this declaration. After stating that it "will always offend" him, he qualifies his absolutism by saying, "I suppose." Lacking any lived experience in a black community, his sense of identity only extends as far as a heightened self-awareness around white people; he remains always alert to how people react to him as a black man, but that consciousness is not offset in any way by a feeling of community shared with other African Americans. Although he has dark skin and labels himself and is labeled by others as "Negro," he has no sense of belonging to any "club," white or black.

As a result of his inability to fit into either the black or the white world, Chelsea suffers from an enduring sense of restlessness and ambivalence. Boles associates it directly with double consciousness when Chelsea questions his own reactions, asking, "Is that the Negro of me or the American?" (*C* 91). He divides himself into the categories articulated by W. E. B. Du Bois when he said that as an African American, "one ever feels his twoness—an American, a Negro" (*Souls* 5). For Du Bois, as for Chelsea, the categories seem mutually exclusive; yet, like Du Bois, who envisions the possibility that these identities might eventually be merged into a "better and truer self" that combines both, Chelsea concludes, "Maybe the two cannot really be separated. The country is young, mad, innocent and very corrupt. I am not as young as I used to be and am none of the others. Like all of the others it was a fact I whittled in trying to chart my position so that I could move freely and defend myself" (*C* 91–92). Within his deep uncertainty about his place in the racial order, Chelsea simply desires the ability to "move freely" and to resist the tendency of others to categorize him, as a liberal cause or as a potential threat. Although one might read this resistance as a sign that he rejects his black ancestry, it reflects the belief that he does not belong anywhere. He remains outside of accepted racial categories, but rather than finding that position liberating, he experiences perpetual liminality. As a result, Chelsea greets even the most life-altering events—when he discovers the dead homeless man or kills the pickpocket—with a lack of emotion that matches the frigid Boston winter. At the novel's end, he simply concludes that the desire for contentment might be delusional and continues with his life as before.

Chelsea seems at odds with the growing black nationalism and atmosphere of social protest of the mid-1960s. His friends, with their highly formal manners and class consciousness, seem to be the product of an earlier decade. Even within that conservative social context, however, Boles portrays Chelsea as deeply conscious of the cultural moment: "The world was obviously awry. America was awry. It had erupted the previous year with the assassination, with murders of civil rights workers by men, whom, if brought to trial at all, would be acquitted" (*C* 86). At the same time, Chelsea does not feel a part of that moment, a sentiment revealed when he imagines striking up a conversation with a black stranger he passes on the street. "What would I tell him? I don't know where I stand in this country? I don't know who to believe? I don't know who to fight?" (*C* 89–90). At an increasingly combative time, he feels pressured to take a side, but his divided consciousness makes it impossible to identify strongly with either group. Chelsea's quandary resembles that of integrated, upwardly mobile African Americans whose new access to formerly exclusive white privileges still does not guarantee their belonging. Middle-class and upper-class African Americans existed before the civil rights movement, but they previously established their affluence in segregated communities and in a context of widespread and often institutionalized racism. The civil rights movement brought about affirmative action programs, hiring initiatives, and access to education that benefited middle-class African Americans (Kelley 287). Historian Charles Banner-Haley identifies the passage of the Civil Rights Act of 1964 and the Voting Rights Act of 1965 as especially influential for fostering the growth of the black middle class and leading to expanded educational opportunities as well as better jobs. At the same time, however, those changes prompted concerns among some newer members of the black middle class that they might lose their sense of racial identity (Banner-Haley 39–40). Burlingame embodies these concerns. His rise in social class is abrupt as a result of his adoption, as he almost instantaneously achieves full integration into an upper-class white community. Boles uses this unusual position to explore the more subtle implications of integration for individuals who were among the first to experience it, including discomfort in the workplace and as a token in white social settings. Although the changes in the black middle class would continue to develop over the course of the 1970s and beyond, Chelsea Burlingame clearly stood on the cusp, and through him, Boles cautions that opportunities for success in the white world would not necessarily erase the bigotry people would face.

Boles imagines integration through adoption to show the psychic cost of moving into a community that remains, at best, uncomfortable with the idea of social equality for African Americans; through Burlingame, he expresses the loneliness that comes from being an outsider. That said, Curling is not a statement against integration and in favor of separatism, since Chelsea's deep ambivalence gets in the way of any strong political stance. Furthermore, his close relationship with his recently deceased brother clearly shows the potential for positive connections across racial lines. Part of his inertia, in fact, comes from his reluctance to mourn his brother, to confront the extent of the loss he feels at the death of perhaps the only person who understood his alienation. In his last letter, which Chelsea can barely bring himself to read, his brother says,

I'm beginning to see what hell it must have been for you. . . . You got by with a hell of a lot because every member of the family wished, in a way, to discredit you, to let you hang yourself. The thing was, they all loved you, too. At least I thought they did. . . . I don't know what I'm trying to say to you. You have always been a father-confessor to us all, in a way. You've seen the best and worst of us. And you've never been a part of us. You have been the mirror for all of us. (*C* 108)

Although this letter recognizes Chelsea's struggle, it also confirms the degree to which Chelsea is less a member of the family than a social experiment. That he serves as the family's "mirror" is an intriguing observation, suggesting that his presence forces them to see themselves in an unflattering light, a light that reveals "the best and worst" of the family. It is not hard to see this relationship as analogous to the national one; in the 1960s, the claims for equality made by the black community reflected back to many white Americans an image of the nation that did not measure up to the mythology. This recognition prompted some whites to advocate for change and others to bunker down and fight to retain supremacy. In many respects, however, the equality earned by African Americans had a steep price for many. Even if it does not reject the possibilities of integration, *Curling* suggests that Chelsea stands alone, without a cohort who can share his experience and through which he might establish a more healthy identity. His elite white family reinforces his sense of alienation in part because it places him at a social level that few, if any, black Americans at the time could have attained outside of the black community. That place in particular emphasizes both the extent to which he has been incorporated into the "white" world and the magnitude of his alienation from it and from African American life.

In terms of its representation of adoption, *Curling* is almost prescient, offering an early depiction of a transracial adoptee's experience just as the practice was in its ascendancy and, furthermore, anticipating the concerns of those who opposed transracial placements with its frank depiction of Chelsea's racial crisis. For many transracial adopters, incorporating a child of color into an otherwise white family contributed to the integrationist ideals of the early civil rights movement on an individual and highly personal level (Ladner 51; Melosh, *Strangers* 159). While transracial placements had been occurring in small numbers since the mid-1950s, they reached higher rates in the late 1960s. As historian Barbara Melosh emphasizes, these placements were never very high proportionally—only about 1 percent of all adoptions among strangers at the time—but they "loomed large in the symbolic landscape of the late 1960s and early 1970s" (*Strangers* 175). As transracial adoption was gaining popularity among whites, peaking at 2,574 in 1971 (Melosh, *Strangers* 175), the civil rights movement itself was fracturing, and those frustrated with the slow rate of change rejected the integrationist goals that appealed to white adopters and turned toward black nationalism, with its emphasis on racial self-reliance. In that context, transracial adoption was read by some African Americans as symptomatic of the failure of white institutions to serve black families (Melosh, *Strangers* 175), as white intervention into the autonomous lives of black Americans (Satz and Askeland 54), and as the exploitation of black families in crisis to serve the needs of white adopters who, in light of declining relinquishment rates, could no longer easily find white infants ("NABSW" 133). Arising out of these sentiments, the NABSW issued a statement in 1972 opposing the practice of transracial adoption, initiating debates that have occurred periodically ever since.

As the most formal, public objection to transracial adoption practice, the NABSW statement reinterprets the early integrationist impulse of white adopters and labels transracial adoption as an assimilationist act certain to erase black cultural specificity. The statement argues that the transracially adopted child grows up white identified and will assume the white family's "posture and frame of reference, different from and often antithetical to that of his ethnics which can only result in conflict and confusion when he does become aware of the social system in which he lives" ("NABSW" 132–33). Moreover, the NABSW also worried that transracial adoptees will be internally conflicted because of their visible racial differences from their families. Finally, the statement argues that white families are not equipped to teach African American children the kind of coping mechanisms necessary for navigating a racist culture ("NABSW" 133). The reaction to the NABSW statement was swift; the numbers of transracial adoptions dropped precipitously in the following years, and as Barbara Melosh argues, many cite the statement as the cause. However, some scholars have also speculated that this drop occurred less out of respect for the feelings of advocates of race matching and more because social workers actually preferred same-race placements all along and only facilitated transracial ones at the instigation of white adopters (Melosh, *Strangers* 176–77). Although some researchers have concluded that the fears that transracial adoptees might feel a sense of racial alienation have been overstated and that transracial adoptees adjust at rates similar to those of other adoptees, such concerns continue to dominate discussions of transracial adoption.[4]

Representing Chelsea Burlingame's fractured racial identity through adoption, as Boles does, anticipates many of the NABSW's concerns. Chelsea's alienation and lack of positive racial identity clearly reinforce the worries of those who oppose transracial adoption. He has absorbed the "posture and frame of reference" of his white family to the degree that he cannot identify at all with African American culture. Additionally, he suffers from internal conflict that results in a crippling sense of double consciousness, and any skill he developed to combat racism comes from personal experience, not from the guidance of his family, who has implicitly discouraged him from disclosing the racist encounters he has (*C* 156–57). With so little information about Robert Boles or criticism on his two novels, it is difficult to draw strong conclusions about the degree to which *Curling* conveys Boles's own concerns about the practice of transracial adoption as such. Most likely, adoption provided him with an expedient thematic device to explore the implications of the struggle for integration by imagining it in the intimacy of an individual family. At the same time, *Curling* can clearly be read for its portrayal of transracial adoption, giving fictionalized voice to those who experienced it and anticipating the perspective of those who were just being adopted in the late 1960s, people who would otherwise not have an opportunity to speak for themselves until much later.[5] In these ways, *Curling* nicely previews how fictional representations of adoption would begin to merge with public discourses of the practice itself in the late twentieth century. With each passing decade, readers would approach the metaphor of adoption in literature with their own perceptions of adoption as a lived experience, perceptions formed not only through controversies like the one raised by the NABSW statement but also through media representations, the political activism by adoption rights activists, and autobiographies by adoption participants.

Even in the midst of this growing public discussion, however, authors still turned to adoption, not because they had a personal stake in it or hoped to shape the public perception of it, but because it served the thematic needs of their work. Toni Morrison's *Tar Baby* is an example of adoption in contemporary literature serving a largely metaphorical function. In *Tar Baby,* adoption facilitates Jadine Childs's ability to cross racial boundaries, serving as the vehicle through which Morrison comments on the pressures brought to bear on upwardly mobile black women in a newly integrated society. Like Chelsea Burlingame, Jadine finds herself in a state of identity crisis. Unlike Chelsea, however, Jadine does not become stagnant in her sense of division but responds to it with acts of self-fashioning that assert her autonomy from the identities prescribed for her.

In *Tar Baby,* Jadine takes temporary residence on the Caribbean island that is home to her aunt and uncle on her father's side, Sydney and Ondine Childs, and to their employers, Valerian and Margaret Street. Orphaned at age twelve, Jadine is adopted formally by her aunt and uncle and informally by the Streets, who help pay for her elite education and encourage her successful modeling career in Paris. After a string of professional and personal successes—including the completion of a degree in art history at the Sorbonne and a cover photo in the French *Vogue*—Jade finds her sense of identity challenged when she encounters a beautiful African woman in a Paris grocery store. Jade follows her, and the woman looks back at her and spits on the ground. Believing that the woman has disparaged her, Jade feels "lonely and inauthentic" (*TB* 48), becomes restless and full of self-doubt, and retreats to the island to regroup. There she meets Son, an African American man who has abandoned the ship he was working on to make his way back to the rural Southern community that he left behind. Falling in love with Jade, Son wants to impart his cultural values to her, to offset the European influences that he feels make her too white-identified. At the same time, Jade sees Son's traditional values as restrictive for women. This conflict over racial and gender roles eventually destroys the relationship, and the couple breaks up. Jadine returns to her modeling career in Paris, "to begin at Go" (*TB* 290). In the novel's last scene, Son departs into the wilderness of the island in what appears will be a fruitless search for her.

On the surface, Jade's circumstances in *Tar Baby* depart from the criteria that govern most of the adoption narratives included in this study. Jade is formally adopted by kin—her uncle on her father's side and his wife, who are both African American—and that fact distinguishes her from characters formally adopted by people of a different race. But Jade also has a second set of adoptive parents in the Streets, who become "patrons"; they care for her material and educational needs, provide her a home wherever they are, and take an interest in her future. Neither family provides her with a great deal of emotional support, a fact that accounts for her sense of insecurity in the novel; nevertheless, each set of parents helps shape her identity and encourages her professional endeavors. Despite these categorical differences, Jadine fits thematically with the other adoptees discussed in this study. Her adoptive status encourages her to move in both black and white worlds, even as she does not feel completely comfortable in either; through her, Morrison explores the meaning of belonging in the decade after integration, a cultural moment that offered unprecedented professional and material opportunities for African American women. As metaphors for postintegration race relations, orphancy and adoption communicate ambivalence about the source of identity, undercutting the novel's essentialism by challenging the discourse of biological kinship on which it depends. Adoption also allows a more nuanced reading of Jade, who is often dismissed by critics as, at worst, self-loathing and, at best, self-absorbed. Foregrounding her family status offers the potential to read her behavior differently; even if it does not fully mitigate her self-absorption, this frame emphasizes her choice to reject traditional conceptions of family, as well as rigid racial categories to which she does not ascribe.

Tar Baby appears to designate race and gender as inherent qualities by locating them in ancestral lines. It begins with a dedication to Morrison's female relatives and ancestors, "all of whom knew their true and ancient properties," a phrase that indicates that these properties are inherited traits, located in the family line and passed from generation to generation. The epigraph continues the idea of kinship by quoting First Corinthians: "For it has been declared unto me of you, my brethren, by them which are of the house of Chloe, that there are contentions among you." The reference to Morrison's given name, *Chloe*, positions that dissent within her individual family, but the events of the novel extend it to the black community and create an associative continuum from the individual to the family to the race. The novel reinforces a connection between essential racial qualities and kinship through characters' names. Ondine and Sydney Childs and Son all evoke kinship through their names, and all possess a strong sense of racial identity and commitment to family. Additionally, the novel's iconic figure of authentic identity, the woman in yellow, is characterized as a "woman's woman—that mother/sister/she" whose gender identity is inextricable from familial roles (*TB* 46). This language further establishes racial and gender identity as inherent by associating it with the normative biological family. Morrison's extratextual statements in a related essay titled "Rootedness: The Ancestor as Foundation," written shortly after the publication of *Tar Baby*, extends this association further. She there discusses the importance of ancestors in African American literature, asserting that their absence in certain novels results in chaos for individual characters: "The point of the books is that it is *our* job [to remain connected to ancestors]. When you kill the ancestor you kill yourself. I want to point out the dangers, to show that nice things don't always happen to the totally self-reliant if there is no conscious historical connection. To say, see—this is what will happen" (344). A consciousness of ancestors signals a recognition of history and one's place in it, Morrison argues, and that recognition, in turn, will secure an identity capable of withstanding the assaults of racism. This logic suggests that identity is inheritable, establishing biological kinship as a prerequisite for a healthy racial identity. While this emphasis on ancestors may be a powerful tool for building an identity that can resist racial stereotypes, it also poses a problem for those whose ancestors are obscured or from more than one racial or ethnic group.

These essentialist markers have led some critics to locate the novel within a binary opposition of cultural rootedness and self-denial. A few adopt Morrison's language of kinship to support the argument that Son, associated with nature and family throughout the novel, is the exemplar of tradition, while conversely, they interpret Jade as rather shallow, possessing little interest in or connection to a cultural past.[6] Moreover, they interpret Jade's choice to return to Europe at the novel's end as a gesture of self-denial. Judylyn Ryan comments on Jade's upward mobility and her desire to have Son become more educated and cosmopolitan, which Jade calls "rescue": "Indeed, the novel convincingly discredits Jadine's agenda for a 'rescue,' not because financial security is to be disdained, nor because it is maliciously intentioned, but because it is undergirded by a materialist and self-alienating consciousness which recommends selling one's cultural inheritance and 'birthright for a mess of pottage'" (617). Alluding to the biblical reference to Jacob and Esau by James Weldon Johnson's "ex-colored man," who expresses regret for choosing to abandon his black identity and live as a white man (Johnson 154), Ryan equates Jade with a race passer. Ryan frames Jade's choice for professional success in terms that suggest selling out not only her culture but also her familial inheritance, her birthright. Critic Marilyn E. Mobley makes a similar rhetorical move, calling Jade a "contemporary black female hero" who "happens to be a cultural orphan, one whose sense of self is based upon a denial of her own cultural heritage and an identification with one that is not her own" (761). Both critics also use language associated with family—the terms *birthright* and *orphan*—to illustrate the high stakes of Jade's choice, by making it equivalent to rejecting family.

Even though these assessments employ the language of orphancy, they fail to recognize that orphancy is not simply metaphorical. By making Jadine a literal orphan and an adoptee, Morrison plants the seeds of her own critique of the relationship between identity and ancestry. As someone adopted by two families and brought up in both "black" and "white" contexts, Jade raises the question of what, exactly, constitutes "her own" racial group? To whom is she disloyal? The inclusion of orphancy and adoption also challenges the reliability of ancestry as a foundation for identity, by removing the continuity of a biological family line. Without it, the very notion of authenticity grounded in ancestry becomes destabilized, and by extension, so do essentialized definitions of identity. This disruption opens up space for other ways to create and sustain a sense of identity. *Tar Baby* offers the possibility, even within the novel's strong argument for ancestry and cultural awareness, that not everyone fits so neatly into predetermined categories.

These questions are easier to address after establishing how Jade's experiences as an orphan and adoptee shape her identity as a whole. Her family status has implications not only for racial and gender identity but for her overall sense of personal security and, in turn, for how readers can understand her choices. Adopted at the age of twelve, Jade is old enough to have a memory of her birth parents yet young enough to need nurturing from her adoptive ones; however, her aunt and uncle do not really provide that nurturing, since she only lives with them part of the time and, more important, since they do not see her as a daughter. Ondine remarks that Jadine is "a 'child' whom she could enjoy, indulge, protect and, since this 'child' was a niece it was without the stress of a mother-daughter relationship" (*TB* 96). Perhaps inevitably, the bond they might have had is diminished by Jadine's age at adoption, yet Ondine's clear distinction between "daughter" and "niece" creates emotional distance that becomes recognizable in the way their relationship plays out in the novel. It causes Jade to establish boundaries between her and the couple as an adult, as when she says, "Nanadine and Sydney mattered a lot to her but what they thought did not" (*TB* 49). At the end of the novel, Ondine herself eventually recognizes that her attitude might have been a mistake: because she did not teach Jadine how to be a "daughter," Jadine now does not defer to her aunt and uncle the way they think she should (*TB* 281). Layered on top of this detached adoptive relationship is Jadine's somewhat undefined affiliation with the Streets. Jade sleeps upstairs with the Streets, and her aunt and uncle occupy the servants' quarters. She dines with the Streets while her uncle serves them, and she calls the Streets by their first names, while her aunt and uncle address them more formally. At the same time, Jade hesitates to consider the Streets family, referring to them instead as "almost family," while she puzzles over the protocols for gift giving, unsure if it would be "appropriate" for her to give the Streets' son a gift (*TB* 90–91). The Streets' attentiveness distances her from her adoptive parents, yet they do not fully accept her into their family. Although Jade does not fully belong to either family, she is clearly influenced by both, sometimes in ways that reinforce the values of each couple and sometimes in contradiction of them. As a result of her division between these two families, she possesses little sense of familial connection, a condition that determines her identity and many of the choices she makes.

The two families shape her racial consciousness, but the combination of their influences also means that her approach to race may depart from theirs as a result. From Sydney and Ondine, she acquires a desire to work hard and advance professionally. The two pride themselves on their work ethic and remain loyal to the Streets, who they consider to be good employers, and they are at peace with their role as servants, even as it seems retrograde to Son and Jade's generation. In an interview, Morrison called Sydney a "good old Uncle Tom" but also said that she had "tremendous respect for him. He is a man who loved work well done" ("Interview" 423). The Childs have a strong sense of racial identity, attuned to bigotry and proud of their family's accomplishments. Ondine, for instance, is clearly invested in Jadine's racial and gender consciousness, as indicated by her regrets about Jadine's inability to be a daughter. From the Childs, and from her other life experiences, Jadine develops a racial consciousness that allows her to recognize when people stereotype her. For instance, Jade is sensitive to what she perceives as Margaret's racializing tendencies, which "stirred her into blackening up or universaling out, always alluding to or ferreting out what she believed were racial characteristics" (*TB* 64). She also wonders about her French boyfriend "if the person he wants to marry is me or a black girl" (*TB* 48). In addition, she resists being placed in racialized gender roles, as when Son calls her "white girl" and, later, when he wants her to embrace a more traditional role as a black woman.

Beyond helping to shape Jade's identity, this characterization of Sydney and Ondine also complicates Morrison's exploration of racial identity. Although their perspectives differ radically from that of Son, the apparent standard-bearer of black identity in the novel, they do have a legitimate racial identity that should be acknowledged. At the same time, they have their own blind spots, treating the inhabitants of the island with disdain, as if they are beneath the Americans. These divergences undermine monolithic definitions of black identity and expose the dissent in "the house of Chloe" that derives from the variety of forms of black identity available to Jadine. Her subtle characterization also reinforces the notion that identity cannot be articulated in simple black/white binaries, despite the fact that the narrative, on the surface, seems to set readers up to do so. The Childs' commitment to education and advancement collaborates with the Streets' willingness to educate Jade. Though it might be easy to decide that Jade's education and social status are simply signs of white identification, she is, in reality, a product of the complex intersections of race, class, gender, family, and nation that make it difficult for her to fit into any single prescribed identity category.

Even though she identifies as a black woman, Jade feels almost as comfortable in a white world as in a black one and perhaps more so, a result of her proximity to the Streets and of her European education and lifestyle. She knows how to navigate cosmopolitan environments like New York and Paris with ease, feeling at home in the predominantly white world of modeling and the Sorbonne, and there are signs that the racial and class influences of her life sometimes lead her to ascribe to white elitist values without questioning them. For instance, she volunteers her belief that Picasso was a genius for having recognized the artistry in the masks he adapted from African folk art, yet she dismisses the artistic value of the originals (*TB* 74). Moreover, the attitude behind her first thought (noted by the narrator) upon seeing the woman in yellow's body—"too much hip, too much bust. The agency would laugh her out of the lobby" (*TB* 45)—suggests an internalization of white European standards of beauty. The paradoxical combination of her detachment from a strong sense of kinship and the multiple racial influences on her highlights the degree to which identity is constructed within and against familial contexts. Given her two adoptive families, Jade's tendency to identify with both white and black worlds is, perhaps, the most "authentic" option available to her, one that does not seem acceptable to other characters in the novel—her aunt and uncle and Son—who want her to be more "black," in whatever terms they define it. Jade's tangled family influences yield a correspondingly complex sense of self, one that Morrison depicts as flawed and messy yet subtly legitimizes.

In the context of Jade's unique family situation, some actions that critics point to as evidence of her rejection of black identity actually derive from her experiences as an orphan and an adoptee. For instance, her encounter with the woman in yellow, widely interpreted as evidence that Jadine does not have an authentic racial identity, also manifests insecurity, the perception that she does not belong in her family. Jadine interprets the woman spitting in her direction as a judgment of her and her racial identity, when, realistically, the woman knows nothing of Jadine at all. The gesture makes her feel "lonely and inauthentic," and Jadine later wonders "why the woman's insulting gesture had derailed her—shaken her out of proportion to the incident" (*TB* 47). The basis for this disproportional response may lie more in the feelings of loneliness the woman evokes than in racial authenticity. Without a strong family network and living far away from the country she knows, Jadine probably feels vulnerable. With this point in mind, Morrison's assessment of the woman in yellow as "a real, a complete individual who owns herself" adds important insight ("Interview" 422). Jadine does not feel a sense of self-ownership, perhaps because she lacks a strong racial identity, but just as plausibly because of the circumstances of her birth.

The sensation of being judged that Jade has with the woman in yellow becomes more acute in her reaction to the "night women," the elders associated with strong black womanhood who seem to haunt her while she is in Eloe. A sign of essential femaleness, these women stand over her while she makes love with Son. She feels singled out: "The night women were not merely against her (and her alone—not him), not merely looking superior over their sagging breasts and folded stomachs, they seemed somehow in agreement with each other about her, and were all out to get her, tie her, bind her. Grab the person she had worked hard to become and choke it off with their soft loose tits" (*TB* 262). To her, these women, all characterized by the essential properties Morrison refers to, seem to draw her back into a traditional gender role that she does not want and to suffocate her with their idea of womanhood. But her anxiety about them extends to something deeper when she responds to her own mother's presence among them: "how could you Mama how could you be with them. You left me you died you didn't care enough about me to stay alive you knew Daddy was gone and you went too" (*TB* 261). Her resistance to the night women stems from her sense of abandonment by her mother and the feeling of being judged for not fitting the traditional construction of black womanhood in Eloe. These responses are also framed by the way that racial identity in the novel is both gendered and linked with motherhood. Without a consistently present mother, she does not respond to these associations the way that others might.

Critics who dismiss Jadine as not black enough obscure the real source of conflict in the novel: the fact that Jade refuses to conform to other people's definitions of black womanhood if they do not match her own self-perception. As John Duvall points out, for Jade, "to commit to the community of Eloe and the enactment of female identity represented by the night women . . . is to acquiesce to a form of patriarchal agrarianism that strictly limits women's role to the natural creation of motherhood" (340). Not only is gender an issue generally, motherhood also becomes implicated in Jade's struggle for self-definition. What initially draws her to Son is his willingness to nurture her, to "unorphan" her, as she calls it, but that impulse is, ironically, the undoing of their relationship (*TB* 229). For Son, "unorphaning" her means making her more "authentic" by encouraging her to embrace his idea of healthy black identity; but as a consequence, he also becomes a parent to her, which may be the bigger challenge to an identity built around her detachment from family. Missy Dean Kubitschek recognizes family as the source of Jadine's problems: "Literally an orphan without a family, Jadine is symbolically a cultural orphan. With no sustaining culture, Jadine rejects any traditional idea of family ties" (98). While I do not entirely agree that she has no culture, I do see how culture and family ties are intertwined. Without traditional family ties, she cannot develop a sustaining sense of culture if it must be rooted in ancestral consciousness and biological kinship.

All of Jade's familial influences—the Childs, the Streets, and Son—encourage her to adopt an identity to which she cannot fully ascribe. For her aunt and uncle, it is "daughter"; for Margaret Street, it is stereotypical black womanhood; and for Son, it is a Southern, rural "earth mother." Throughout the novel, Jadine attempts to form an identity within and against these pressures, but in returning to Paris, she really begins that process in earnest. Rather than a sign of self-abnegation, her choice to leave conveys the desire to reinvent herself on her own terms. She plans to "tangle with the woman in yellow—with her and with all the night women who had *looked* at her" (*TB* 290), to challenge a symbol of black womanhood that excludes her. She does not reject black identity; she expands the options available to her, returning to "tangle" with the woman in yellow rather than to ignore her. The text also suggests that this decisive move is only the beginning of a long process. As John Duvall explains, "The logic of the plot implies that Jadine, as an African American woman, has not yet achieved racialized adult identity but that an important precondition of that identity has been reached: namely, she recognizes that black female identity need not accept its construction by black men when that construction is complicitous with the assumptions of white patriarchy" (332). Duvall rightly singles out Son as one of the people constructing Jadine's identity, but clearly he is not the only one.

Jadine's act of self-fashioning comes with a high cost. When she concludes that "she *was* the safety she longed for" (*TB* 290), she recognizes that there is no safety in others; the only shelter is a strong sense of self. In another context, Morrison showed that there are clear limits to being responsible only for oneself; it can result in the "dangerous freedom" experienced by *The Bluest Eye*'s Cholly Breedlove, utterly detached from any accountability to others (*Bluest Eye* 159). At the same time, Morrison seems to validate Jade's choice by showing the precedent in nature for independence. The third-person narrator, who, at this point, seems to occupy Jadine's subject position, ruminates on the soldier ant, who responds to "some four-million-year-old magic she is heiress to, that it is time" to reproduce (*TB* 291). The soldier ant draws on a stash of sperm stored from mating once in the past and, from it, creates a kingdom without men. This natural precedent for Jade's solitude and independence situates her back in the realm of authenticity, ironically, just as she rejects it by leaving behind the pressures of prescriptive identities. This move legitimizes her choice by making it, too, seem "natural," claiming a black female identity on her own terms. John Duvall says this scene "reiterates the notion of self-reliance while insisting upon female fecundity" (346), a combination that allows Jade to possess the nurturing qualities of black womanhood without sacrificing her values. In leaving, she may achieve the status of owning herself that Morrison attributes to the woman in yellow ("Interview" 422), although Morrison also suggests that Jade is still only approaching that status and has not yet achieved a complete sense of self-worth ("Interview" 424).

Ending on this note reinforces the ambivalence about the importance of essential identities that pervades the novel. The solitude of the female soldier ants—their instinct to mate once—suggests that Jade's falling out with Son and her decision to go back to Paris alone is part of a larger natural system. At the same time, Morrison's impulse to validate with nature indicates the difficulty in completely abandoning nature as a means of defining identity. Moreover, the novel also shows that employing nature as a model does not work for everyone, particularly for those whose lives are deemed "unnatural." Obviously, this status applies to adoptees, but it also extends to others who fail to fit into traditional categories—the multiracial, gays and lesbians, and orphans, to name just a few. Margaret Homans assesses the novel's approach to authentic origins when she observes, "Morrison's adoption novel reveals both the appeal and the risk of romantic fictions of racial origins; the adoption narrative licenses the novel to denaturalize origins, to expose their fictiveness and the ways in which they might both serve and fail to serve the present." Indeed, as I have argued here, adoption clearly destabilizes the idea of racial origins in the novel, introducing space to consider other routes to establishing a racial identity. Homans goes on to say, "Morrison does not suggest that authentic origins could be retrieved or restored; fictive origins are the only origins there are" ("Adoption Narratives" 16).

Yet the clear tensions in the novel between Jadine and the rest of the characters, who are both invested in and representative of identities grounded in authentic origins, suggest that the opposite is equally true. The belief in their very existence and their power to authenticate individual identity sustains all of the main characters and, to a certain extent, Morrison herself. While Morrison's statements in interviews suggest sympathy for Jade, she does not back away from her own investment in an awareness of ancestry as a central facet of a healthy racial identity. In this way, Morrison's novel offers important insight into the idea of the "emotional truth" of essential identities, echoing the point made by Jane Jeong Trenka's The Language of Blood (discussed in chap. 1). Embracing inherent qualities—the power of "blood"—to ground identity can be empowering, but what sustains one person may not work for another. Identity is, as Linda Martín Alcoff reminds us, highly subjective (92), and Jadine goes against the tide of essential identities that carries the other characters. For this reason, I posit that Jade survives not because she realizes that all origins are ultimately fictional but because of the tremendous effort she expends to overcome the self-doubt cultivated by those deeply committed to their own belief in authentic origins. The possibility that origins are fictional does not do Jade much good if everyone else remains invested in them, and the consequences of this discovery are high. In embracing her act of self-fashioning, Jade must leave behind the people who she originally considered her refuge, because they ascribe to a standard of cultural consciousness located in the authority of the roles of "wife" or "daughter," to which Jade does not have access. In this novel, the price for recognizing the fictionality of origins is paid almost exclusively by the adopted. Homans may be correct that even Son, the character most invested in the authenticating power of origins, finds that they are not as stable as he would like to believe ("Adoption Narratives" 15); nevertheless, the confidence in origins as a source of cultural authenticity remains at least partially intact for Son, for many characters and critics, and, to some degree, for Morrison herself.

In *Tar Baby*, as in *Curling*, transracial adoption offers a vehicle for addressing the challenges of sustaining a healthy racial identity in the post–civil rights era. Both texts, in their own ways, reflect ambivalence about what role race should play in defining the self, particularly as African Americans gained more access to previously exclusive white professional institutions. For Boles, the double consciousness that can result from integration is almost crippling, but for Morrison, it opens the door to new ways of challenging racial and gender norms—both constructed within black communities and imposed externally. Morrison in particular engages with essentialism in a way that shows how it can legitimize identities in flux, a characteristic of the novel's cultural moment. In *Tar Baby*, essentialism functions as an authorizing force, yet the novel subtly shows just how easily it becomes a tool for creating divisions, disempowering or delegitimizing other experiences and perspectives. Both the power of essential identities to define the self in opposition to cultural bias and the ambivalence that underlies such efforts arise again in the following chapter. Although the cultural context for the works under discussion there is quite different (focusing on the ways in which transracial adoption speaks to the relationship between American Indians and white America), adoption continues to allow the authors to explore the meaning of personal and collective authenticity.

CHAPTER 5

Captivity and Rescue in the Fiction of Dallas Chief Eagle, Leslie Marmon Silko, Barbara Kingsolver, and Sherman Alexie

By the last decades of the twentieth century, Americans had become familiar with adoption as a practice. The debates over the transracial adoption of African American children in the early 1970s contributed to this consciousness, as did the growth of the adoption rights movement (ARM) that arose in the late 1970s. The ARM identified problems with midcentury adoption practices, particularly the secrecy of closed-records adoptions. Although the movement itself is beyond the scope of this study, it had a profound effect on the way that Americans came to understand adoption by the end of the twentieth century,[1] which, in turn, shaped its representation in fiction. Activists often used autobiographical narratives to advocate for the opening of records, and through them, Americans learned that many adoptees wanted information about their birth families and, moreover, that the lack of knowledge could be traumatic for some (Melosh, "Adoption Stories"; Modell). Furthermore, media accounts of adoptees searching for birth families, along with psychological impact studies of adoption, contributed to the public consciousness of adoption practices. As a consequence, adoption became familiar to the general public, and its representation in literature began to be evaluated in terms of its accuracy. But despite the concerns raised about traditional adoptions and the controversy surrounding the transracial adoption of African American children, many Americans still perceived of it as a benevolent act, particularly when the adoptees in question were identified as "children in need" and came from developing nations or, at times, marginalized groups in the United States. These contradictory perceptions of adoption as at once problematic and essentially benevolent made it possible to interpret a single adoption scenario in vastly different terms, depending on one's perspective.

By the time Barbara Kingsolver wrote *The Bean Trees* (1988), one of the best-known fictional depictions of transracial adoption in contemporary American literature, readers and critics brought to it this somewhat paradoxical perception of adoption. Many responded favorably to the novel's depiction of a single woman who adopts an abused Cherokee child, goes to great lengths to maintain custody of her, and develops an awareness of social justice as a consequence of their relationship. This adoption, represented in terms of "rescue," helps manifest Kingsolver's vision of multicultural coalition that is a theme in the novel. Others, however, saw in the novel an inaccurate portrayal of the transracial adoption of American Indian children. It failed to acknowledge the Indian Child Welfare Act of 1978 (ICWA), which prohibits the adoption of Native children without the permission of their tribe. It also failed to consider Turtle, the Cherokee child, in terms of her cultural identity, using her instead as a vehicle for addressing her white adoptive mother's development.

Several novels that followed *The Bean Trees* effectively revise Kingsolver's original depiction to more accurately reflect the cultural history of American Indian child custody. Taken together, *The Bean Trees*, Kingsolver's sequel *Pigs in Heaven* (1993), *Gardens in the Dunes* (1999) by Leslie Marmon Silko (Laguna Pueblo), and *Indian Killer* (1996) by Sherman Alexie (Spokane/Coeur d'Alene) participate in a collective conversation about American Indian adoption outside of the tribe. They comprise a unique but telling example of how fictional representations of adoption can shape perception of policy and cultures while also serving as a vehicle for examining concerns about cultural belonging. In *Gardens in the Dunes*, Silko depicts some of the historical precedents that led to the enactment of the ICWA, by situating the informal adoption of her protagonist, Indigo, within the context of the boarding school movement. Paired with one another, these child welfare policies illustrate how adoption, which seems like a benevolent act in certain contexts, can also be damaging to individuals or, in the case of tribes, whole cultures. In *Pigs in Heaven*, Kingsolver herself deliberately attempts to represent the objections to adoption raised by tribes, while maintaining the image, offered in *The Bean Trees*, of cross-cultural cooperation achieved through adoption. Alexie, in contrast, uses *Indian Killer* as his own corrective to positive images of adoption outside of the tribe; in focusing on its psychic impact on an individual adoptee, he treats extra-tribal adoption as one of many damaging appropriations of Native culture by white Americans.

These texts are exceptional, not only because Kingsolver chose to write another novel to correct the impression created by the first one, but because they so clearly engage one another—implicitly and sometimes, in the case of Alexie, quite explicitly—as they attempt to define the meaning of American Indian adoption. In this way, they are also exceptional in the degree to which adoption as a metaphor became entangled with its representation; these authors grapple in fiction with the real-world perceptions of the practice that individual readers bring to the text. Because these perceptions are shaped by personal experience and cultural backgrounds, fictional adoptions prompt larger concerns for these authors, particularly the American Indian ones, about what constitutes an authentic representation of American Indian experience and who is authorized to offer those representations. I position Kingsolver's first novel at the center of this discussion, not because her portrayal is superior or more authentic than others', but because both *The Bean Trees* and *Pigs in Heaven* have become two of the best-known representations of transracial adoption in contemporary American literature.[2] Given the criticism that *The Bean Trees* and *Pigs in Heaven* have garnered, I use Kingsolver's work as a point of departure to explore alternative portrayals in texts that not only address the implications of real-world adoption practices involving American Indians but also use it metaphorically, to access issues related to tribal identity and authenticity.

Adoptive relationships have figured heavily in American literature's treatment of Native people since the first contact. One of the first literary forms developed by European settlers was the captivity narrative, which usually refers to accounts by white women of their abduction by tribes as acts of war. Early examples from the colonial period, such as Mary Rowlandson's 1682 narrative of her abduction and captivity, are spiritual autobiographies meant to affirm Christian faith that was tested against the heathen "other." Not all captivities, however, ended with release; some taken in acts of war, such as Eunice Williams and Mary Jemison, remained "unredeemed" and willingly chose to stay even after their kin came to reclaim them.[3] Some were captured with the express purpose of replenishing the tribe after the death of members, which also meant permanent adoption for captives.[4] Incorporating captives into the tribe was part of larger Native kinship patterns that centered around the extended family and close members of the community and did not necessarily privilege biological kinship in the ways European Americans did. Mark Jerng identifies kinship as one foundation on which national identity was established in the nineteenth century. Beginning with Americans' anxiety over stories of the colonial period's "unredeemed" captives who preferred living with their adoptive families in the tribes to returning to white American life, Jerng explains the distinction between American Indian and American approaches to adoption and the ways authors negotiated differing kinship practices in literature. Native adoptions involved complete substitution, incorporating the adoptee into the tribe without concern for his or her race or ancestry, while the codification of adoption practices in the American legal system, which began in 1851, constructed adoption "as if" it were like blood kinship, with consanguinity remaining the privileged form of kinship. Jerng elaborates on the implications of this distinction.

> This form of [Native] kinship is so threatening because adoption here completely changes the adoptee's social status and affiliation. If one child can just as easily substitute for another, then he or she can take on different attributes and characteristics—be they national or racial. Substitutability means that borders between peoples dissolve. The sentimental construction of "as-if" kinship on the other hand relies on the unchanging origins of a child no matter where or what position she is in. It relies on the child's uniqueness and unsubstitutability, maintaining firm boundaries between one family and another: we love you as if you were one of our own. It thus allows for adoption but uses the sentimental family form in order to preserve distinctions between peoples. (21)

Jerng argues that American authors in the nineteenth century attempted "to secure the psychic and imaginative borders between Native Americans and white settlers" by rewriting the kinship bonds in ways that prevented any kind of identification between the two groups (8). Defining adoption, in other words, became a means of asserting American national identity.

In contemporary literature, definitions of adoption are still at issue, even as the terms of the debate have shifted as a result of historical developments. Contemporary narratives about American Indian adoption are informed by the earlier trope of captivity, while they are often also shaped by the concept of rescue, which arose around adoption as it began to be viewed in sentimental terms beginning in the nineteenth century. In a contemporary context, adoption is perceived as saving "problem children," and the language of child saving implicitly equates the adopters' privilege with moral authority to deliver adoptees into better lives (Dorow 50–57; Solinger, *Beggars* 20–32). That attitude quietly implies a hierarchy of power relations along racial, class, and—in the case of international adoption and autonomous indigenous tribes—national lines. This motif nearly always appoints the white, affluent parents as "rescuers" and the poor child of color as the "rescued." The contemporary narratives discussed in this chapter engage in other negotiations of identity—American Indian as well as American—that are framed in competing terms of captivity and rescue.

A historical novel by Sioux author Dallas Chief Eagle offers a particularly compelling example of how even a single act of adoption can be configured as captivity or rescue, depending on the context in which it is viewed. *Winter Count* (1967) imagines the years preceding the Wounded Knee massacre in 1890, as the federal government encouraged assimilation by, among other things, moving tribes onto reservation lands. Chadwick Allen, in an introduction to *Winter Count*, posits that despite its setting in the past, the novel is "an artifact of the times in which it was written and first read" in its "insistence on articulating a Native perspective" (ix). Its depiction of a series of adoptive relationships helps to emphasize that perspective by exposing the divergences between tribal understanding of kinship and the dominant culture's. In this way, *Winter Count* cannot be read apart from another aspect of its historical moment: the child welfare crisis of the 1950s and 1960s, which removed thousands of American Indian children from their tribes for adoption or foster care, in a challenge to tribal sovereignty akin to the push toward allotment and reservations in the late nineteenth century. While not *Winter Count*'s main focus, adoption is a recurring theme, and I discuss it briefly here to call attention to the novel as a relatively unknown adoption text and to flesh out some of the dynamics of captivity and rescue as contested terms in adoption.

As small children, Turtleheart and Evensigh, the protagonists of *Winter Count*, were found at the site where four adults, presumably their respective parents, were murdered. Turtleheart's physical characteristics mark him as "Indian," though his tribal affiliation is unknown, while Evensigh is clearly white. Drawing a distinction between Indian and American codes of honor, a tribal elder observes that the murderers could not have been Indians, because Indians would not have left behind helpless babies (*WC* 135). Taken in as an explicit act of rescue, both children join the tribe with equal standing, despite the differences in their race. As Allen observes, "Their relationships to their families, to their band, to the Sioux Nation, and to the larger confederacies of Plains Indians are primarily cultural rather than biological" (introduction xii). The fact that both are adopted by the chief's family—Evensigh goes to his sister and Turtleheart lives in the chief's own lodge—speaks to the collective aspects of the tribe's kinship patterns; as the tribe's leader, the chief incorporates the children not only into his own family but into the tribe as a whole. When they grow up, the two fall in love and marry, though shortly after, they are ambushed by a group of gold miners who brutally beat Turtleheart and leave him for dead.

Presuming that Evensigh has been stolen by Indians, they take her to a white settlement, despite her protests that she wants to be returned to her Sioux family. What the whites assume is an act of rescue is, in her eyes, a form of captivity. A military commander rules her wish to return to the tribe "out of the question" (*WC* 21) and determines that Evensigh should be adopted by a white couple whose daughter recently died. Although she begins to assimilate to American culture, Evensigh never stops mourning her husband or loses her longing to return to her tribal family. On the verge of remarrying—to a white man—she decides to make a final visit to Indian territory, to see for herself how the tribe is faring, after she reads alarming stories about the Indian removal in the newspapers. Discovering that Turtleheart survived their attack, she remains with her husband on the reservation, until both perish at Wounded Knee, leaving behind their infant son.

Evensigh's circumstances allow Chief Eagle to make a number of important observations that contrast her life in white America to her time with the tribe, and they show how captivity and rescue are very much in the eye of the beholder. Although the original circumstances in which she is seized are an unequivocal kidnapping, Chief Eagle depicts her subsequent "captivity" with the white family with more nuance. For instance, *Winter Count* assesses white culture through Sioux eyes (Allen, introd. xiii), as in Evensigh's observation that there is a commonality between the cultures in their belief that a strong work ethic will earn community respect (*WC* 67). At the same time, Evensigh has the opportunity to explain certain Sioux practices to her white family, the Callahans, which makes her something of a cultural emissary. Furthermore, her exemplary white adoptive parents become a corollary to her generous, beloved Indian parents; each has something positive to offer her. By aligning the two families this way, Chief Eagle illustrates that, all things being equal, a seemingly "white" woman would still prefer to be with the tribe; culture wins out over race. Evensigh's movement between two adoptive families replicates that of Donald Glover in Chesnutt's *The Quarry;* this shift contrasts the two cultures and shows that loyalty and love, not racial ancestry, dictate one's affiliations. As with Glover—and in the tradition of the marital kinship drama discussed by Sollors—Evensigh must choose between two different spouses; one will grant her access to the privileges of whiteness, and the other enables her to return to the band and family who nurtured her. The novel closes with one final act of adoption that illustrates the rapid decline of the tribe's fortunes while holding out faint hope for the future. As he is dying after Wounded Knee, Turtleheart staggers to the priest who has taken up residence on the reservation, and he places his infant son in the man's arms. Turtleheart, who had previously refused to convert, has relinquished his son to almost guaranteed assimilation, yet as Allen reads this scene, Turtleheart's choice to wrap his son in his personal "winter count"—a traditional Sioux calendar marking the accomplishments of each year—suggests that some aspects of tribal culture will endure (introd. xiv).

In *Winter Count* and in the other texts discussed in this chapter, rescue and captivity serve as a kind of shorthand in depictions of American Indian adoption, and they carry attendant meanings that are informed by cultural history and personal experience. The conversation that takes place among these novels illustrates that adoption in literature functions as a powerful trope, a metaphor expansive enough to communicate a variety of sometimes conflicting visions of American Indian and American identities. At the same time, by the end of the twentieth century, it could not function in literature solely as a symbol. Representation matters, and it, too, determined how these texts were received, as can be seen in Kingsolver's *The Bean Trees*. Kingsolver used adoption as a metaphor, depicting it as a vehicle toward cross-cultural connections between American and indigenous people, both domestic and international. In this way, it replicates captivity narratives in the colonial period that offered "the enticing if threatening possibilities of cross-cultural kinship ties" (Strong, "To Forget" 468). When read absent of any larger historical context, adoption seems like an explicit act of rescue, not only for the adoptee, but for the adoptive mother as well.[5]

The Bean Trees is the story of Taylor Greer, a young working-class woman from Kentucky who wants to get away from her small town. On her journey west, an abused Cherokee toddler is handed to her by a stranger in a parking lot; not knowing what else to do, she continues on with the baby. She names the child Turtle, since she has the tenacious hold of a snapping turtle. The pair end up in Arizona, where they make friends, including a single white mother of a Chicano child, an elderly woman who runs a sanctuary for refugees, and the indigenous Guatemalans that the woman shelters. As their lives become more entwined, Taylor awakens to a greater sense of her and her country's place in the world. The novel culminates in Taylor's attempt to formalize her adoption of Turtle by asking the Guatemalans to pose as Turtle's birth parents in the office of a notary public. The "relinquishment" successful, the novel ends with the mother-daughter pair in a quasi-legal adoption. This novel advocates for a strong community, one, I argue, that is envisioned through the act of adoption; moreover, Taylor's movement away from individualism occurs only after her recognition of her own privilege as a white woman and as an American, a discovery linked to her new motherhood.

Kingsolver uses Taylor's relationship with her daughter to illustrate her growing consciousness of her own and other people's biases. Early in her parenthood, Taylor faces questions about the visible differences between her and her child. A coworker says, "You know, your little girl doesn't look a thing like you. . . . I mean, no offense, she's cute as a button," to which Taylor responds, "She's not really mine, she's just somebody I got stuck with" (*BT* 52). The comment implicitly inquires about how Taylor comes to have a dark-skinned child, but Taylor, unprepared for curiosity, has no adequate response, and what she chooses to say simply diminishes their relationship. Later, having faced similar questions and become more comfortable in the role of mother, however, Taylor plays with inquisitive strangers by manipulating the latent anxiety over race mixing that sometimes underlies their remarks. Asked if Turtle's father is Native American, Taylor responds by saying, "Her great-great-grandpa was full-blooded Cherokee. . . . On my side. Cherokee skips a generation, like red hair. Didn't you know that?" (*BT* 71–72). In contrast to the previous scene, Taylor now claims Turtle as her own biological kin. In addition, she eschews the notion of the child's father altogether, redefining the question by designating Turtle's American Indian heritage matrilineal. The statement is partially accurate, as earlier in the novel, Taylor and her mother, Alice, talk about their genealogical claim to Cherokee status (*BT* 13). Furthermore, her statement shows Taylor purposely aligning herself with her daughter's nonwhite ancestry to challenge the potential judgment of others.

Kingsolver employs the trope of adoption as a means of creating even broader cross-cultural coalitions, by including a Guatemalan couple who confronts Taylor's privilege as a white American. Taylor's Guatemalan refugee friend Estevan must explain the reasons for his marginalization, as an indigenous person and as an activist in a democracy movement challenging Guatemala's American-backed military regime. Taylor learns from Estevan how members of his organization were tortured with equipment provided by the U.S. Army. Unaware of any of this history, she responds to his criticism of the United States by saying, "You think you're the foreigner here, and I'm the American, and I just look the other way while the President or somebody sends down this and that, shiploads of telephones to torture people with. But nobody asked my permission, okay?" (*BT* 135). Although this comment seems to deny the possibility that she might have any complicity in U.S. actions abroad, her actions in the rest of the novel illustrate that her relationship with the Guatemalans and the sanctuary movement has led her to disidentify with American imperialism and to take risks on behalf of the Guatemalans to achieve social justice. To do that, she drives the Guatemalans to a safe house across the country, asking them to pose as Turtle's birth parents along the way so that Turtle may be "officially" relinquished and then adopted by Taylor herself. This emotional scene is the climax of the novel,[6] bonding Estevan and his wife to both Turtle and Taylor in what Kingsolver calls "a strange new combination of friends and family" (*BT* 216). Through this adoption, the group achieves a cross-cultural, international coalition, a family created not by biology but through nurturing and willing affiliation.

In *The Bean Trees*, Kingsolver's vision of cross-cultural coalition is enabled by her portrayal of adoption as an explicit act of child rescue. Turtle's status as both helpless child and victim of abuse makes it easy for readers to override any misgivings they might otherwise have about Taylor's decision not to report Turtle's abandonment to authorities. Legal studies scholar Ilene Durst, for instance, places Taylor's choices, including taking Turtle with her, in the category of "an ethic of care": "Under Taylor's decision-making process, the desire not to sacrifice herself or her most intimate relationships trumps any other imposed rule. Accordingly, Taylor refuses to abide by the limitations of the law's construction of justice in order to abide by her moral responsibilities" (sec. 1). Understanding Taylor's actions in terms of justice also derives, I believe, from the pervasive association of adoption with rescue, particularly when it involves children of color and those from developing nations. The novel clearly plays into this association through Turtle's vulnerability. Taylor's decision to take Turtle with her is figured explicitly as rescue, especially since the more logical response would have been turning the child over to authorities right away. At least one reviewer talks about Turtle's adoption as "a rescue from abuse" (Solomon), and virtually all mention Turtle's status as an abuse victim before noting, without comment, Taylor's choice to leave with the child. The perception that this action is heroic accounts for the novel's largely positive reception by critics and readers. She prevents a child from being abused further, something very difficult to argue against. At the same time, the notion of rescue functions another way, appearing to benefit Taylor, too, as she is delivered into greater social consciousness by choosing to adopt. Kingsolver injects into the novel a conceptualization of adoption as an act of mutual rescue, an approach characteristic of early twentieth-century orphan stories in which sheltering an orphan also offers adoptive parents a better life (C. Nelson 69). Taylor's relationship with her daughter saves her from ignorance, making her more attuned to cultural difference and more willing to take risks on behalf of those with whom she might previously have felt no sense of affiliation.

Despite the overall positive reception of the novel by white American critics, this privileging of whites as rescuers of the abject resonated much differently for other readers, who brought to the text their own perception of adoption. For those familiar with the way that the U.S. government used Native children as pawns in its political relationships with tribes, the representation of adoption in this novel is less about multicultural coalition and more about the undermining of American Indian families and tribal sovereignty. American Indian children have often been the first target of U.S. government policies to assimilate tribal members. Those policies began in 1819 with the Civilization Fund Act, meant to educate American Indian youths into the "arts of civilization," and continued in the early twentieth century with the mandatory placement of Native children in boarding schools that isolated them from their families and cultural heritage (Mannes 266). Families who failed to comply would find their children abducted by government agents to enact the policy. The U.S. government attempted to foster assimilation in other policies directed at Indian families, too, particularly the implicit encouragement of marriage between Indians and other Americans.[7] By the mid-twentieth century, the Indian Adoption Project and other policies removed Indian children from their families, with an estimated 35 percent of children on reservations separated from their families and placed with white foster and adoptive parents (Matheson 233). This long history blurs the boundaries among captivity, kidnapping, adoption, and education, casting adoption in a much different light.

Evidence of the truth in the idea that one person's child rescue is another's child "snatching" (quoted in Ladner 57), Kingsolver's representation of adoption prompted criticism from Laguna Pueblo author and activist Leslie Marmon Silko, who reads the adoption scenario in *The Bean Trees* as a reinforcement of negative stereotypes about American Indians.

> Books were and still are weapons in the ongoing struggle for the Americas. Only a few years ago, a best-selling novelist breathed new life into old racist stereotypes with a portrayal of the Cherokee reservation people as pitiful drunks and child abusers whose children are better off with any white woman who comes along. Such sentiments soothe the collective conscience of white America. The subtext of such stereotypical portrayals is: Take the children, take the land; these Indians are in no condition to have such precious possessions. ("Books" 155)

Silko's criticism places the adoption into a larger cultural context of detribalization. More than just a narrative about family, this novel is, for Silko, a "weapon" wielded against tribes attempting to maintain their autonomy. King-solver's few depictions of the Cherokee are indeed stereotypical, from the drunk, abusive boyfriend who causes Turtle's aunt to give her away to a stranger to Taylor's characterization of tribal lands as "not a place you'd ever go to live without some kind of lethal weapon aimed at your hind end" (*BT* 13). Although she softens this attitude somewhat when Taylor returns to Oklahoma to for-malize the adoption, the novel never really treats the American Indian charac-ters as having any subjectivity, except in relation to Taylor's Guatemalan in-digenous friends, when she mentions that they seem more relaxed among the Cherokee (*BT* 204). Silko argues that representations such as the one she notes in *The Bean Trees* have a real-life impact on the general reading audience's un-derstanding of tribal cultures. Her comments echo Dallas Chief Eagle's multi-faceted depiction of adoption as both captivity and rescue, showing not only that the form itself can be used for a variety of discursive purposes but that the same text that may be seen by one set of readers and in one situation as ad-vancing a critique of white privilege and American imperialism could be un-derstood by another set of readers as a colonialist text itself.

In her novel *Gardens in the Dunes,* written after both of Kingsolver's adop-tion novels, Silko goes further to offer a depiction of adoption as something more akin to captivity than rescue. While adoption as such is not a central con-cern of the novel, it does provide important historical perspective to inform contemporary discussions of adoption outside of the tribe. The novel focuses on a girl, Indigo, and her older sister, Sister Salt, two of the few remaining Sand Lizard people, a fictional tribe in the desert Southwest nearly eradicated by dis-ease and encroachments on their land. The girls are largely raised by their grandmother, who teaches them the tribe's ancient traditions of farming and weaving, and when she dies, they are both seized by authorities. Indigo is sent to a government boarding school, while Sister Salt, deemed too old to be edu-cated, is forced into domestic labor on the Parker reservation. Indigo runs away from the school and takes refuge in the yard of a house owned by a white cou-ple, Hattie and Edward. Determined to eventually return Indigo to the school, the couple nevertheless keeps custody of her for the summer and takes her with them to the East Coast and abroad. By the time they return to the United States, Hattie has had a change of heart and refuses to send Indigo back. Instead, she helps her to locate her sister. The novel ends with the sisters reunited in the gar-dens in the dunes, along with Sister Salt's young son, the next generation of Sand Lizard people.

In this novel, Silko aligns the boarding school movement to adoption as acts that deprive children of their families and culture. The quasi mother-daughter pair of Hattie and Indigo provide a useful foil for Kingsolver's Taylor and Turtle, emphasizing important perspectives lacking in *The Bean Trees*. Both relationships begin as "rescues," but in *The Bean Trees* (and largely in its sequel, *Pigs in Heaven*, as well), the narrative point of view is located with the white adoptive mother, not the child. This choice encourages readers to identify with Taylor and to let her perspective define the terms of their relationship, particularly since Turtle is so young in *The Bean Trees* that she cannot speak. In *Gardens in the Dunes*, both characters' perspectives are included, but the novel begins and ends with Indigo and her family, positioning her at the narrative's center; more important, her age makes her old enough to articulate a response to her situation. What we learn is that while Indigo feels affection for Hattie, she never considers their relationship a permanent one. Instead, she continuously dreams of being reunited with her sister and mother and plots ways of escaping back to them. This perspective of an older child also calls attention to how much Indigo's survival is a consequence of her highly developed sense of identity as a Sand Lizard (Li 27). On the day she escapes from the school, Indigo "took off running, just as she had the morning she and Sister Salt escaped the soldiers and Indian police who pursued the Messiah's dancers at Needles. Sand Lizard people were not afraid of capture because they were so quick. Grandma Fleet taught the girls to wait and watch for the right moment to run" (*GiD* 69). Employing her grandmother's wisdom and linking it to a skill shared with members of her tribe, Indigo has the confidence to escape. Her relationship with her maternal relatives also gives her the strength to resist, as she places herself in what Stephanie Li calls a "preexisting cultural narrative; although she is physically alone, she is part of a larger historical legacy of survival and resistance" (Li 28). Comparing the two novels, Deborah A. Miranda (Esselen/Chumash), concurs with Li, saying, "A white woman does not save an Indian girl child from the degeneration of her race, as in Kingsolver's plot; instead, Silko creates an Indian girl who holds her own with white culture while drawing strength and power from her own" (145). The difference in adoptive mothers is telling, too. When placed together, Hattie's and Taylor's divergent fates speak to the limits of Kingsolver's fantasy. While Taylor is understood as redeemed from loneliness and ethnocentrism by her relationship with Turtle, Hattie does not get to fulfill a growing sense of nurturance by adopting Indigo, though she does remain deeply sympathetic to the fate of Native Americans. After she willingly facilitates Indigo's return to her family, she is brutally raped and beaten by white townspeople as a consequence of her affiliation with the Indian sisters, who then nurse her back to health. Her fate marks a dubious kind of rescue. While she, like Taylor, may have come to a greater understanding of herself and the world through an act of adoption, that knowledge comes at a very high price.

The matrilineal family portrayed by Leslie Marmon Silko in *Gardens in the Dunes* shows the power of relationships created through common culture and kinship, yet her choice to set them against the larger backdrop of the history of tribal disenfranchisement and systematic exploitation emphasizes the complexity of adoption. There are clearly points of connection across the boundaries of culture, as illustrated in the relationship between Hattie and Indigo, in which Frederick Aldama observes an "unspoken understanding" between the two characters. He goes on to conclude, "Home for Silko is not about racial solidarity. It is about seeking out like-minded peoples who are open to new visions and to change, and who share a deep commitment to the earth and the human spirit" (458). At the same time, the common commitment to the earth shared by Hattie and Indigo—both gardening enthusiasts—is an individual solution, one that cannot resolve the larger forces that threaten to destroy the girls' family and have already eradicated most of their tribe. The connection between boarding schools and adoption implicitly critiques the American Indian adoption policies that would follow in the midcentury. The cumulative effects of adoption as a systemic "solution" to American Indian child welfare problems were just as devastating as the boarding schools. By ending the novel with Indigo and Sister Salt reunited in their ancestral home—despite the clear challenges ahead—Silko reiterates a point made clear by Dallas Chief Eagle: culture and family will win out over the perceived material benefits of mainstream American life.

Silko is not the only author who attempted to widen the lens through which readers view the adoption of American Indian children. Kingsolver herself felt chagrined at the limitations of her representation of tribal issues and adoption in *The Bean Trees*, and she wrote its sequel, *Pigs in Heaven*, as a corrective, an attempt to incorporate Turtle's birth family and culture into her relationship with Taylor. Explaining her return to the mother-daughter pair in a second novel, she stated, "I realized with embarrassment that I had completely neglected a whole moral area when I wrote about this Native American kid being swept off the reservation and raised by a very loving white mother. It was something I hadn't thought about, and I felt I needed to make it right in another book" (Perry 165). In another interview, she said, "I didn't even stop to think when I was writing *The Bean Trees* that Turtle was being stolen from her tribe, essentially. Not stolen really, but lost to her tribe" (quoted in Gilbert). In this way, Kingsolver shares the position taken by Silko that literature influences readers' understanding of culture. In *Pigs in Heaven*, representation and practice become explicitly intertwined; adoption still functions as a metaphor for multicultural coalition, but the novel is also explicitly didactic, attempting to address the issues of cultural identity and tribal autonomy embodied in American Indian adoption that Kingsolver overlooked previously. The novel returns to the theme of community, which Kingsolver locates in tribal cultural practices and juxtaposes to the individualism promoted in mainstream American ideology.

Pigs in Heaven revisits Taylor and Turtle three years after Turtle's adoption. When Turtle witnesses an accident and saves a man's life, mother and daughter end up on *The Oprah Winfrey Show*, where a Cherokee tribal attorney, Annawake Fourkiller, sees them; she decides to investigate the adoption, believing that it was arranged in violation of the Indian Child Welfare Act. Most of the novel is an extended debate about the merits of each side of the custody case, pitting the "best interests" mandate of mainstream American child welfare practice, represented by Taylor and her family, against the more collective approach undertaken in some tribal cultures, as advanced by Annawake Fourkiller. Kingsolver depicts this polarity as virtually irreconcilable, building a powerful case for overturning the adoption by explaining how American Indian children have been taken from their tribes, the consequences of that removal, and why the ICWA should exist. Although the novel creates the expectation that the adoption cannot stand, Kingsolver achieves a compromise by returning to the idea of adoption as mutual rescue, casting a wider net this time to include both white and tribal characters whom the adoptive relationship redeems. That redemption becomes a crucial component of the custody compromise.

Early in the novel, virtually all of the characters are alienated from their families to varying degrees, but Turtle's adoption—despite and sometimes because of the custody challenge—eventually helps to reposition them more fully into a familial context. Taylor is the most obvious example of this phenomenon. After being alerted to the possibility that the adoption might be challenged, Taylor takes Turtle on the lam. She essentially abducts her in order to avoid the tribe's challenge. This development restages the scene in which Taylor chooses to take Turtle with her in *The Bean Trees*, but this time, the consequences are somewhat different, as she displaces Turtle and herself from their support system. This "abduction" subtly echoes the fact that Turtle herself was removed from a community when Taylor originally took her. Without the double-income household and shared babysitting agreements that she relied on in Tucson, Taylor sinks into poverty, unable to care for Turtle effectively. Separated from the people who have served as her informal family, Taylor recognizes that she does not want to live independently, that her community is necessary for her family's survival. Having initially believed that the most important thing was keeping custody of her child, she discovers, as she says, "I love her more than I can tell you, but just that I love her isn't enough, if I can't give her more. We don't have any backup. I don't want to go through with this thing anymore, hiding out and keeping her away from people. It's hurting her" (*PiH* 321). After this realization and the recognition that she may not be equipped to raise a child of color without the experience and insight of the tribe, she decides to visit the Cherokee Nation and face the custody challenge.

As with Taylor, the characters Cash Stillwater and Alice Greer in *Pigs in Heaven* both find redemption and deliverance into stronger family relationships through adoption. At the beginning of the novel, Cash, Turtle's biological grandfather, lives in Wyoming, having left the reservation after the death of his wife and daughter. He works in a health food store and also assists a friend whose job is to make traditional Indian beadwork while displaying herself at her trade in the window of a shop. Alienated from his culture—a point emphasized as he watches his friend perform Indianness for tourists—he returns to the tribe and initiates a search for his missing granddaughter. Back in Oklahoma, circumstances and orchestration throw him together with Taylor's mother, Alice, who has arrived in Cherokee territory to visit a cousin and, at the same time, quietly gather information about the tribe's claim to Turtle. Alice, too, is delivered from loneliness through her relationship to adoption. Recently divorced from a man who paid little attention to her, she is attracted to Cash because he listens. Their decision to marry coincides with the custody agreement forged between Taylor and the tribe, leaving Cash reconnected with his biological family line through his legal guardianship of Turtle, and both Cash and Alice are rescued from the loneliness of their previous lives.

Adoption is, ironically, the novel's central conflict and its ideal solution. The illegal adoption of Turtle causes the custody dispute in the first place, yet the resolution is facilitated by embracing adoption as a means of creating community, albeit in somewhat different terms than in the first novel. An agreement devised by Annawake Fourkiller makes Cash Turtle's legal guardian while granting Taylor partial custody, in an arrangement that requires Turtle to live with the Cherokee Nation part of each year and to learn about Cherokee culture. The marriage of Cash and Alice greatly facilitates that agreement, smoothing over any awkwardness in sending a child to live with a relative she has only just met. The combined marriage and adoption plots reinforce one another, creating a number of interconnected quasi-nuclear families that emphasize kinship by consent. Turtle and her coparents, Cash and Taylor, comprise a symbolic nuclear family. Blood and constructed kinship merge, as Cash is both parental guardian by law and grandfather by biology. Furthermore, Cash's marriage to Alice also provides Taylor with a father figure for the first time. Cash, Alice, and Taylor form another nuclear family, one reinforced by the "peculiarly identical" expressions on Cash and Taylor's faces that one character notes in passing (*PiH* 339). This commonality suggests another figurative bond, a variation on the physical resemblance that so often indicates a family connection shared across generations.

Pigs in Heaven revises the depiction in *The Bean Trees* of adoption as a symbol of coalition, maintaining its emphasis on cross-cultural cooperation but more attentive to the integrity of tribal cultures. It details the rationale of the Indian Child Welfare Act, not only explaining the history behind it, but also adding emotional dimensions, through Turtle and by tying Annawake's choice to pursue the case to the trauma suffered by her twin brother when white parents adopted him. Didactic in nature, the novel communicates this history explicitly through conversations involving Alice, Jax (Taylor's boyfriend), and Annawake and indirectly through the lessons Taylor learns about racial difference, symbolized somewhat facilely through Taylor's failure to recognize that her daughter is lactose intolerant. These experiences are meant to be instructive about the general lack of knowledge that most whites have about Indian concerns. In this way, the novel offers a stronger statement on white privilege than does *The Bean Trees*. Although Taylor's privilege is challenged in *The Bean Trees,* she does not have to sacrifice any of her own power to advance the well-being of the marginalized people with whom she interacts. In fact, Taylor's status as a white woman helps them, as illustrated by the ease with which the notary accepts her word that the Guatemalans are Turtle's parents simply because she is white (*BT* 214). In *Pigs in Heaven,* however, being part of a cross-cultural coalition, such as the one established at the end of the novel, requires her to relinquish some of her privilege to comply with a resolution meant to rectify historical power disparities. A much more optimistic solution than an absolute disruption of the adoption, shared custody still forces Taylor to give up some of her power to someone she barely knows: "Taylor can still remember the day when she first understood she'd received the absolute power of motherhood— that force that makes everyone else step back and agree that she knows what's best for Turtle. . . . But giving it up now makes her feel infinitely small and alone. She can't even count her losses yet; her heart is an empty canyon" (*PiH* 341). The happiness that accompanies the marriage and the custody agreement tends to gloss over the fact that shared custody represents a loss of parental privilege for Taylor. As Marianne Novy puts it, "While the ending may be utopian from Turtle's point of view, or from the allegorical perspective that it joins Native Americans and whites, Taylor's point of view is different. She is losing the unique maternal power and position that is so important to her" (*Reading* 210). Aside from this sacrifice, however, the main values of cooperation and coalition achieved through nurturing relationships endure, and adoption is, at least for the individuals involved, generally a positive thing.

The novel's conclusion with compromise has been met by critical responses ranging from dissatisfaction to outright derision, as Novy's allusion to criticisms about a "utopian" ending suggests. One critic said that it "trivializes" the cultural conflict because "the reader is invited to believe that the world is inhabited by moral, ethical folks who get along socially" (A. Nelson). Another argued that it is "unrealistic—and dishonest—that this disquieting dilemma is resolved so neatly" (M. Ryan 79). Given the task that Kingsolver undertakes in returning to a beloved mother-daughter pair and then threatening to disrupt their relationship, plus the added burden she builds into the text by showing cultural differences as deeply polarizing, we should not be surprised that the novel garners criticism. Certainly, the marriage of Alice and Cash and Alice's Cherokee ancestry—which facilitates the resolution—feel contrived. Under these circumstances, critics have a point about the conclusion's dependence on coincidence, but such criticisms also reveal something important about the assumptions that they, as readers, bring to the text. Claims that the custody agreement is unrealistic or that custody battles cannot be resolved through compromise reflect the influence of media representations of disrupted adoptions and custody disputes based on race and/or culture, which were particularly prominent in the 1980s and 1990s and still appear periodically today; they, in part, have created the expectation that such conflicts are irresolvable. My point is not to diminish the fact that adoptions are sometimes disrupted and often so under the circumstances similar to those in the novel, which features an inappropriately administered—and, frankly, fraudulent—adoption. Instead, I am interested in how the media's obsession with disrupted adoption might create the false expectation that compromises can never happen. In fact, two important test cases for the Indian Child Welfare Act, *In re Halloway* (1986) and *Mississippi Band of Choctaw Indians v. Holyfield* (1989), resulted in compromises similar to the one depicted in *Pigs in Heaven*. As Christine Metteer explains, in *Halloway*, the six-year-old Navajo child remained a "ward" of his adoptive parents, and his birth mother was appointed his legal parent with visiting rights, while in *Holyfield*, the tribal court eventually approved the adoption of the children involved (Metteer 230). In both cases, when given the authority, tribal courts preserved existing adoptive relationships outside of the tribe, and both cases attest to the realism in Kingsolver's solution. Moreover, as Marianne Novy suggests, we, as critics, might trust readers a little more: "Readers of *Pigs in Heaven* will not expect that transracial adoption issues will be solved in life by allowing transracial adoption only to people with parents related to the nonwhite group who will marry into it if the adoption is contested. 'Utopias' need not be read in such a literal way" (*Reading* 210). The fact that idealized solutions, like the one in the novel, seem so out of the question attests to the prominence of the disputed adoption in the media, what Kingsolver herself refers to as the almost iconic figure of the adoptive mother forcibly losing custody of her child (quoted in Karpen); this narrative makes it difficult to accept that compromises can sometimes happen.

In focusing on the realism of the resolution, critics might be distracted from the more crucial aspect of verisimilitude at stake in Kingsolver's novels, involving the accurate representation of American Indian experiences and political concerns. To what extent does adoption fiction—indeed, any fiction— need to be "true"? More important, what are the grounds on which we evaluate their authenticity? Clearly, Leslie Marmon Silko, the critics who responded to *Pigs in Heaven*, and even Kingsolver herself all feel that veracity is important in depicting adoption, since fictional representations help to shape public perceptions even when they are not necessarily intended as statements on the practice. The heightened awareness of adoption as an individual experience and as a social issue accounts for the privileging of accuracy and raises the additional question of who is authorized to address these issues. Members of the adoption "triad" (birth parents, adoptive parents, and adoptees) have been particularly sensitive to the way each point of view is or is not represented in fiction and nonfiction alike.[8] Silko's critique of *The Bean Trees* also asks who can speak in regard to cultural difference. Sherman Alexie takes this question up directly. He advocates vigorously for authenticity in the representation of Native experiences, something that he strongly implies can only be achieved by American Indian authors. In *Indian Killer*, he uses adoption to frame the issues of cultural authority and subject position. Like Silko and Kingsolver, Alexie clearly believes that fiction defines public perception of cultural difference. In an interview, he

said, "All too often when non-Indians write about Indians they get authority.
... Their work becomes substitute [sic] for work by Indians. Barbara Kingsolver
writes utterly safe literature. It's good. But it's not going to challenge anybody's
expectations of what everything is, of what's Indian. That's the job of the
writer—to challenge. We're not out to be class president" (Ibold). Alexie
equates the power of literature to activism; it cannot simply reassert traditional
power dynamics but, rather, has to challenge them directly. As in this statement,
Barbara Kingsolver often figures prominently in his critique of white authors
who write about American Indians. For instance, he directed this comment toward her: "When you finish writing about Indians, you get up from your type-
writer and you're still white. When I finish, I have to go out and buy groceries,
as an Indian" (quoted in Egan). He stresses the importance of subject position,
that whiteness gives authors certain privileges, not only in publishing, but in
everyday life. Underlying these statements is the implication that he or people
like him are better arbiters of Indian experience than a white author like Kingsolver. While surely someone with lived experience as an Indian will have a better sense of the community's concerns, his statements do not necessarily clarify
the criteria for an authentic Indian experience. After all, Alexie himself has been
subject to criticism similar to that which he levels at Kingsolver, about inauthenticity in his own depictions of tribal experiences, a point I will return to
later.

I highlight these issues about authenticity and representation not to arbi-
trate which position is right but, instead, to call attention to the rhetoric of authenticity and the way it functions in Alexie's adoption novel, *Indian Killer,* and,
indeed, underlies the subtle conversation among the novels discussed here. An
alternative to the adoption story lines in *The Bean Trees* and *Pigs in Heaven, Indian Killer* uses transracial adoption as a vehicle for critiquing white appropriations of Native cultures. His depiction of John Smith, an American Indian
adopted by white parents and raised with a destructive lack of identity, rewrites
Kingsolver's American Indian transracial adoptee by portraying adoption as an
act of genocide, rather than a problematic but ultimately benevolent experience. Through John Smith, Alexie links adoption to a larger pattern of exploitation—of tribes' cultural practices and of the authority to represent Indian experiences—that he sees as disempowering Indians themselves. *Indian
Killer* is as much a polemic as *Pigs in Heaven,* albeit with different aims. It argues against white incursions into Native cultures, through explicitly essentialist language that authorizes Indians alone to document their experiences. Much
like the overt essentialism in Morrison's *Tar Baby,* however, this position con-

tains the seeds of its own critique, as it remains in productive tension with Alexie's portrayal of Indian identity as constructed in multiple contexts and often in resistance to prescriptions from both within and outside Native communities. This strategy suggests that Alexie's notion of inherent identities functions strategically rather than monolithically, as a way of preserving a sense of cultural autonomy.

The novel, a thriller, centers around a series of murders in Seattle and their effect on white and American Indian characters. The main suspect appears to be John Smith, an unfortunately named American Indian of unknown tribal affiliation adopted by white upper-class parents. Although they try to foster a sense of Indian identity in their son, Smith's parents fail to provide him with a sustaining sense of self, causing Smith to internalize his anger at the lack of knowledge about his ancestry; eventually, his sense of fractured identity manifests as schizophrenia. As the murders attributed to the Indian Killer begin to accrue, racial violence and fear increase, culminating in John Smith's kidnapping of author Jack Wilson, a white American who claims obscure but undocumented Native ancestry and writes mystery novels featuring a shaman who is also a private eye. Throughout the novel, Wilson and Professor Clarence Mather, a white professor of American Indian studies, are the targets of criticism from Marie Polatkin, a Spokane Indian student and activist who challenges their representations of tribal cultures as inauthentic and exploitative. Feeling a need to act against the growing hatred of Indians in Seattle, John Smith takes Jack Wilson to the construction site of Seattle's last skyscraper and tells him to "let us have our own pain" before leaping to his death. Although posthumously identified by some, including Wilson, as the Indian Killer, John Smith is clearly not the murderer, and indeed, the Indian Killer is never caught. The novel's final scene features the killer singing and dancing, joined by other Indians in an allusion to Wovoka's Ghost Dance (*IK* 419).[9] The scene lends a note of magical realism to the novel's conclusion and suggests that the Indian Killer is a mystical manifestation of righteous vengeance on behalf of all Native people.

In *Indian Killer*, Alexie removes adoption from Kingsolver's discursive frame of a loving family and redefines it as a militaristic abduction. With little information about his birth parents, John Smith can only imagine the circumstances surrounding his adoption, which he does in vivid detail. After his barely teenaged mother gives birth, the infant John Smith is whisked away by a faceless man in a white jumpsuit who arrives in a helicopter. As it lifts off, "suddenly this is a war. . . . The helicopter gunman locks and loads, strafes the reservation with explosive shells." Some Indians scatter but others remain "unperturbed by the gunfire. They have been through much worse" (*IK* 6). In Smith's fantasy, his relinquishment becomes a military action with the cinematic qualities of a Vietnam War movie. The Indians around the hospital are treated as hostile combatants who threaten the retrieval of the precious cargo. The helicopter's gunfire extends the violence enacted against John Smith and his family to the entire tribe and suggests that individual acts of adoption affect the tribe and, moreover, that this adoption is merely one of the many other atrocities committed against its people. This scene perverts the notion of adoption as "rescue"—as the helicopter swooping in is often associated with rescue in war films—by showing it as a violent abduction. Here adoption is not an image of cross-cultural connection; it becomes an act of war and, for Alexie, a vehicle through which to critique the colonization of tribes.

Not only does the novel challenge the idea of adoption by whites as a benefit to Indian children, but it specifically critiques the practice of cultural preservation advocated by adoption professionals as a way of offsetting adoption's losses by creating a sense of cultural identity. A consequence of the transracial adoption debates of the 1970s and the more recent activism of some adoptees and adoptive parents, cultural preservation practices include exposing children to their birth culture and teaching them that culture's language and customs in order to make them feel connected. As the next chapter discusses further, these efforts have grown into a cottage industry, particularly in international adoption. Alexie alludes to such strategies when he shows Smith's parents offering a hodgepodge of stories about American Indians, blurring tribal cultures in an ineffectual effort to provide a sense of connection for Smith. The novel juxtaposes these efforts to the child's name, which his adoptive father chooses in order to honor his own grandfather, noting to himself the irony that his grandfather was an immigrant but failing to recognize the larger irony that "John Smith" is also synonymous with colonization and the displacement of Indian tribes. The end of Smith's relinquishment fantasy symbolizes the inadequacy of these cultural preservation efforts, when Olivia, his adoptive mother, puts the infant John to her "large, pale breasts" that cannot provide him nourishment (*IK* 8). The lack of information about his origins—exacerbated by his adoptive parents' inability to help him develop a sustaining sense of identity, to nurture him physically or culturally—leaves John Smith constantly seeking a past that can never be located. It also creates a paralyzing condition of double consciousness that devolves into schizophrenia and, ultimately, suicide.

Through John Smith and his adoption, Alexie speaks to other acts of cultural appropriation that threaten tribal cultures. Throughout the novel, Alexie sustains a dialogue about authenticity, positioning the most culpable white characters, author Jack Wilson and professor Clarence Mather, against Indian activist Marie Polatkin, who challenges both characters on their exploitative behaviors. She voices the novel's most overtly polemical points. For instance, Marie protests the fact that Mather, a white man, is teaching a Native American literature class, arguing, "Well, when I take a chemistry course, I certainly hope the teacher is a chemist. Women teach women's lit at this university, don't they? And I hope that African-Americans teach African-American lit." When Mather replies, "I have been involved with Native Americans longer than you've been alive," she responds, "As long as I've been alive, I've been an Indian" (*IK* 312). Marie's argument about professors' subject position collapses gender and cultural identity (women's studies) with professional training (chemistry), creating a rather simplistic equivalency between lived experience and learned knowledge. Perhaps Alexie intended Marie to be an unapologetically radical college student, but since her statements so closely resemble his own—as in his comment, directed toward Kingsolver, that he must go to the grocery store as an Indian—her positions risk making his authorial argument seem rather one-dimensional, too. Moreover, as critic Louis Owens (Choctaw-Cherokee) notes, for all her demands for authenticity, Marie herself is not exactly as "authentic" as she would like others to be: she "organizes protest after protest but almost never returns to her own reservation community (or does so secretly by night) and shows no sign of being a product of any coherent community, Indian or otherwise. All Marie knows how to do is protest the existence of white people" (78–79). But this contradiction may not be a flaw; in fact, the irony that her public statements do not match up with her lived experience may actually be the point and is, perhaps, one of the novel's strengths. The contradictions in Marie's character subtly undercut the novel's essentialist language and "flat-footed," to use Owens's word (78), didacticism, to offer a more complex position on identity that can accommodate a diversity of lived experiences that could qualify as "Indian."

Marie's vocal activism derives from her own feelings of inauthenticity, a situation that allows her to serve as an important corollary to John Smith. In some ways, she resembles *Tar Baby*'s Jadine, whose identity does not conform to the roles made available to her, though Marie seems even more alienated. While Jadine resists essentialist definitions of identity, Marie employs them strategically, as a tool that can compensate for her precarious sense of identity. Marie's alienation results from several factors. Her parents have chosen not to teach her the tribal language, believing that it will not serve her in the wider world (*IK* 33), and they encourage her to pursue a path off the reservation, where her peers have either lost interest in their education or have devoted themselves to their culture, speaking Spokane, traveling the powwow circuit, and settling down on the reservation. Considering herself an outcast from her tribe (*IK* 38), she does not feel comfortable in the largely white world of the university either, engendering hostility from some whites on campus for her outspoken advocacy for Indian issues. Her insecurity makes Marie constantly conscious of the spectrum of Indian identity, "with the more traditional to the left and the less traditional Indians to the right. Marie knew she belonged somewhere in the middle of that spectrum and her happiness depended on placing more Indians to her right" (*IK* 39). Under these conditions, maintaining an essentialist stance on Indian identity serves to confirm her position on that continuum and to compensate for the ways that she might otherwise depart from traditional values.[10]

The novel's militant tone also disguises the degree to which Marie and, by extension, Alexie, struggle to redefine the meaning of Indian identity in reaction to expectations imposed from within and outside tribal communities. Marie aligns herself with urban Indians, "an amalgamation that included over two hundred tribes in the same Seattle area where many white people wanted to have Indian blood." This community is comprised of outcasts who were forced out or never lived on the reservation in the first place; despite this displacement, they still identify with their tribes (*IK* 38). Marie's identity also extends beyond Indians as such to include the urban underclass of the homeless more generally, whom she sees as their own kind of tribe, treated as Indians often are (*IK* 146). This surprisingly expansive definition accounts for her general impatience with stereotypical "Indian" things, which she defines as "spider this, spider that" (*IK* 247) or "dancing half naked and pounding drums": "Marie knew there were hungry people waiting to be fed. Dancing and singing were valuable and important. Speaking your tribal language was important. Trees were terrific. But nothing good happens to a person with an empty stomach" (*IK* 331). In this view, an American preoccupation with the idealized signifiers of Indianness—as represented by Mather and Wilson, the characters who "go native"—completely overlooks the lived experience of the Indians that Marie knows, people who are homeless and sometimes physically and mentally ill. These attitudes also offer a definition of Indian identity that departs from Marie's strident statements about authenticity. Beyond familiarity with cultural practices or native languages (though these things are not necessarily a prerequisite), being "Indian," in Marie's mind, is a lived experience, a consciousness of the struggles and triumphs of individual Indians, many of whom are defined as much by mainstream American popular culture as by tribal practices. In this novel, as in much of Alexie's work, Indian identity involves certain values—humor, a commitment to family, generosity, and a lack of class consciousness. Perhaps it is telling that Marie is one of the only Native characters in the novel to have grown up on the reservation, yet her identity is not focused there. This recognition of the plight of urban Indians and the homeless points to new strategies for establishing more satisfactory identities that respond to individuals' unique experiences. Marie ultimately understands identity as something to be sought, not automatic or guaranteed, and also as something constructed in more than one location. While it is attached to the body, it is not limited to it, even if much of the language in the novel might seem to suggest otherwise.

The definition of Indian identity established by Marie's thoughts and actions, rather than her words alone, suggests a multifaceted and variable combination of lived experience, physical traits, cultural practices, and a general sense of alienation. When aligned with Marie's, John Smith's identity problems seem decidedly less singular. As children, both attempt to wipe their dark skin away—Marie because she wanted to be white (*IK* 232), John because he wanted to look more like his parents (*IK* 306). John's fantasy reservation life strongly resembles Marie's childhood. She had all of the things he dreams about but still felt alienated from her peers, which suggests that the things he desires would not necessarily guarantee happiness. It further demonstrates how John creates an illusion of Indian life that is as unrealistic, perhaps, as Jack Wilson's fiction. John is not in a position to recognize that even a relatively positive life cannot grant a secure identity. That John Smith's identity problems are not as unusual as they initially seem is even more apparent when he is paired with Father Duncan, the Jesuit priest and Spokane Indian who mentors Smith as a boy. Like Father Duncan, Smith suffers from a divided consciousness. As an Indian and a Jesuit, Father Duncan is affiliated with the colonized and the colonizer simultaneously, as is John Smith, a member of a white family. Both eventually commit suicide. Grouping Marie, Father Duncan, and John Smith in this way highlights one of the novel's many ironies: that John Smith, in his extreme alienation, is more Indian than he ever realizes.[11] His adopted status divides him psychically and culturally, which means that he never recognizes that he actually does belong to a community.

Although consistent with themes of hybridity in contemporary American Indian identity that appear in Alexie's other writing, *Indian Killer* lacks the nuances of his other work. He mentions in an interview that this novel has a particular hold on him: "It's sold by far the least of all my books. Indians didn't like it. It was the book that was hardest to write, that gave me the most nightmares, that still, to this day, troubles me the most because I can't even get a grasp on it. It's the only one I re-read. I think a book that disturbs me that much is the one I probably care the most about" (Campbell). Recently, he has backed away from the novel, calling it a "very fundamentalist, binary book, the product of youthful rage" (Jaggi). In 2003, Alexie published "The Search Engine," a short story that, in an interesting corollary to Kingsolver's pair of adoption texts, seems to be a corrective to *Indian Killer*'s representation of adoption. In it, Alexie revisits not only *Indian Killer*'s issues of authenticity and representation but also the characters of Marie Polatkin and John Smith and offers a less tragic outcome of American Indian extra-tribal adoption. In the story, college student and Spokane Indian Corliss Joseph stumbles across a book of poetry written by Spokane Harlan Atwater in the early 1970s. Intrigued by his writing and the fact that no one on the reservation knows who he is, she eventually tracks him down to Seattle. She learns that he was adopted as a child, claimed an Indian identity in the 1960s until he felt like a fraud, and spent the rest of his life in a blue-collar job, taking care of his (adoptive) parents. As a young man, Atwater suffered from uncertainty about how his ancestry fit into his personal identity, particularly when he was writing poetry, and as an adult, he still has not entirely resolved those issues, yet he also seems to have had a satisfying life. There are clearly psychological costs to his adoption, but he does not end up schizophrenic and dead by suicide, as John Smith does. Like Marie Polatkin, Corliss Joseph possesses a precocious intellect, a sense of alienation in her family as result of that intellect, and a proud cultural consciousness. But while Marie is extremely self-protective and confrontational, Corliss tempers her assertiveness with amused cynicism and a willingness to give the benefit of the doubt to those she encounters, which include a white homeless man; a deaf, elderly white woman who owns a used bookstore; and Harlan Atwater himself. Both Marie and Corliss provide an alternative perspective to their counterparts in *Indian Killer*, suggesting that Alexie's stance on both adoption and authentic identity may be more expansive than the tone of *Indian Killer* might suggest.[12]

The issues of representation and appropriation brought up not only in *Indian Killer* through Marie Polatkin but by both Alexie and Silko in regard to Kingsolver's adoption narratives raise an important question about who should speak about American Indians. Both Alexie and Silko suggest that lived experience—going "to the grocery store as an Indian"—is a crucial aspect of accurate representation, yet Alexie's own critical reception attests to the limitations of that criterion, too. Alexie has, at times, been sharply rebuked by critics who felt that his accounts of tribal life feed white American stereotypes about Indians. Reviewing Alexie's earlier novel *Reservation Blues* (1995), Gloria Bird (Spokane) argues that Alexie's reliance on film references allows him access to a non-Native audience but resonates differently and perhaps not so well with a Native reader: "My concern is with the colonialist influence on the native novel, and how that influence shapes the representation of native culture to a mainstream audience" (48). In other words, Alexie's use of cinematic popular culture—Bird likens him several times to Spike Lee—is ultimately a colonialist approach. Louis Owens also argues that Alexie's work "too often simply reinforces all of the stereotypes desired by white readers: his bleakly absurd and aimless Indians are imploding in a passion of self-destructiveness and self-loathing" (79). Characterizing Alexie's work as stereotypical and colonialist, these critics encourage us to reposition the initial conflict between him and Kingsolver in a broader context, one of constant negotiation to define the meaning of Indian identity at a time when American Indians are variously idealized, demonized, or presumed extinct. *Indian Killer* captures the tensions for individuals attempting to forge a satisfying personal identity in the face of conflicting definitions of authenticity. Ironically, despite its essentialist rhetoric, *Indian Killer* makes a reasonable, if veiled, argument for a more expansive definition of tribal identity that might make space for a self-defined identity in resistance to ascribed ones. Like Toni Morrison's *Tar Baby*, *Indian Killer* emphasizes both the value of essential qualities to define identities and their limits. Essentialism works strategically to ground identities that are threatened or at risk, serving as a powerful means of asserting a collective identity. Biology ascribes permanence, immutability, and stability to identity, yet as the adoptees and some of those affiliated with them, like Marie Polatkin, show, these qualities create rigid categories for those whose sense of self or personal experiences do not permit them to fit easily into biogenetically defined categories. The result is an ambivalence about what constitutes authentic identity, an ambivalence communicated through narrative tension, as seen in Alexie's *Indian Killer*.

The degree to which these fictional narratives raise the question of veracity, on an individual and cultural level, illustrates the merging of narrative metaphor and lived experience at the end of the twentieth century. As this chapter shows, the largely metaphorical and plot-driving function of adoption in *The Bean Trees* could not stand once it was placed in the larger context of cultural practices and adoption policy, a context partially fleshed out in *Winter*

CHAPTER 6

Adopting Ambivalence in the Fiction of Sui Sin Far, Anne Tyler, and Gish Jen

In the previous two chapters, transracial adoption challenged the propensity to ground identities too firmly in implicitly or explicitly biological explanations for difference. In Toni Morrison's *Tar Baby* and Sherman Alexie's *Indian Killer*, in particular, essentialist rhetoric employed as an assertion of strong racial identity actually masks a degree of ambivalence about what exactly makes a person culturally or racially "authentic." In the contemporary fiction discussed in this chapter, however, ambivalence takes center stage. Ambivalence is the point of departure for creating a healthy sense of identity for the adopted and nonadopted alike in the context of transnational migrations that include adoption. Contemporary international adoption causes a series of ruptures—familial, cultural, and national—that obscure personal origins, perhaps even more so than domestic transracial adoption in which, at least theoretically, the adoptee participates in his or her national culture of birth, if not a racial or ethnic one. Attempts to compensate for the losses experienced by international adoptees include cultural preservation practices such as language classes and culture camps, as well as other ways to help adoptees feel connected to their birth culture. As Anne Tyler's *Digging to America* (2006) and Gish Jen's *The Love Wife* (2004) illustrate, these strategies may do some good for helping adoptees establish a healthy sense of identity in a nation still preoccupied with race, but they do not and perhaps cannot restore origins lost in the adoption process. These novels demonstrate that a middle space exists between overprivileging the importance of origins and effectively undervaluing them by focusing too closely on their fictive qualities.

The relationship between immigration and adoption in these texts helps to illustrate how origins are implicated in a variety of early twenty-first-century experiences, but before turning to the contemporary texts that are the main focus of this chapter, I want to begin with an early example of how transracial adoption pairs with immigration, in this case to interrogate the tensions in the intolerance toward immigration and racial difference in the United States. "Pat and Pan," a short story published in 1912 by Chinese American author Sui Sin Far,[1] depicts the transracial adoption of a white boy by Chinese American parents and the subsequent disruption of that adoption by white authorities. Pat is the birth son of a destitute white woman who falls ill and leaves him in the care of her Chinese American friends, who later conceive a daughter, Pan. The two children are devoted to one another, as indicated by the opening scene, in which they lay "sound asleep in each other's arms. Her tiny face was hidden upon his bosom and his white, upturned chin rested upon her black, rosetted head" ("PP" 160). The sleeping children catch the eye of Anna Harrison, a white missionary, who is informed that Pat is the son of the local Chinese American jeweler, and she protests, saying, "But he is white" ("PP" 160). Pat speaks no English and is thoroughly embedded in Chinese culture until Anna Harrison encourages him to attend the nearby mission school; she allows his little sister to attend only to ensure that he will go. After a couple of years, community gossip about the white boy becomes intense, resulting in Pat being taken from his home by a "comfortably off American and wife who were to have the boy and 'raise him as an American boy should be raised'" ("PP" 164). Initially Pat protests, saying, "I am Chinese too!" But he eventually grows into his position as a white boy, while Pan observes with sorrow. In the story's final scene, Pat is with a group of white boys and rejects his sister—"the China kid"—outright, to which she responds, "Poor Pat! . . . He Chinese no more" ("PP" 166).

Because it features a white child adopted by parents of color, the adoption scenario sketched out in "Pat and Pan" is unusual even for today, when Americans have otherwise grown accustomed to multiracial families created through adoption. In Far's time, this arrangement of a white child being raised by Chinese American parents would have been beyond the pale, as indicated by the crisis it raises for the community. She uses this adoptive family to show how white America polices the boundaries of the color line through individual families. Biographer Annette White-Parks sees Sui Sin Far's fiction as a calculated attempt to fight racist policies directed toward Chinese Americans. These policies took a variety of forms, from the Chinese Exclusion Act of 1882 (which prohibited the immigration of Chinese laborers and made the Chinese ineligible for naturalized citizenship), to discriminatory tax and landownership laws, to social segregation and victimization in the form of racially motivated violence against people of Chinese descent.[2] In contrast to other fiction of the time that perpetuated hostility toward the Chinese through gross stereotyping, Sui Sin Far places Chinese Americans at the "center of her fictional vision" (White-Parks 215). In doing so, she gives voice to her marginalized characters, who then illustrate the racial oppression inflicted on the Chinese. Far enacted this strategy covertly, by featuring children as both subjects and intended audience in many of her stories. It fit her vision of humanity as "'one family,' a kind of ultimate sense of human community that transcends all contrived groupings" (White-Parks 211). Children and families were also appropriate subjects for a woman writer at the turn of the century. "Children's literature" at that time "aimed not to entertain but to instruct and control" (White-Parks 208). These methods created space for her to publish fiction that subtly challenged the dominant view of the Chinese in both Canada and the United States.

The transracially adoptive family in "Pat and Pan" is just one example of how Far attempted to subvert stereotypical cultural roles; through it, she juxtaposes the Chinese American community's response to Pat and Pan's mixed-race family with that of the white community, in order to critique white America's obsession with race. Chinese culture and white racial origins are not mutually exclusive, nor does racial difference preclude cultural commonality, at least for the Chinese citizens of the community, who see the child as "white; but all the same, China boy" ("PP" 160). This expansive understanding of Chinese American identity contrasts with Miss Harrison's determination that "for a white boy to grow up as a Chinese was unthinkable" ("PP" 161). By her logic, "white" and "Chinese" are inherently different and cannot be bridged on the level of either family or nation. Far's characters also subvert presumptions of white supremacy by refusing to fulfill the stereotypes of the time. Rather than stock predatory and immoral characters,[3] the Chinese Americans in this story, as in the majority of Far's fiction, are good yet not paragons. Pan in particular challenges stereotypes applied to both women and the Chinese. Although younger than her brother, she is brighter than he, excelling at school while he struggles with basic concepts. This may be another, more subtle inversion. Pat's white mother is abject and destitute, and Pat himself seems lacking in innate intelligence. All of these characteristics were presumed by eugenicists at the time to be inherited weaknesses, and Far may be using white supremacist logic to challenge claims of racial superiority. Astute, Pan seems to recognize the threat posed by Anna Harrison and acts as a mediator between her and her brother to protect him. The positive traits of the Chinese Americans stand in contrast to the white mission woman's disregard for Chinese culture ("PP" 162) and people, signaled by her interest in luring Pat away to the white world.[4] But perhaps the most pointed indictment of characteristics associated with whiteness comes from Pat's final assimilation to the white world, signified by his repudiation of Pan in the final scene. Being white means rejection of everything Chinese, even family.

Mrs. Harrison's status as a missionary is also significant because it communicates a certain distrust of Christianity as a tactic for colonizing, both in the United States and when attached to American incursions into other countries.[5] Far articulates this skepticism more explicitly in a short essay called "Americanizing Not Always Christianizing," which equates American assimilation with Christian conversion and cautions that "Americanizing does not always mean improving or even civilizing" and, moreover, that not all Christians live up to the values of the faith (257–58). In essence, she warns against assuming an ethnocentric approach to other cultures, even (or especially) in the name of Christianity. White-Parks articulates this issue more explicitly when she observes that "missionary efforts . . . undertaken by white American women in positions of influence over children—social workers, school-teachers, mission workers— were basically designed to squelch [Chinese American] culture by forcing Chinese Americans into the fold of westernization, as interpreted through Christianity" (180). Far's critique of the combined powers of Christianity and cultural assimilation in "Pat and Pan" takes on added significance when viewed in the context of changing adoption patterns at the turn of the twentieth century, when adoption became more institutionalized and professionalized and when its participants responded explicitly to racial differences. In previous decades, adoption was sometimes religiously motivated, a phenomenon seen in the actions of Protestant minister Charles Loring Brace, founder of the Children's Aid Society and the social engineer of the "orphan trains," which in the middle to late nineteenth century moved children, purportedly orphans, across the nation for adoption placement in the West. In Brace's time, religious conversion often trumped racial differences, particularly if the adoptions involved children of color assimilated into white homes.[6] "Pat and Pan" illustrates a departure from that ethos. For one, the white missionary actually imposes racial distinctions, citing them as her justification for removing Pat from his family. Pat's position in a nonwhite and potentially non-Christian home is an unintended manifestation of assimilation achieved through adoption. He might assimilate, but not in the way that white dominant culture would condone, as his placement has made him a "China boy." In showing white society's intolerance of this adoption arrangement, Far undermines the paternalistic rationale for adoption as both a religious conversion and assimilationist strategy. The image of family that Far creates before Pat is removed from his home, however, does anticipate a different kind of conversion narrative that accompanied depictions of international and transracial adoption in the middle of the twentieth century, a point to which I will return shortly.

"Pat and Pan" resembles Charles W. Chesnutt's *The Quarry* and Dallas Chief Eagle's *Winter Count* in its multiple adoptions, the first disrupted by a second that will place the adoptee in a family deemed more racially appropriate by the dominant group. In other ways, it departs from Chesnutt's work and other early twentieth-century instances of transracial adoption by making the racial difference in the family visible. Far's scenario does not encourage the contemplation of racial ambiguity that is prompted by adoptions in the fiction of Chopin, Faulkner, and Chesnutt, yet the problem of racial categorization raised by Chesnutt's accidental passers resonate in this story as well. Sui Sin Far's life concerns resembled those of Chesnutt's racially mixed characters and, indeed, of Chesnutt himself. Eurasian, Sui Sin Far could have passed for white, but she did not. In her nonfiction essay "Leaves from the Mental Portfolio of an Eurasian," she discusses her mixed-race identity and desire to bridge cultures without either having to privilege one over the other or being destroyed in the process: "I give my right hand to the Occidentals and my left to the Orientals, hoping that between them they will not utterly destroy the insignificant 'connecting link'" (230). In a culture both virulently anti-Chinese and antimiscegenation, Far's very existence was transgressive, as she well knew. With this in mind, the pairing of white brother and Chinese American sister in "Pat and Pan" resembles the allusions to miscegenation that appear in the work of Chesnutt, James Weldon Johnson, and Pauline Hopkins. For instance, the opening scene of the children in one another's arms could, in another context, appear to be a postcoital posture, and the narrator also refers to them as "lovers," which characterizes the intensity of their devotion to one another. White-Parks reads these scenes as acknowledging "the potential for sexual relations, childbearing, and marriage. The story addresses fears in the dominant white culture of loss of their 'own' people to those they term 'other'" (225). The presence of transracial adoption exacerbates that image, by constructing through calculated choice the consequences of multiracial sex: Chinese and white siblings. Transracial adoption is, after all, a kind of miscegenation, undertaken without sexual intercourse but accomplishing a mixing of races. Far's transracially adoptive family explicitly rejects the doctrine of racial purity upheld through antimiscegena-tion laws, and, moreover, it illustrates the consequences of fetishizing racial pu-rity for those of mixed ancestry. At the beginning of the story, the children curl up together like two halves of a whole, but by the end, they are completely sev-ered from one another. The possibility for a coherent multiracial identity like that sought by Far herself is refused by the destructiveness of the white com-munity, which is responsible for introducing racial hierarchy into Pat and Pan's harmonious family. Likewise, the potential for the peaceful coexistence of dif-ferent races and cultures seems out of reach.

Considered by many as the progenitor of Asian American literature, Sui Sin Far herself resists a linear narrative suggested by her place as a literary "fore-mother."[7] Although she was born in England, raised in Canada, and wrote and published in both the United States and Canada, Far is characterized as an American author, in part, I suspect, because her life and subject matter embody the kinds of contradictions associated with American identity. In their intro-duction to Mrs. Spring Fragrance, and Other Writings, Amy Ling and Annette White-Parks list some of the conversations that Far anticipated, including those surrounding the meaning of multiracial and transnational identities and, as they mention in passing, the circumstances of international adoptees from Asia (6). While they do not elaborate on that point specifically, it calls attention to how Far's work uncannily foreshadows not only the subject position of inter-national adoptees but fictional representations of them as well.

By the middle of the twentieth century, transracial and international adop-tions were still linked to religion in ways that might have prompted ambiva-lence from Sui Sin Far. On one hand, adoption continued to remain an avenue to achieving religious goals that also encouraged cultural assimilation. On the other hand, the belief that the mixed-race adoptive family was in the image of "God's family" (Jerng 125) would probably have moved Far, who herself be-lieved in humanity as one family. Regardless, there were significant changes from Far's time in the exact dynamics of the relationship between religion and race in adoption, and these changes, in turn, serve as the foundation of the per-ceptions of international adoptions across racial lines that remain influential today. Though religion itself is beyond the scope of this project, this relation-ship provides an important backdrop for the representation of adoption in the fiction of Tyler and Jen.[8] In the immediate post–World War II era, author Pearl Buck advocated for international and domestic transracial adoptions in lan-guage that blended political elements—an antiracist agenda—and religious ones. Adoption could achieve religious goals by explicitly combining races and nations within a single family. This philosophy established what Mark Jerng calls "the sentimental, salvational worldview that dominated practices of transnational adoption and created the conditions of personhood for a whole generation of transnational adoptees. Though Buck herself talked often of needing to value the cultural origins of the child, what attended this political imagination of adoption was an ethos of assimilation and erasure of ties" (127). Jerng goes on to argue that, more recently, international adoptees have achieved "social visibility" in ways that counteract that earlier sentimental narrative, particularly by emphasizing their lost familial and national origins in order to assert a sense of self (128).

Adoption fiction at the turn of the twenty-first century, particularly *Digging to America* and *The Love Wife*, highlights some of the implications of adult adoptees' concerns about lost cultural origins. In response to adoptee activism, adoptive parents have taken up this problem and have sought out strategies to improve their and their adopted children's cultural awareness; this approach has repercussions not only for adoptees themselves but in the ways in which entire adoptive families choose to respond to adoptees' inaccessible origins, a phenomenon explored in Tyler's and Jen's novels. Through international transracial adoption, contemporary American authors address the problems of modern national identity. Tyler's *Digging to America* and Jen's *The Love Wife* use international adoption to explore the significance of individual, cultural, and national origins for establishing belonging. By pairing international adoption from Asia with another form of transnational migration, immigration, both novels express ambivalence about the role of origins in defining identity, particularly when the circumstances of migration prevent individuals from firsthand knowledge of or participation in their cultures of birth. In these novels, the act of adoption, which requires family members to respond to the adoptees' lack of verifiable origins, provides the metaphorical space to address a larger cultural ambivalence about the significance of origins in defining American identity. Those in adoptive relationships model strategies for responding to personal and cultural dislocation, not only for immigrants and their offspring, but also for white Americans attempting to negotiate a multicultural community.

In the United States, origins establish personal identity and locate an individual's place in a national context. As illustrated by the texts discussed in the first half of this book and by Far's "Pat and Pan," origins played a crucial role in categorizing individuals racially in the early twentieth century. While the one-drop rule itself does not dominate the way it once did, most Americans still put a great deal of stock in their sense of heritage, even if they have no lived experience of an ancestral culture or any connection to it. Genealogy is the second most popular hobby in the United States (Novy, *Reading* 6), a testimony to Americans' interest in their individual and cultural pasts. Yet, as Marc Shell argues, consanguinity can sometimes be faked. "Bastardy" and changelings (and secret adoptions) introduce the possibility that those whom we think are blood kin may not be (Shell 4), making origins far less stable than many Americans perceive them to be. Moreover, the origin stories that sustain identity may be accidentally or intentionally inaccurate. The degree of confidence we have in our personal, individual origin stories is often most evident after they are disproved, in the anguish that can occur when, for instance, an individual learns that the man he knows as his father is not. Adoption provides important insight into this cultural paradox, in which origin stories serve to authenticate personal identity at the same time that they may not actually be verifiable truths. Margaret Homans posits that adoption narratives are fixated on the past, on origins that can never be known, but since that past is irretrievable, these narratives actually create something new to serve the present needs of the adoptee ("Adoption Narratives" 7). Rather than asking these narratives to document a past that cannot be located, "the adopted and their families might do better to understand themselves as inventing helpful fictions about those irretrievable historical moments" ("Adoption Narratives" 9). Homans argues persuasively for the productive work that comes from those fictions, and she rightly notes in passing something that should probably remain at the forefront of any discussion of adoptees and origins, the idea that a narrative "absence at the origin" is not necessarily the liberatory condition that some might suggest. In fact, obscure origins position adoptees (and their families) outside the cultural norm, forcing them to find new ways to orient a sense of self, including, but not limited to, the kind of fictional narratives that Homans outlines. They may also assert a sense of self by simply accepting their rootlessness or by developing other paradigms for self-definition, as some of the characters in these novels demonstrate. Both illustrate that the origins problems in international adoption are not simply "cultural"; they are also familial. Both also show that attention to cultural differences sometimes intersects with another process: the development of new strategies for identifying as "parent" or "child" or "sibling" in the absence of blood ties. Sometimes, responding to cultural difference facilitates the building of new bonds in response to familial difference, as is the case in *Digging to America*; sometimes, cultural difference is held responsible when familial relationships are threatened, as happens in *The Love Wife*.

Digging to America and *The Love Wife* place international adoption into direct relationship with the questions of origins that confront immigrants, their children, and white Americans alike. Although participants in international adoption often focus on the birth country's culture, both of these novels redirect attention away from the sending culture and toward cross-cultural relationships in a U.S. context, offering adoption as a model for how nonadopted Americans can confront the absence of origins in their own lives. The term *origins* applies broadly to support this reading and includes the nation or culture into which one is born but no longer lives or, in the case of some adoptees, never did. It extends to idealized family histories that people use to ground their identities as well as to the obscured family histories that shape our lives and of which we have no knowledge. In these disparate contexts, the nonadopted characters' struggle parallels adoptees' attempts to reconcile origins, but with a distinction: adoptees must, from the outset, accept that knowledge of their personal origins is unavailable, leaving them no choice but to find other ways to locate a stable self; in contrast, the nonadopted must relinquish the fantasy that origins can be completely knowable, a realization they eventually achieve expressly because of their relationship with adopted characters.

In Anne Tyler's *Digging to America*, international adoption and immigration inform one another directly. The novel pairs two extended adoptive families—one white American and the other a combination of first- and second-generation immigrants from Iran—who meet at the airport on the day their infant Korean daughters arrive in the United States. The white, U.S.-born couple, Bitsy Dickinson and Dave Donaldson, commit themselves to preserving the culture of their daughter, Jin-Ho, through gestures such as replicating the haircut with which she arrives in the United States and dressing her in traditional Korean clothes, while the Iranian Americans, Sami and Ziba Yazdan, rename their daughter "Susan" and raise her with little attention to her Korean ancestry. The differing approaches to cultural origins in the adoption plot remain a backdrop to and a mirror for the larger questions of cultural traditions and American expectations for assimilation embodied by Maryam Yazdan, Sami's mother and a naturalized immigrant from Iran who vacillates between wishing to be mistaken as American-born and retaining her status as a foreigner.

As with many representations of contemporary international adoption, *Digging to America* exhibits familiarity with some of the logistics of adoption. The novel begins in an airport with both families waiting to pick up their children, a part of the process recognizable to many Americans and one that Tyler witnessed at an airport herself.[9] Even those who have not seen such events firsthand would probably know of them from news media coverage of international adoption and would be familiar with other practices associated with it, such as language camps and classes and strategies to establish for adoptees a sense of cultural heritage associated with their country of birth.[10] While this novel uses adoption to speak to the complexities of immigration, the logistics of international adoption itself also become part of the text. Similar to Barbara Kingsolver's adoption novels, this inclusion raises the problem of the author's responsibility for accurate representations. As different members of the adoption triad attempt to articulate their own experiences, a greater demand for informed representation has arisen, particularly from transracial adoptees who want more consideration of the challenges of adoption, rather than a celebratory treatment of it centered around the adoptive parents.[11] That Tyler purposely chose not to research the matter, as she said in an interview (Gray), accounts, perhaps, for the very limited voice given to the adoptees in this novel, despite her apparent awareness of adoption's cultural preservation practices. As is the case with Kingsolver's *The Bean Trees,* I do not offer *Digging to America* as an example of an "accurate" representation of adoption or because I consider Tyler an authority on the subject. As I discuss later, her narrative choices in representing adoptees certainly reveal her lack of attention to their points of view. But this limitation does not necessarily render her novel moot for the purposes of discussing adoption's function as a literary trope; adoption provides a means of accessing the issues of immigrant identity that primarily occupy Tyler, even if her representation sometimes seems rather shortsighted. If anything, her rather blithe use of adoption draws attention to the way that adoption can be the object of profound public fascination even as the complex concerns of its participants remain obscured.

In *Digging to America,* the adopters respond to their children's cultural detachment not through language classes or culture camp but through an "Arrival Party." This yearly event is devised by Bitsy Dickinson to "commemorate the date the girls arrived" (*DtA* 52), observed with a sheet cake decorated with an American flag, a song about arrival ("She'll Be Coming 'Round the Mountain"), and a screening of the video made at the airport on the day the girls arrive (*DtA* 53). According to Bitsy's plan, the girls will wear traditional Korean outfits and enter the room on cue, as if arriving all over again. Bitsy recruits Ziba and her family to participate for the same reason that she initiates a friendship with the other couple in the first place: "I believe the girls should get to know each other, don't you? So as to maintain their cultural heritage" (*DtA* 19). In this novel, "cultural heritage" serves as a catch phrase for the variety of problems with difference introduced by adoption, and its usage by Bitsy also captures the paradoxical qualities of a focus on culture. After all, while a relationship between the girls might be important because of their common experiences as adoptees, it cannot, strictly speaking, cultivate a heritage that neither child is old enough to participate in or remember. Even as Bitsy conscientiously tries to enact the conventional wisdom of contemporary adoption, the novel indicates that such efforts might actually serve a different function altogether, creating scripts that can facilitate familial belonging in the absence of biological kin connection. As with other forms of transracial adoption, international adoption destabilizes American cultural assumptions about shared origins within families. Even though "cultural" differences are emphasized in international adoption, familial differences remain operative as well, causing a disjuncture in the family that can be mediated through attention to culture.[12]

The Arrival Party provides a collective script that can compensate for the lack of biological and cultural connections between adoptees and parents, yet it also illustrates the difficulties that accompany such efforts. Bitsy's attitude toward "heritage" and her design of the party, for instance, communicate ambivalence about her family's difference. Unequipped to cultivate a heritage that she herself does not live, Bitsy counterbalances the party's Korean elements with what she does know: American culture. The Arrival Party commemorates the day the girls became not just family members but Americans, too, a circumstance reflected in the flag cake. Korean culture signifies a birth history that cannot be accessed, while the flag cake substitutes a physical signifier of national belonging in place of the more abstract quality of familial belonging that still remains somewhat precarious. The perspective of the Iranian Americans illustrates the limitations of this strategy for responding to adoption's difference. As Sami Yazdan remarks privately, Bitsy's Arrival Party is "quintessentially American": "For [their daughter's] birthday they give her a couple of presents, but for the day she came to America it's a full-fledged Arrival Party, a major extravaganza with both extended families and a ceremony of song and a video presentation. Behold! You've reached the Promised Land! The pinnacle of all glories!" (*DtA* 87–88). Sami's comments highlight the cultural politics of international adoption communicated through narratives of upward mobility that privilege American culture over the adoptee's sending country. While one could easily defend the Arrival Party as the parents' way of observing something tangible to them—the arrival—since they had no part in their daughter's birth, Sami's point of view also recognizes that the Arrival Party effaces the child's subjectivity, minimizing the day of her birth and promoting her new Americanness as the event worth observing.

Sami's response to the Donaldsons reflects his own ambivalence as an American-born child of immigrants, and his presence and that of his wife create an important counternarrative to the cultural preservation strategy of managing adoption's difference. Unlike Bitsy, who feeds her daughter "culturally appropriate" soy milk (*DtA* 24), the Yazdans call their daughter "Susie-june," using a Persian diminutive. They grow out her hair, dress her in American clothes, and do not spend much time thinking about her Korean cultural heritage. While Bitsy attempts to preserve Jin-Ho's difference, the Yazdans facilitate Susan's acculturation. Their choices about Susan replicate their own attempts to fit in with American culture, such as Ziba's embrace of American fashion and music after her arrival as a teenager or Sami's tendency to be "more American than the Americans," as his mother describes it (*DtA* 83). As people already marked physically and culturally as "other," they minimize the signs of difference in an effort to fit in. At the same time, however, the Yazdans also fulfill their own project of cultural preservation, raising Susan in an Iranian American extended family that speaks Farsi, cooks traditional food, and observes Iranian holidays. Susan thus picks up enough Farsi to ask her father a question in it and learns to make rice "with the efficient, forward-swooping motion employed by every Iranian housewife" (*DtA* 161). Both families must respond to the obscure past of their adopted children, but the Yazdans must also deal with the loss of their own culture in the act of immigration. While the Donaldsons may for the first time have to consider the implications of being detached from origins, the Yazdans continue with the process of compensating for their own cultural losses and, as a result, instill a cultural tradition into Susan that may not replicate the one she was removed from but may, nevertheless, sustain her.

The videotape of the girls' arrival, shown at each party, captures the deep ambivalences involved in rewriting culture scripts to respond to adoption's obscure origins. The video is actually a series of recordings taken by various Dickinson-Donaldson family members at the airport and spliced together. It begins with a "dated-looking, pale blue watered-silk background [with] copperplate script [that] spelled out *The Arrival of Jin-Ho*" (*DtA* 70). The footage is clearly taken by different people, with the camera at times "swooping" and at other times steadily documenting the events. The tape mediates the arrival and attempts to provide a linear narrative, compensating for what they do not know about Jin-Ho's birth by narrating what is essentially her rebirth in the liminal space of the airport. The contents of the tape reflect the difficulty in such a task. The perspectives shift without warning; at one point an uncle is filming and narrating, then suddenly he himself is in the picture (*DtA* 71). Even as they attempt to capture the moment and give it meaning, the splicing suggests the elusiveness of the experience, its resistance to a fixed narrative. That resistance becomes more evident in subsequent showings of the tape. Initially, the Donaldsons assume that Susan was not captured in their footage, since they did not yet know the Yazdans, yet the first communal viewing of it shows that she, too, appears in this video document. The following year, when the Donaldsons show the tape again, the title has been altered to read "The Arrival of Jin-Ho and Susan" in a different font. The adoption narrative has shifted again, broadened to include the arrival of both children.

While it attempts to compensate for the absence of origins in adoption, the tape also reveals the families' changes over time. As the parties continue annually, the tape fades into the background, no longer formally viewed by the group. Later, as Jin-Ho becomes older (and the novel briefly occupies her subject position), the reader learns that she hates the video—"She never, ever, even once in her life had watched that stupid videotape" (*DtA* 220)—and her grandfather mentions in passing that she "accidentally" drops it in a punch bowl (*DtA* 253). These developments accompany her general rejection of all things Korean: "Jin-Ho was not about to travel to Korea. She didn't even like the food from Korea. She didn't like wearing those costumes with the stiff, sharp seams inside" (*DtA* 220). The family narrative sustained by the video is not complete, taking on new meaning with the introduction of Jin-Ho's point of view. Not celebratory for Jin-Ho, the tape becomes alienating, an emphasis on her difference that collides with her own self-perception. The inclusion of Jin-Ho's perspective and the absence of Susan's illustrate the degree to which the narrative of the girls' difference is established without their consent, a situation compounded by Tyler's unwillingness to dwell too long in the child's point of view. In an interview, Tyler went so far as to say, "My main concern was not having too much of either girl's voice. A little of a child's-eye view goes a long way, in my opinion—you don't want to sound 'cute,' and you certainly don't want to force the reader to stay too long in the terrible country of childhood" (Gray). This narrative choice has a cost, as it allows readers to avoid occupying the subject position of the transracial adoptee, a figure whose experience should be more central to a novel that revolves around adoption. At least a couple of readers have noted that the points of view of the adoptees remain obscured in the novel,[13] and even the brief glimpse into Jin-Ho's thoughts contradicts the rather blithe depiction of adoption offered here. Tyler introduces a tension that she is uninterested in exploring. This hint that adoptees might think differently reminds us that international adoption narratives evolve past the scenarios imagined when the adoptees are children; they remain constantly open to revision as the adoptee matures and reevaluates his or her relationship with the past.

The limitations in Tyler's approach to adoption emphasize the fact that adoption—while important for this particular analysis—is actually secondary to the novel's main plotline, Maryam Yazdan's eventual assimilation to American culture. Yet without adoption as an example, Maryam could not overcome her own ambivalence about cultural origins. She expresses the connection between the social positions of adoptee and immigrant immediately upon meeting her granddaughter, a recognition that elucidates Maryam's struggle to find a sense of belonging in the United States. She feels an instant bond with the child, "something around the eyes, some way of looking at things, some *onlooker's* look: that was what they shared. Neither of them quite belonged" (*DtA* 13). Their common outsider position compensates for the lack of biological kinship ties and parallels their experiences in transnational migration, which depends on the severance of both national and kinship ties. Anthropologist Sara Dorow observes that children become available for international adoption only when they are declared "orphans" by their sending nation, and they can become American citizens upon entry only if one of their adoptive parents is a legal citizen of the United States. Dorow calls these conditions a "kind of serial monogamy of national/familial kinship," which is further compounded by regulations that forbid adoptees' birth families from immigrating to the United States to be with their children (209). International adoptees' citizenship status depends on severing ties to the birth family and establishing a new family relationship in the United States, a deprivation echoed in Maryam's experience, in which the breaking of national connections results in kinship loss as well. Maryam associates her immigration with the separation from family, though her "serial monogamy" (to borrow an apt phrase) functions differently than that of the infant adoptees. Unlike them, she remembers the people she left behind, and they become a force that orients her toward a past she can no longer access. At her greatest moment of alienation, Maryam dreams of traveling back in time to return to her mother (*DtA* 265). She conceives of herself as an orphan, perhaps not surprising for a woman whose parents have been dead a long time, but the orphancy is more than just familial: "She still mourned her mother's death, but she had traveled so far from her, into such a different kind of life. It no longer seemed they were related" (*DtA* 146). As a symbolic (not to mention literal) source of her origin, Maryam's mother represents the losses Maryam experiences as an immigrant to the United States, a movement that disrupts her sense of relatedness—to her homeland, to her mother, and to her new nation.

Such a loss also has consequences for how Maryam conceives of family more generally. Immigration and adoption collaborate to complicate the meaning of ancestry for those permanently detached from their original cultures. This point becomes abundantly clear late in the novel, when Maryam shares with Susan a family photo album. After pointing out a picture of Maryam's father, she tells Susan, " 'He would be your great-grandpa.' But would he? The words sounded untruthful the instant they slipped from her mouth. Close though she felt to Susan—as close as any grandmother could possibly feel—she had trouble imagining the slightest link between the relatives back home and this little Asian fairy child with her straight black hair, her exotic black eyes, her skin as pale and opaque and textureless as bone" (*DtA* 257). The problem is a combination of cultural, racial, and familial ruptures that confound the logic of genealogy, which traces generations through shared blood. These ancestors, by virtue of Maryam's position as Susan's grandmother, are also Susan's ancestors. But what does ancestry mean when Susan does not share the "blood" of any of the people in the photo album? While the constructed kinship of adoption certainly makes sense in the context of immediate, proximate family members, such as Maryam and Susan, it does not adequately address the problem of ancestry. Without personal relationship or blood connection, who are those people to Susan but strangers? Ancestry also poses a problem for Maryam, who, like the adoptees, stands on the threshold of two different cultures and two different conceptions of family. Part of the reason that she cannot imagine the thread connecting them is because she, too, is tangential to that thread herself. While she feels as close to Susan as any grandmother could, she represents one of the only strands that link these families together, a blood connection from previous generations and a relationship constructed through mutual affection that links her to her granddaughter. The genealogical—and presumably "blood"—line she documents through the photo album stops with her son, Sami, and in a sense skips a rail to become a constructed link, which will be sustained through Susan and any future generations that come from her. Those who preceded Maryam share familial blood and racial and cultural heritage. The line that comes after her will be not only of a different race—and an exoticized one, as her language "fairy child" suggests—but of a different nationality as well.[14]

The novel's conclusion intimately binds adoption and immigration through the traditional marital kinship drama (Sollors, *Beyond* 165). Throughout the novel, the Dickinson-Donaldsons and Yazdans have shared a series of life experiences that bring them closer: the death of Bitsy's mother from cancer; the adoption of the Donaldsons' second child, Xiu-Mei from China; Bitsy's breast cancer diagnosis; and the courtship, brief engagement, and break up of Maryam and Dave Dickinson, Bitsy's father. The novel concludes on the day of yet another Arrival Party. The format of the party has changed; rather than a fancy Iranian meal as they had in the past, they take out sushi from a restaurant. In place of the Stars and Stripes sheet cake, dessert is a traditional Middle Eastern dish, baklava, with a couple of miniature paper flags stuck in it. The shift reflects the gradual melding of cultural traditions, those long established and those innovated in response to adoption—a new, seemingly more organic script that arises out of the families' blending their interests and responding to current needs. The party is almost ruined, however, when Maryam fails to show up. The Dickinson-Donaldson family senses that her reluctance to attend stems from her broken engagement to Bitsy's father, and all of them go to Maryam's house to plead with her to join them: "We can't have the party without you. We need you!" Hidden from view, Maryam watches as they turn around, disappointed by her lack of response. At that moment, Maryam chooses to cast her lot with the Dickinson-Donaldson family: "Maryam thought of Bitsy's hopefulness, her wholeheartedness, her manufactured 'traditions' that seemed brave now rather than silly. The sudden wrench to her heart made her wonder if it might be Bitsy she loved. Or maybe it was all of them. . . . 'Wait!' she called. 'Don't go! Wait for me!' . . . They stopped. They turned. They looked up at her and they started smiling, and they waited for her to join them" (*DtA* 277).

This last scene dramatizes Maryam's willingness to join American culture. Her hesitation and then effort to call the family back puts the emphasis on her, on the fact that it is her choice and perhaps her responsibility to give up some of the foreignness she has reserved for herself throughout the novel and join them. The implied marriage at once replicates and offers variations on the kinship drama model of the early twentieth century in which an immigrant chooses an American identity over an Old World one by taking an American spouse. By marrying Dave, Maryam will, symbolically, choose an American spouse over the ancestors pictured in the album she shows Susan. Her relationship with Dave represents her commitment to being an American in spirit as well as in name. This scene signals more than a completed transition for Maryam, however. The family's arrival also gives them a role in the process by requiring them to include her. Moreover, when the family arrives, it is Bitsy that Maryam singles out and wonders if she might love; she does not mention Dave. Throughout the novel, Bitsy has represented a specific kind of American entitlement that Maryam resents. While politically conscious and attempting to be culturally aware, Bitsy is also overbearing, imposing her own views without regard for how they might affect others. To identify Bitsy as the one Maryam loves signals her acceptance of the unpleasant parts of American culture that have held her back previously; it also provides another, more generous interpretation of Bitsy's and the culture's flaws. In this way, the conclusion winks at the classic "comedy" ending of marriage yet departs from it, emphasizing that the connections forged at this moment extend beyond marriage. The efforts of the family and Maryam's acceptance complete the consensual kinship initiated through improvised scripts that link the two families. More than the traditional kinship drama that forges bonds through marriage or the adoptive kinship drama that connects through adoption, this novel models, much like Barbara Kingsolver's *Pigs in Heaven*, multiple connections across families with no formal kin relationship. Their kinship is cultivated through collective effort.

The novel ends happily, with Maryam's self-imposed isolation relieved through her relationship with the Dickinson-Donaldsons. While the gesture they make to include Maryam suggests the efforts required of white Americans to help facilitate the process, the novel puts the burden of establishing belonging on immigrants, encouraging them to give up their sense of foreignness, which may be the only identity to remain after leaving their countries. In an interview, Tyler implied that the novel's ending is not the last word on Maryam's belonging: "But because I agree with Dave [Bitsy's father] that we all feel the others belong more, I don't think a single one of these characters will ever reach the point where he or she would say, 'I've succeeded; I'm in. I can sit back and breathe easy now'" (Gray). Despite this message, the text implies a shift in thinking on the part of newer, nonwhite immigrants that is not demanded as much of the white Americans.

Digging to America synthesizes immigration and adoption, representing both as manageable experiences; even as Tyler herself hints at unresolved issues, the novel depicts closure after struggle. In this sense, Gish Jen's *The Love Wife*, although its publication precedes that of *Digging to America* by a few years, is its antithesis. In *The Love Wife*, confronting absent origins does not lead to resolution but instead remains a lifelong state of negotiation. The novel depicts a multiracial and adoptive family who must enact the terms of Mama Wong's will. Family matriarch and immigrant to the United States from China, Mama Wong dictates that her son, American-born Carnegie Wong, and his wife, Janie Bailey ("Blondie," as Mama Wong and the rest of the characters call her), sponsor a female relative from China who will live with the family and ensure that the children learn Chinese. In return for sponsoring Lan for two years, the family will inherit "the book" that documents the Wong family history. The

rest of the family includes Lizzy, a foundling who looks "Asian" but has no documentable ancestry; Wendy, an adoptee from China; and Bailey, the biracial
birth son of Carnegie and Janie. They represent a full spectrum of familial,
racial, and cultural identity issues. The arrival of Lan into the family foregrounds its racial and cultural differences, as Carnegie becomes interested in
the Chinese culture he previously eschewed and as Janie must respond to her
position as the only non-Asian person in the family. The tensions between culture and race, nurture and nature, overwhelm and threaten to destroy the family. The novel ends with hope, suggesting that the family's commitment to one
another—their participation in consensual familial and cultural relationships—will overcome the strains they experience; nevertheless, those tensions
do not actually dissipate. Instead, ambivalence becomes perhaps the strongest
thread in the fabric of their relationships, something to be accepted because it
cannot be fully resolved. In *The Love Wife*, as in *Digging to America*, international adoption serves as a backdrop for the experiences of immigrants, their
children, and native-born Americans struggling to negotiate a sense of identity.
Different from the family in *Digging to America*, *The Love Wife*'s Wongs are
more mixed, a complicated combination of immigrant and native-born Americans formed through mixed-race marriage, domestic adoption, international
adoption, and biological conception. Within this milieu, the kinds of closure
offered by *Digging to America* are less attainable and, as *The Love Wife*'s conclusion suggests, perhaps not even desirable.

This novel's unusual structure creates the narrative conditions that reinforce its affirmation of ambivalence. The first-person narration switches from
one character to another, sometimes in the middle of a conversation in what
one reviewer calls a "choral manner" (Kakutani), though it also possesses qualities of a documentary film, as if some characters were addressing a silent audience located just off camera.[15] Laid out like a play, the novel signals the character's point of view by introducing it with the speaker's name. In addition, the
immigrant characters, Mama Wong and Lan, also get two forms of narration,
one in regular font that signifies them speaking English with occasionally
strained syntax, the other in italics, suggesting the use of their native language.
This structure resists a dominant narrative point of view or ideology, uniquely
depicting individual experiences with difference as fluid and highly subjective.
Many events are simultaneously narrated from different characters' points of
view, allowing for instantaneous alternate reactions, as in the following scene
when various family members discuss adoption.

WENDY / . . . . It's not fair, says Lizzy. It's not fair that Wendy's adopted from China and speaks Chinese, while nobody even knows what I am or where I came from. I hate being soup du jour . . . . It's probably how come my real mother abandoned me, don't you think it's how come?

—No, says Mom. I think she left you at the church because she loved you and knew she couldn't parent you.

LIZZY / It was like some present she popped out of her pocket all wrapped up but that you know she didn't wrap herself. . . .

—You're just saying that! I said. How do you know? You're just saying what it says in the adoption books you should say. . . .

—It's not out of a book, said Dad, walking by.—It's out of the adoption video. . . .

WENDY / Anyway, he's calmed Lizzy down a little, Mom just wishes she could talk like Dad sometimes. But she can't, it's like her mouth just doesn't move that way, I know because in that way I'm just like Mom. Even if she isn't my birth mother, I'm like her anyway. (*LW* 211–12)

This scene highlights the polyphonic nature of the text, with dialogue juxtaposed against various characters' interpretation of the scene. This narrative strategy also allows for a critical exploration of transracial adoption's complexities. In this scene, one of many in which the adoptees react to the lack of information about their origins, the advice of adoption specialists—offered by Blondie when she says that Lizzy's birth mother "knew she couldn't parent you"—is immediately confronted by Lizzy herself, who complains that such a response seems artificial or prepackaged. It is, as Carnegie points out and Blondie admits in another part of the novel (*LW* 107).

This brief interchange exposes some of the flaws in adoption's conventional wisdom, not just in how to explain it, but also in the emphasis on culture to provide a sense of connection for international adoptees. In many ways, Lizzy and Wendy Wong are *Digging to America*'s Jin-Ho and Susan all grown up and, in the case of Lizzy, angry. Their parents' attempts to make them comfortable with their otherness often fail because such pro forma responses are inadequate to address not only the specific needs of each individual adoptee but also the complex circumstances of adoption itself, which resists easy answers. Because the text provides alternating points of view, Lizzy's anger, which sometimes appears whiny and self-involved, also becomes understandable when informed by her parents' ineffective attempts to meet her needs, especially since, as Margaret

Homans points out, Carnegie and Blondie have "clumsily required Lizzy to identify as Chinese, because it is convenient to have two girls that 'match'" ("Origins, Searches" 71). Lizzy's anger gains further dimension when offset by Wendy's more tempered commentary. These two characters seem to be an answer to the call for more complex representations of adoptees' points of view. Even though Blondie's strategy fails, the conversation among family members suggests different means of responding to the absence of origins; in this case, it is Lizzy's speculation that her birth mother abandoned her at a church because she is "soup du jour," the family's shorthand for racially mixed. As Margaret Homans suggests, origin stories are sometimes constructed to meet the present needs of the individual ("Adoption Narratives" 5). Lizzy looks for the best explanation she can find for her abandonment, and a story that implies rejection supports her carefully cultivated persona as an outsider.

The novel suggests that these cultural preservation strategies fail because the questions that the girls have about their personal circumstances simply cannot be answered. Although the parents create "a veritable Chinatown tchotchke shop" in Wendy's bedroom to celebrate her Chinese ancestry (LW 206), no amount of material objects can tell the girls who gave them up or why. The emphasis on "culture" fails to substitute for loss of biological kin. Instead, the girls enact other strategies of self-fashioning derived from their obscure origins. Ambiguity becomes the source of identity, as Sandra Patton explains: "By their very absence, these mysteries of heritage construct our selves as much as our known families do, for the sense of being without a 'true' family history and identity—in a society that defines familial 'truth' through biology—shapes our vision of our selves and our place in our families and in society" (7). Drawing on her difference, Lizzy adopts the persona of a maverick, through her confrontational behavior and her personal style: bleached blonde hair, creative vintage clothing, and henna tattoos. Wendy responds to her adoptive status and uncertainty about her past by becoming a social chameleon, fitting in to any situation. Wendy is an observer, a gatherer of information who can assume multiple perspectives on every issue. Blondie identifies that empathy when she considers Wendy's chessboard, "on which she was playing a game against herself. That being the sort of thing Wendy could do—take both sides of something, and play it right out!" (LW 206). This capacity to see both sides, to put herself in other people's shoes and to draw lines of affinity across boundaries resonates with Sandra Patton's description of adoptees as participant-observers. "We live our lives," Patton says, "at the margins of difference—perpetually crossing borders, we are both insiders and outsiders, both natives and foreigners" (7). For both sisters, responding to their lack of origins involves consciousness of it. They talk about it constantly, both with their parents and privately, keeping one another company in their unique position.

The novel sets up a contrast between the adoptees' conscious efforts to develop a sense of self in the absence of important personal information and their parents' lack of insight into their own relationship with origins, with which both are, in their own ways, unhealthily absorbed. Blondie and Carnegie's central problem is that they fail to recognize the commonalities that they have with their daughters. They, too, experience precarious kinship ties—as a result of death, marriage, and adoption—and that instability forces them, in turn, to overemphasize racial and cultural origins to compensate for what they have missed in their family relationships.

Blondie initially responds to the lack of biological ties with her children by focusing on difference as something to celebrate, only to find that her attitude toward it changes as her family ties become tenuous. Initially, she derives a sense of self-worth from her position as an adoptive mother of a child of color.

> When people asked, *Is she yours?* or, *Where did you get her?* I would laugh and feel proud—of myself, of my family. It was a species of vanity. . . . I had always drawn strength from the fact that my hair next to Lizzy's should be a picture that challenged the heart. Now I drew on it purposefully, the way other women drew on the knowledge that they were intelligent or thin. I had had the heart to take these children in, after all. Had I not loved them deeply and well, as if they were from the beginning my own? (*LW* 133)

Her sense of self comes from what she perceives other women could not do, adopt a child, a racially different child at that, which makes her seem, at least to herself, more accepting than others. The contemporary discourse surrounding international transracial adoption reinforces Blondie's rather self-congratulatory stance by articulating the practice in terms of rescue and heroism.[16] As she feels herself increasingly alienated from her family, laudable "cultural" difference devolves into the immutable foreignness of "race." Blondie observes the family at the dining room table, all of whom, except Bailey and her, have Asian features, and thinks: "If I had beheld our family's reflection from the doorway, I would have thought it a testament to human possibility. . . . But if I thought about this being the group that would gather around my deathbed . . . I thought of myself as dying abroad—in the friendly bosom of some foreign outpost" (*LW* 248). Despite the fact that the rest of her family would be considered out-

152 / KIN OF ANOTHER KIND

siders in white American culture, Blondie feels outnumbered within their household, her family a "foreign outpost" bound together by an essential Asianness she does not share.

The catalyst for Blondie's alienation is Lan's arrival from China, which destabilizes the family. She joins them ostensibly because Mama Wong wants the children exposed to Chinese culture, though Blondie suspects it is because Mama Wong wants Lan to be Carnegie's Chinese mistress, his "love wife." As a result of her presence, the children become interested in all things Chinese, privileging Lan's ideas because they seem more authentic than their parents' experiences with China. Equally important, Lan disrupts the family's status quo by creating a more fun maternal alternative to whom Wendy and Lizzy turn, an adult ally for the girls. In response, Blondie falls back on white privilege when confronted by the realities of an increasingly multicultural society. Feeling threatened, she wonders, "How different it would feel—I could not help but feel how different—to be, say, a white couple with one Asian child" (*LW* 247). Under those circumstances, Blondie would not feel "outnumbered" as she currently does, nor would she doubt her own self-perception as a virtuous adopter. Blondie's fantasies of privilege illustrate Shu-ching Chen's reading of the novel's racial politics: "While multiculturalism seeks to incorporate racial differences, the terms in which racial differences are accepted and codified are often laid down by the hegemonic mainstream" (22). Although Chen views multiculturalism in *The Love Wife* as an oppressive force, Jen's depiction of Blondie's situation offers a nuanced picture of multiculturalism as at once flawed and desirable, a practice with real costs for those who embrace it. In another text, Blondie might become a caricature of the elitist white adopter whose liberal self-satisfaction is challenged by her mixed-race family. Instead, Jen makes her a complex figure, sincerely committed to cultural sensitivity and genuinely curious about Chinese culture—long before she met her husband and much more than he himself is, at least initially. Blondie studied Asian languages in college, speaks Mandarin, and lived in China, while Carnegie does not speak any Chinese languages and has little interest in the culture until his mother dies.

The present circumstances of Blondie's life, however, make the sometimes-abstract ideals of liberal multiculturalism tangible, with losses not only for transnational migrants and their children but for someone in a dominant position as well. Blondie's perception of her marginalization within her family represents the larger issues facing the United States at the beginning of the twenty-first century. Efforts to advance multiculturalism bump up against deeply embedded insecurities about the importance of common origins in establishing group belonging. The presence of immigrants and the growing populations of non-white Americans further challenge the national self-perception. Blondie's exposure to upwardly mobile, energetic immigrants such as Mama Wong and Lan, for instance, makes her self-conscious about her own family's history and gives her the sense that families like her own are on the wane. Relative to earlier generations of Baileys who were abolitionists and suffragettes, Blondie's generation "felt ourselves to be votive lights at best, if compared with the original bonfires" (*LW* 75). Lan, the immigrant deposited within the American family, draws attention to the limitations of American multiculturalism and to the sense that white America is losing its dominance. Immigrants function as mirrors to white America. "You make their reflection look small, look weak, look not so smart, not so hardworking, they do not like you," as Mama Wong tells Carnegie (*LW* 72). This fear that a multicultural United States means the loss of white cultural dominance informs Blondie's attitude toward her multiracial family.

If Blondie represents white hegemonic American culture reacting to its changing composition, then Carnegie stands for second-generation Americans trying to navigate their identities as both American and other. Carnegie's obsession with origins results from destabilized family ties following the death of his mother. During her lifetime, he defined himself in opposition to her, the mother who had wanted him to be "real Chinese" but complains, "Still you grow up American" (*LW* 374). Describing Carnegie as "neither happy nor unhappy," Blondie thinks that he "cared about a certain small vengeance," expressed through his insistence that his mother is wrong (*LW* 38). After her death, Carnegie invests himself in Chinese culture. He learns the language and begins to read Chinese poetry; moreover, he prepares himself to unearth the family narrative contained in "the book," a lengthy family history written in Chinese. The family first learns of the book when a relative in China informs them that Mama Wong left a will with two stipulations: that they will host a relative—Lan—and that Wendy, "the only real Chinese in the family," according to Mama Wong, should inherit the book after the relative has spent some time with them (*LW* 192–93).

The book functions like the arrival video in *Digging to America*, as an artifact of the past that resists the clarity it is expected to provide; its significance in Carnegie's mind illustrates the paradox of origins, at once crucial and unattainable. The book represents essential origins, the "truth" of Carnegie's family's past, and this information—as well as the physical object itself—becomes inextricably linked to Carnegie's precarious sense of cultural identity, one further undermined by the death of his mother. When Blondie asks him whether a book written in Chinese that he cannot read might not make him feel "plain American" rather than connected to China, he rejects that notion, saying, "It's all I have. I have no sisters, no brothers, no uncles, no aunts. I am as on a darkling plain. Of course the book matters to me. I have no family" (*LW* 200). Referencing the alienation described in Matthew Arnold's "Dover Beach," Carnegie overlooks the family he has created with Blondie to orient his identity around a familial and cultural past. He dwells on the dimensions of the book until its physical qualities evolve to embody a fantasy of his ancestral past: "His certainty was so substantial that he could almost have stood it, in place of the book to come, on the bookshelf" (*LW* 202).

In the abstract, the book signifies Carnegie's belief in a definable past, but its arrival illustrates that the answers only yield more questions, leaving the truth of personal origins out of reach. The book, written completely in Chinese, arrives with a note in English from a Hong Kong relative; it says, "Unfortunately, you are not in it, because you were adopted in the United States. Anyway you were not born yet when the book was updated. However your older sister will be happy to see her name, the only child in her whole generation" (*LW* 369). This revelation that Carnegie was adopted and that Lan is actually his half sister through adoption, though not by blood, is the only information that Carnegie can read on his own. He does not exist, at least according to the book that he expects will document his personal history, nor can he read it without the help of an interpreter, which renders his personal history—something in which he has placed great stock—literally inaccessible to him. Considering his newly discovered status as an adoptee, one has to ask, does this family history, in which he does not even appear and to which he is not linked by "blood," qualify as "his" in any way? As in the case of Susan and Maryam in *Digging to America*, adoption challenges the principle of documented bloodlines that constitute genealogy. Homans insightfully traces the shifting meaning of authenticity that also results from the book, as Carnegie seems stunned that he is not Mama Wong's "real" son while Lan is her "real" daughter, yet the book reveals several adopted ancestors, which "grants him more ancient Chinese family authenticity, not less, even as it radically redefines authenticity to include the made-up, what appears in the modern US context as the inauthentic" ("Origins, Searches" 73). Yet the significance of his adoptive status in the context of his family line remains lost on Carnegie. His daughter tries to help him process the new information about his birth by employing the same adoption platitudes that he and Blondie always give her. "How lucky!" says Wendy. "Second choice doesn't mean second-best. . . . It's just how things happened" (*LW* 370). In this context, those truisms seem even more hollow than they do when applied to the girls. Although they now share this recognition that one may never know the truth of one's origins, Wendy and Carnegie differ, since Wendy has spent her whole life acknowledging this fact, whereas Carnegie experiences the sudden trauma of learning that the origin story he grew up with is not true and, perhaps worse, that there is no way to know who his birth parents were or why his adoptive parents chose to adopt.

In an American culture that locates identity in "blood" and understands origins as verifiable truths, a discovery such as Carnegie's can completely destroy one's sense of self, an effect signaled by the heart attack that Carnegie suffers shortly after he receives the book in the mail. In a semiconscious liminal space between life and death, Carnegie has an unexpected (and possibly hallucinated) conversation with Mama Wong. Regardless of how literally we are meant to interpret her return, Mama Wong becomes Carnegie's guide to resolving the identity crisis that ensues when he realizes that his past and his family are not what he believed them to be. Justly criticized as somewhat contrived by reviewer Michiko Kakutani, who sees the ending as "melodramatic plot gymnastics" and "hokey plot high jinks," this set of events nevertheless leads to an important commentary about the reliability of origins. Reviewer Jeffrey F. L. Partridge challenges Kakutani's assessment by pointing out the value of Carnegie's discovery, which disputes various family members' obsession with what is "natural." With Carnegie's discovery, "the fantasy of primordial culture vanishes" (Partridge 250), and leaves in its place a sometimes discomforting ambivalence. When Carnegie confronts Mama Wong with the newfound knowledge that she adopted him, she provides no explanation of how she came to be his mother and instead defines their relationship in contradictory terms. Carnegie declares, "I'm not even your son," and Mama Wong responds, "Who are you if you are not my son?" but shortly after, she states the opposite, saying, "How can you be my son?" Frustrated with her responses, Carnegie says, "I see and I don't see," and Mama Wong instructs him to embrace that paradox: "Good! See and don't see, say and don't say, know and don't know. That is the natural way." She goes on to reassert the contradiction at the center of their relationship: "I was not your mother. You were not my son." "But that's not true," Carnegie protests. Then she says, "Okay then. I was your mother. You were my son." Again, he starts to say, "That's not true," when she answers, "Exactly!" signifying that both statements are false and, paradoxically, true as well. Judged within the paradigm of blood kinship and biological conception, Mama Wong and Carnegie are not kin, yet in lived experience, their ties are as close as any mother and son. Mama Wong, refusing to embrace one view over the other, characterizes the ambivalence surrounding the idea of what constitutes a "real" family in the context of adoption.

Mama Wong embraces contradiction as a strategy for navigating the competing polarities that define identity in the twenty-first century. Martha Minow calls it "practice with paradox" and argues that embracing identity as a priori paradoxical is to counteract the tendency to locate individuals and groups in either-or categories. It is, in other words, a way for Carnegie to get around the contradiction that he both is and is not his mother's son. As a result of seeing it as paradoxical, identity becomes a process, a continuing series of negotiations (Minow 50). Minow claims that

> every person lives and operates within degrees of freedom and constraint. Yes, people who have relatively more power or enjoy its privileges can place others in oppressive conditions and even seem to define the identities of those so placed. Yet, the powerless people have more control than observers may think, because they have power to shape their identities, and to take advantage of the space between their assigned identities and their own aspirations and alternate conceptions for themselves. . . . Through an ongoing process of negotiation, identities, even group identities, constantly change. (51)

Minow's point about the space between assigned identities and individual aspirations rings especially true in the case of adoption, in which participants must identify themselves within and against the narrow definition of blood kinship. Carnegie's fixation on the past and on the truth of his origins distracts him from recognizing the possibilities that come from acknowledging contradiction and constructing new categories of his own, a practice already undertaken by his daughters.

Accepting paradox in the realm of adoption translates to the problem of ethnic and national origins as well, as Mama Wong hints that Carnegie's cultural past is both important and ultimately unknowable. Carnegie, trying to navigate through the new revelations about his adoption, informs his mother that the book says he is not her son, to which she replies, "Only an American boy would read something and think, Oh, that must be true. As if truth is that simple!" After labeling him "American" for believing too much in an authentic past, she also applauds him for being "like real Chinese" when he accuses her of wrecking his life (LW 376). Just as he is at once her son and not her son, he is also, at once, American and Chinese. This attitude reflects her own approach as revealed through Carnegie's memories of her, demanding that he retain Chinese practices of filial piety while expecting that he invest himself in the same American vision of advancement through acquiring wealth that she embraces. Furthermore, she herself models the image of American ethnic identity as a practice in paradox, and she imparts that wisdom to Carnegie. Lest this ending seem too celebratory of paradox, however, the circumstances of Mama Wong's life also suggest that real losses do accompany it. Mama Wong dies while suffering from Alzheimer's; her struggle to remember and the effect of her diminished mental capacity on her family imply that the loss of origins can have an almost pathological effect at the same time that—like the debilitating disease that symbolizes it—it cannot be prevented.

In her approach to identity, Mama Wong resembles the novel's adoptees much more than she does her own son and his wife, both of whom invest themselves strongly in the idea of essential identities. If Mama Wong advocates a practice with paradox, accepting that biological and social constructionist arguments for identity can both be true, then Wendy Wong, drawing on her adoptive identity, pushes that philosophy one step further. In response to her older sister's attempts to make Wendy resent her younger brother because he is "bio and a boy and a Bailey [meaning he looks white], not like us," Wendy rejects that notion completely. Recounting the conversation, Wendy says, "'He's soup du jour, like you. He's just been like more adopted by Mom than by Dad.' Lizzy laughs when I say that. 'How can he be adopted, she says, he's natural.' 'He is, I say. You're just jealous because you think he's more adopted than you'" (*LW* 363). Wendy's paradigm resembles the paradoxical relationship outlined by Mama Wong: one can be both "bio" and adopted. By this definition, adoptive status comes to resemble a Kinsey scale; everyone is adopted, in a matter of degrees. Underlying Wendy's understanding of kinship is the notion that all family relatedness is constructed; our relationship to one another gains meaning not from some inherent substance but from our willing performance of the roles of parent, child, or sibling. More provocatively, Wendy's theory suggests that kinship is a matter of affinity, its meaning defined by the degree of effort we invest in it. Such an idea puts the responsibility on all family members equally to determine the degree to which they adopt one another, but it also implies that we might simply care for some family members more than others. In that sense, considering everyone "adopted" in some way is no less precarious than the other depictions of kinship discussed in this study; it simply distributes the uncertainty more evenly among family members.

All three narratives discussed in this chapter demonstrate attempts to reconcile the paradoxical nature of American identity. The crises depicted in both *Digging to America* and *The Love Wife* are emblematic of that paradox. In a nation in which origins are not supposed to matter, they nevertheless take on greater significance, until they become authenticating documents of belonging. That paradox remains largely hidden until the unusual conditions of adoption bring them to light, as the narratives in this chapter demonstrate. Furthermore, these texts are remarkable for how they depict transracially adoptive families against the norms of adoption practice—both in Sui Sin Far's time and in the contemporary period—as they serve as vehicles for exploring individual and national identity. While Sui Sin Far's "Pat and Pan" resembles her contemporaries' depictions of transracial adoption as largely a narrative trope to facilitate certain plot developments, she also departs from the tendency to downplay racial differences in favor of religious conversion that sometimes occurred in adoption practices of the late nineteenth century, by using a fictional transracial adoption to critique the assimilationist agenda of religious missionaries. The contemporary narratives discussed here also represent a new literary turn. They illustrate an acute awareness of adoption that corresponds to its recent prominence in the public consciousness, an awareness reflected in the detailed account of certain practices—the airport arrival in *Digging to America* and the trip to China to pick up the child in *The Love Wife,* among others. In their depictions of contemporary adoption, they also respond to these practices in ways that challenge them. By creating nonwhite adoptive parents, for instance, both authors confront assumptions about race and culture in the adopted family and, as I have argued, negotiate other issues of national identity. *The Love Wife* goes further in challenging the conventional understanding of international adoption by allowing the younger generation of adoptees to talk back, not just to their parents, but to the dominant discourses that have inadequately shaped their lives. In this way, these texts, more so even than Barbara Kingsolver's and Sherman Alexie's, illustrate the interdiscursive nature of contemporary adoption fiction. Even in texts in which adoption functions metaphorically, the very representation of adoption practices has the power to challenge dominant discourses. These texts, in other words, function as the kinds of adoption plots that Marianne Novy discusses in *Reading Adoption*, plots that shape the public understanding of adoption. In that way, their representations of adoption do something quite exciting, offering ways of expanding the perception of adoption as a complex and, indeed, paradoxical practice for those who may have little other lived contact with it.

Conclusion

In the texts discussed in this study, fictional adoptions serve as sites for negotiating and resisting normative social identities anchored in biology. Both *The Love Wife* and *Digging to America* problematize biology as the source of connection among individuals in families and communities, and they both suggest that an overreliance on prescribed identities of any kind can be detrimental, not only for those whose lives do not fit into established categories, but for anyone attempting to navigate an increasingly diverse American culture. The texts included here encourage a broad definition of "diversity," one that encompasses the mix of races, cultures, and ethnicities in the United States, as might be expected, as well as a wide range of family configurations within which we locate ourselves.

Even as many fictional transracial adoptions challenge the notion that biology is the source of belonging, none of the texts analyzed here will actually discard it outright. For Faulkner and Chopin, race ultimately remains an immutable quality, a stance that seems to reinforce the status quo of white supremacy. Several other texts, however, acknowledge biology's power as a rhetorical tool for resistance, particularly Toni Morrison's *Tar Baby* and Sherman Alexie's *Indian Killer*. Both novels advance a nationalist position that locates identity in essential qualities. As Morrison's interest in ancestry as an element of "rootedness" indicates, essentialist language articulates the endurance of a people and designates a collective within which individuals can locate themselves in opposition to negative stereotypes. This political value explains, in part, why such language lingers in adoption discourses. Beyond the strategic power of essentialism, however, treating individual identity as something inherent has an emotional value that cannot be denied. It may seem obvious, but it bears mentioning that essential identities are appealing expressly because of their immutability, because they secure identity at moments of precariousness, a feature that Alexie and Morrison emphasize in their depictions of Marie Polatkin and Son, respectively. Their attachments to inherent qualities as more "authentic" reflect the insecurities of their lives. *The Love Wife*'s Carnegie Wong demonstrates this point as well, as he fixates on the family book as an artifact of identity as a response to his mother's death. I have argued in this study that adoption disputes the very notion of inherency, but as these texts also demonstrate, it does not necessarily eradicate the tremendous appeal of inherent identities. If anything, adoption may make that appeal stronger. As Jane Jeong Trenka's *The Language of Blood* suggests, this allure of stable origins is one reason why real-life adoptees, the ones who must actively undertake the self-making that adoption allows, are sometimes the least enthusiastic about the potential for adoptive self-fashioning; for us, it is not optional. Immutable qualities contain what Trenka calls an "emotional truth" that is hard to reject, especially since so few, except the adopted, are asked to do so in actuality.

Yet despite the rhetorical and emotional power of biology to articulate a positive sense of self, adoption in these texts also illustrates how too much of an investment in biologically based authenticity can be detrimental to those who deviate from their community's norms. For them, adopting the language of biological essentialism to sustain collective identities can be almost as restrictive as when biological differences become grounds for discrimination, as it was in the era of eugenics. Toni Morrison's Jadine Childs and Alexie's Marie Polatkin are two important examples of this point; both occasionally take refuge in essentialist thinking, yet it does not provide what they need, and in fact, it encourages them to conform to prescribed roles that do not fit their personal experiences. The tensions surrounding adoption in both novels extend beyond individual characters and suggest that despite the overtly essentialist statements these authors make in their work, neither feels entirely comfortable choosing to privilege biology over socially constructed, individually negotiated identities.

Ambivalence about biology, a defining element of the transracial adoption texts discussed in the present study, could easily be misunderstood as narrative incoherence, a misreading that may explain why so many of these novels are considered "lesser works" in the authors' canons. Chesnutt's *The Quarry*, for instance, went unpublished in his lifetime, a sign that it did not meet the standard set by his earlier novels, *The House Behind the Cedars* and especially *The Mar-*

row of Tradition. John Duvall notes that *Tar Baby* is "somewhat marginal" in Morrison's canon; it is "less frequently taught and receives relatively less critical attention than her other novels" (325). Robert Boles's *Curling*, while deemed promising by critics when it was published, went out of print shortly after publication and remains so now. Sherman Alexie has himself claimed that *Indian Killer* is the novel that troubles him the most (Campbell), and even *Light in August*, while one of Faulkner's prominent novels, does not receive the scholarly attention of *The Sound and the Fury* or *As I Lay Dying*. One thing these texts all have in common, besides adoption, is the degree to which they do not definitively resolve the complex identity issues that they raise. Instead, the pervasiveness of essentialism coexists with the individual characters' power to resist ascribed identities. Reading them through adoption, however, provides that missing coherence by encouraging us to acknowledge the importance and even the usefulness of the contradictions that these texts embody. In this way, the anomalies that seem to weaken these texts for readers looking for unambiguous statements about the meaning of racial identity can actually be understood as one of their strengths, encompassing the contradictory options for identity that exist in our national culture. When taken together, the early-century texts discussed in the first half of this book allude to this contradiction, as adoption allows authors to, in the case of Chesnutt, speak to the constructedness of racial identities, while a very similar adoption scenario accommodates Faulkner's and Chopin's implication that race is an immutable quality. The texts discussed in the second half of the book make the paradox of origins even more explicit, as they waver between essentialist and social constructionist approaches to individual identity. These narratives suggest that American culture could be characterized in part by a paradoxical attitude toward origins, and so, perhaps, could its national literature. But without attending to adoption, we may miss the fact that the anomalies embodied by these texts may actually be one of their greatest assets.

Along with exposing contradiction as a subtle characteristic of American fiction, reading through adoption also offers an explanation for some of the more confounding aspects of these novels. For example, focusing on adoption can reveal the stakes of characters' choices, so that Joe Christmas's seemingly inexplicable willingness to get caught by Percy Grimm and his squad at the end of *Light in August* makes more sense, attached, as it is, to Christmas's status as an adoptee and his insistence on self-definition at odds with the community's pressure to make him choose a race. He embraces death over being categorized in a way that contrasts with his own self-image. Similarly, Désirée in "Désirée's

Baby" commits suicide not simply because she assumes that she is black but because her precarious family situation, without social status of her own, becomes too much to bear. In another example, Jadine Childs, a character often dismissed by critics as racially self-loathing, seems much more sympathetic when framed by her adoptive status. As an adoptee raised in both white and black families, the authenticity of her racial identity is as much contingent on her position as an orphan and an adoptee as it is on the standard for authentic blackness by which she is usually judged. Finally, the mysterious beyond-the-grave conversation between Mama Wong and Carnegie that ends *The Love Wife* makes at least a little more sense when attached to adoption, which has already rendered most of the family's origins fictive. Mama Wong's ghostly appearance is an extension of that impulse.

Adoption also complicates interpretations that tend to focus on race or gender or cultural differences alone as the root of narrative conflict. Because biological kinship upholds our assumptions about the heritability of race, racial problems can also be family problems. For instance, Chelsea Burlingame, in Robert Boles's *Curling,* suffers from a racial identity crisis, uncertain of where he fits in his community. Clearly, race is one of Chelsea's problems, but it is not the only problem, and it may not even be the most important one. Raised from birth in an emotionally distant white family, Chelsea lacks not only a strong sense of racial identity but also a determining sense of family identity. As in the case of Jadine Childs, attributing his crisis only to race overlooks an equally defining experience of being without strong family ties. In a somewhat different manifestation of this phenomenon, both Dallas Chief Eagle and Leslie Marmon Silko show that family and culture are inextricable, as both characters who are "adopted" into the white world return to their people, a move that both authors emphasize is primarily about love and loyalty to family. In Gish Jen's *The Love Wife* and Anne Tyler's *Digging to America,* race and family also intersect explicitly, as racial and cultural problems serve as proxies for tenuous familial bonds. In *Digging to America,* the white American characters work hard to cultivate a cultural identity for their adopted Korean child, a strategy that subtly serves the larger purpose of establishing narratives of cultural connectedness that can substitute for the absence of authenticating "blood" kinship. This strategy occurs in *The Love Wife,* too, though with less idealistic outcomes, as cultural identity problems are not as easily resolved as they are in *Digging.* In many of the texts discussed in these chapters, characters turn to culture to reinforce tenuous kinship ties.

Beyond highlighting the often unacknowledged existence of anomaly in

American literature and providing important insight into plot and characterization, adoption in literature can also shed light on a more prominent characteristic of American culture: the belief in the potential for individual reinvention. Carol Singley notes that cultural ambivalence toward adoption comes from the tension between origins and "an ideological commitment to severing all genealogical ties, starting over, and creating oneself and one's nation anew" (79). This potential for self-fashioning is a major concern for the authors discussed in this study. For some, like Charles W. Chesnutt, the displacements of adoption offer liberatory potential to define oneself in opposition to prevailing social codes, yet in most of these authors' texts, the desire to fashion the self in opposition to normative categories is, at best, a struggle. For characters like Chelsea Burlingame, Marie Polatkin, and Maryam Yazdan, the process of self-definition is thrust on them by circumstances—adoption or cultural dislocation or immigration—and it is often undertaken in resistance to ascribed roles that do not fit their unique experiences as participant-observers in the worlds of family and culture. At its most extreme, self-fashioning is an impossibility, as is evident in Chopin's "Désirée's Baby" and Faulkner's *Light in August*. In these texts, individuals who attempt to define themselves contrary to normative racial categories face punishment and death, a clear message about the ability of individuals to forge their own, independent identities. Taken together, these narratives illustrate a clear investment in the American mythology of reinvention, but virtually all depict it as an act of sheer will, one with significant losses for those who attempt to make themselves anew. They suggest varying degrees of interest in the potential of self-fashioning but reveal an underlying skepticism that even the radical displacements that accompany adoption can permit significant change.

This study illustrates some of the ways in which adoption in American literature taps into the culture's broader concerns with the source and substance of identity. Although this fact has often been overlooked, adoption can help illuminate established American mythologies in new ways. For these reasons, both literary and historical research that takes a long view on adoption, looking at its representation and evolution throughout American history, will continue to be important. As the field of adoption studies grows, research by Marianne Novy, Margaret Homans, Claudia Nelson, Mark Jerng, and Carol Singley in American literature, along with histories by E. Wayne Carp, Barbara Melosh, Ellen Herman, and Julie Berebitsky, offer important opportunities to place adoption practices and their fictional representations in proper historical context. Doing so allows us to see how certain current discourses—such as the rescue motif so common in contemporary transracial and international adoption—have roots in earlier eras of child welfare, as indicated in Nelson's work on adoption as a form of "mutual" rescue for parents and children in the late nineteenth and early twentieth centuries and in Jerng's research on adoption in captivity and slave narratives. This awareness will not only help in understanding the evolution of fictional adoptions but might also inform how we talk about adoption in its everyday practice. Likewise, awareness of adoption as it is discussed today, in fiction and in real life, can shape how we approach earlier representations of adoptive and quasi-adoptive relationships in fiction, even as we remain attentive to the unique historical conditions of earlier adoption practices. Reading back can expose dynamics that might otherwise go unnoticed, as in the case of early-century representations of multiracial families created through volition, such as those by Chesnutt, Chopin, Faulkner, and Sui Sin Far, among others. Because transracial adoption was not even legal at the time, these adoptive relationships might be overlooked for what they are: kinship formed consensually, if at times unwittingly, across race lines. Read in relationship to current adoption practices, they reveal important commonalities in how Americans respond to race mixing when it occurs in the intimacy of families.

Exciting research is taking place in both the humanities and the social sciences, and the two fields of study intersect in ways that might positively affect future studies of adoption in literature. Current research on international adoption in the social sciences—sociology and ethnography—utilizes narrative analysis strategies that can apply to the study of fiction. The work done by Sandra Patton, Sara Dorow, and Toby Alice Volkman, for instance, reveals important insights about the construction of narrative conventions around adoption and the discursive shorthand that implicitly shapes how we understand it. As my readings of Gish Jen and Anne Tyler suggest, attending to the discourses that circulate around adoption can supplement our reading of fiction, which is both a participant in advancing those discourses and a venue for challenging the conventional wisdom that sometimes surrounds transracial adoption. Likewise, I think the narrative discourses in fiction, documented by Novy, Homans, and Jerng, can inform the analyses undertaken by social scientists, by showing how narrative conventions are reinforced—or undermined, for that matter—in the realm of fiction. As Novy illustrated in *Reading Adoption* and as my reading of Barbara Kingsolver, Leslie Marmon Silko, and Sherman Alexie further demonstrates, fiction and nonfiction discourses are mutually informative, and the concomitant development of these fields of study will continue to improve our understanding of adoption.

The final chapter of the present study examines the ways in which international adoption evokes larger cultural concerns about the meaning of personal and collective origins. It only begins to explore the possibilities for further study that these elements of contemporary adoption introduce. The concerns about origins will become greater as reproductive technologies continue to extend the range of possibilities for creating families. As E. Wayne Carp's recent studies on adoption have suggested, the voices of individual adoption participants have an important role in shaping both the perceptions of the practice and the policies that govern it. For that reason, autobiography and life writing by Betty Jean Lifton and Florence Fisher helped to alter midcentury adoption policies favoring closed records (Carp, *Family* 138–66), and the self-presentations of international adoptees such as Jane Jeong Trenka, Amy Robinson, and Jae Ran Kim have also affected how international adopters approach the task of parenting their children. Unlike adoption participants, the children of newer reproductive technologies have not yet begun to express themselves in any sustained way, but as their stories are told, new paths for study will be forged.

More immediately, however, another underrepresented group involved with adoption has begun to gain a voice, as gay and lesbian adopters articulate their family experiences. Just as studies of queer kinship patterns have helped to widen our understanding of the limitations of linking biology to kinship, so may these families' representations of their own experiences help to expand our understanding of adoption. Dan Savage's two autobiographies—primarily *The Kid: What Happened When My Boyfriend and I Decided to Go Get Pregnant,* but also, to a lesser extent, *The Commitment*—begin that process. In *The Kid,* Savage sets out to make a claim for the legitimacy of gay adoption; at the same time, he also provides important insight into the ways in which the nontraditional gender roles in gay parenting can mediate the tensions of heterosexual adoption and perhaps circumvent them altogether. Coming at parenthood from a nonnormative place already, Dan and Terry create an adoptive relationship that eludes some of the traps of stereotypical family roles and truly challenges the lingering biocentricity of contemporary adoption. They do so not by ignoring their son's birth parents and thus burying the complexities of their kinship but, rather, by acknowledging the importance of the blood tie. They create a model of kinship that values their own legally and emotionally formed family unit at the same time that they unite their son's families across the lines of blood and social construct. In this way, they collectively manifest what Savage calls "the most plural definition of every plural pronoun" (*Commitment* 35).

A very small percentage of Americans has any personal involvement in

Notes

1. Historians have recently argued that adoption helps to frame debates about the meaning of motherhood in the early twentieth century, to elucidate postwar attitudes toward single parenthood, and to trace the evolution of adoption rights activism out of the identity movements of the 1960s and 1970s. See Berebitsky; Solinger, *Wake Up;* and Carp, *Family Matters.* For studies of adoption in literature, see Novy; C. Nelson; Homans, especially "Adoption Narratives" and "Origins, Searches"; Jerng; Singley; Melosh, "Adoption Stories"; Askeland, "Informal Adoption"; and dissertations by Askeland, Deans, and Callahan. Anthropologists, ethnographers, and sociologists place contemporary adoption in a variety of other contexts, including transnational migration, domestic race relations, and nonnormative kinship, and they rely on personal and collective narratives to interrogate the social position of adoption and to expose the assumptions embedded in its practice. See Dorow; Volkman, *Cultures;* Yngvesson and Mahoney; and Patton. In their focus on the importance of narrative in creating cultural meaning and on adoption's larger cultural contexts, they serve as important critical foundations for this study.

2. To further elaborate, Sollors says, "In American social symbolism ethnicity may function as a construct evocative of blood, nature, and descent, whereas national identity may be relegated to the order of law, conduct, and consent. Writers and theorists participate in the delineation of a conflict between contractual and hereditary, self-made and ancestral, definitions of American identity" (*Beyond* 151). This "social symbolism," articulated in kinship terms, captures a central dilemma of American identity: what makes us American?

3. "Race" is especially problematic when applied to Native Americans since it has often been deployed to recast and contain tribal claims for sovereignty (Berger), and sometimes threatens to obscure the specificity of American Indians' social status, which exists apart from the paradigms created by slavery and immigration, which define other American "minorities" (Allen, *Blood* 110–13).

1. Quiroz is not the only person to make this argument. Dorothy Roberts advances a similar point, but she comes at the topic from a slightly different angle, looking at the

conditions that place African American children in foster care in disproportionate numbers. Color-blind placement advocates often cite this issue to justify making transracial adoptions easier. The National Association of Black Social Workers in their 1972 statement against transracial placements also questioned white adopters' motives for adopting transracially (133). The statement is discussed later in this chapter and again in chapter 4.

2. Herman notes the growth of "second-parent" adoptions, which allow "two individuals of the same sex to simultaneously occupy roles as legal parents" (293). On one hand, as Herman points out, these arrangements testify to the ways in which gay families are already legally recognized—even as opponents of gay marriage attempt to exclude them from legal and social equality. On the other hand, the extra effort to achieve second-parent adoptions—each parent must go through the process as opposed to a straight couple adopting together—indicates the additional challenges that gays and lesbians must face. See also Hollinger on second-parent adoptions.

3. Schneider focuses his study on mainstream American culture, across regions and religions, though he does not take into consideration the kinship patterns of tribal cultures nor does he account for racial or ethnic differences or those related to sexual orientation. Despite these limitations, Schneider's work remains valuable for this study.

4. "Race has become a trope of ultimate, irreducible difference between cultures, linguistic groups, or adherents of specific belief systems which—more often than not—also have fundamentally opposed economic interests. Race is the ultimate trope of difference because it is so very arbitrary in its application" (Gates 5).

5. See historian Stephanie Coontz, who describes the family as a place where individuals are socialized into certain roles but where they can also renegotiate them (2). Social historian Betty G. Farrell also talks about the political effects of the family: "one meaning of the family as a central institution of the social order is that it reinforces the political and economic status quo. Families ensure that the distribution of resources both to the advantaged and disadvantaged will remain relatively stable, since the transmission of wealth, property, status, and opportunity is channeled along the lines of kinship" (7).

6. Homans explores the degree to which adoption culture, on one hand, puts a high premium on "knowledge of personal (familial, genetic) origins" while, on the other hand, such knowledge is often inaccessible to adoptees and their families ("Adoption Narratives" 4). Arguing through narrative and trauma theories, Homans suggests that "the adopted and their families might do better to understand themselves as inventing helpful fictions about those irretrievable historical moments" ("Adoption Narratives" 9–10). While the singular experiences of adoption highlight this response to absent origins, anyone, as Homans argues, could benefit from approaching origins as constructs rather than innate. See also "Origins, Searches" and for a detailed discussion of essentialism in the discourses surrounding international adoption see "Adoption and Essentialism."

7. William H. Tucker captures the range of people implicated by eugenics, which included "the so-called feebleminded, the insane, alcoholics, certain criminals (the 'delinquent and wayward'), epileptics, the diseased (including those with tuberculosis), those with impaired vision or hearing, cripples, and the dependent—'orphans, ne'er-do-wells, the homeless, tramps and paupers' (a definition that, as the English geneticist J. B. S. Haldane pointed out, would include Milton, Beethoven, and Jesus)" (61).

8. These include families left behind by passers who must distance themselves from anyone who could mark them as black (Chesnutt's *The House Behind the Cedars*, Jessie Fauset's *Plum Bun*); families disrupted by children switched at birth and raised to assume the other's racial position (Twain's *Pudd'nhead Wilson*); families conceived by white men with black women, whose children could not inherit their father's wealth or name (a particular concern of Chesnutt, treated in both *House* and *The Marrow of Tradition*).

9. For discussions of passing's subversive potential, see Ginsberg; Kawash; and Sollors, *Neither*.

10. Solinger's *Wake Up Little Susie* is a comparative study of black and white women's divergent experiences with single pregnancy before *Roe v. Wade*.

11. Reliable statistics about adoption in the last few decades can be difficult to find. While statistics about contemporary international adoptions are generally quite reliable since the state department monitors and reports international adoptions, domestic adoption statistics through foster care are sometimes maintained by individual states, with no centralized national data. Furthermore, national data on "stranger" adoptions, domestic adoptions conducted privately or through agencies, was last collected in 1975. While the 2000 Census had a question about adopted persons living in households, it did not distinguish between stepparent and stranger adoptions or domestic and international. Tentative adoption statistics can be found at the Evan B. Donaldson Adoption Institute's Web site.

12. Moreover, in the 1990s, the "color-blind" argument prevailed, resulting in the Multiethnic Placement Act of 1994, which prohibits adoption agencies from factoring race into their child placements. See Patton's analysis of the events leading up to this bill and Roberts's discussion of the way that pro-transracial adoption legislation can weaken black families.

13. For instance, one exception to the tendency to argue in terms of culture is the Oglala Sioux, which used explicitly racial language in a resolution protesting adoption and foster care outside of tribes ("Oglala Sioux" 88).

14. See Carp, *Family*; Melosh, *Strangers*; and Wegar.

CHAPTER 2

1. Werner Sollors explores the connection between miscegenation and incest prevalent in the literature and cultural discourse of the late nineteenth century and early twentieth century in *Neither Black nor White*, chap. 10.

2. Two narratives that confront the repercussions of passing in family relationships are Jessie Fauset's *Plum Bun*, in which Angela Murray must distance herself from her sister in order to pass and finds that it is not worth the loss of her family, and Langston Hughes's "Passing," an epistolary short story in the voice of a man passing for white who refuses to acknowledge his mother and abandons his siblings financially in order to achieve his ends. The dynamics of family relationships and passing appear but are not directly engaged in Larsen's *Passing*, Johnson's *Autobiography*, Pauline Hopkins's *Of One Blood*, and Chesnutt's *Paul Marchand, FMC* (1999, ca. 1921).

3. For discussions of passing's subversive potential, see Eileen Ginsberg's introduction to *Passing and the Fictions of Identity*, Samira Kawash's *Dislocating the Color Line*, Gayle Wald's *Crossing the Line*, and Sollors on passing in *Neither Black nor White*, chap. 9.

4. Anthropologist Judith Modell posits that adoptive family relationships are modeled on biological kinship, with adoptive family members behaving "as if" birth kin (2). She argues that making adoption like biological kinship "is a powerful fiction, but certainly not a new idea. A British jurist in the nineteenth century, asserting that adoption should not be a distinct kind of kinship, wrote: 'We must try to regard the fiction of adoption as so closely simulating the reality of kinship that neither law nor opinion makes the slightest difference between a real and an adoptive connection' (Maine 1861, 239). No one doubted, then or now, that the 'real connection' was the genealogical connection" (2).

5. In *Reading Adoption*, Marianne Novy briefly discusses the Freudian family romance in literature; some nonadopted people fantasize that they were actually adopted from a different, more appealing family (6). This narrative element sometimes involves discovering that the birth parents are of a higher social class—"rich nobility"—while the adoptive parents are "poor commoners." As Novy notes, in real life adoption, socioeconomic circumstances are frequently the other way around (131).

6. Du Bois used the term "talented tenth" to refer to the most educated and established members of the African American community, who he charged with guiding the black masses ("Talented").

7. I address Chesnutt's position as an author before and during the Harlem Renaissance in an article, "The Confounding Problem of Race."

8. See Sollors on the "throwback" in *Neither Black nor White*, chap. 2.

9. An important exception is Langston Hughes's short story, "Who's Passing for Who?" (1952), in which a couple claims to be passing, first for white and then for black, leaving the story's narrator uncertain of his companions' race.

CHAPTER 3

1. Student readers, for example, generally assume that Désirée must be white, as do literary critics. For instance, Emily Toth describes the story by saying, "in the final ironic reversal, then, it is Armand—the master of the plantation—who is black" (205). Likewise, Catherine Lundie reads the ending as Désirée "somehow vindicated of a charge" when Armand's ancestry is revealed (132). Sollors (*Neither* 68) and Peel (233), however, suggest that Désirée remains uncategorizable.

2. Byron Bunch repeats the claim that the man was black but with no clear evidence. Doc Hines "knew somehow that the fellow had nigger blood. Maybe the circus folks told him. I don't know. He aint never said how he found out, like that never made any difference" (*LiA* 374). Mrs. Hines recalls that the circus owner "come back and said how the man really was a part nigger instead of Mexican, like Eupheus said all the time he was, like the devil had told Eupheus he was a nigger" (*LiA* 377). This statement is the closest to a definitive rendering of Christmas's father's race, and even it is tenuous, since the claim is thirdhand and the circus owner no more likely to know the man's racial identity than anyone else.

3. See *Birth Marks*, chap. 1. In Patton's own case, her Jewish ancestry was not disclosed to her adoptive parents, presumably for fear it would discourage them from adopting (43).

CHAPTER 4

1. In an article on Charles Wright's *The Messenger,* W. Lawrence Hogue includes Boles's work in a list of black writers he categorizes as existentialist, and both in theme and style, *Curling* demonstrates obvious existentialist influences.

2. Critics cite, with varying degrees of emphasis, the novel's elliptical style as a flaw, but all suggest that the novel's unusual perspective provides an important insight into racial identity. See Dempsey; Watkins, "Caged"; Cassill; and an unsigned review called "Beyond Race Cliché."

3. A 1981 article in the *New York Times* includes Boles among a number of authors who were "critically acclaimed" in the late 1960s but disappeared by the early 1980s as the publishing industry took fewer risks on black, experimental writers (Watkins, "Hard"). Along with the two novels mentioned in the text, Boles published at least two short stories under the name "Robert Boles," "What's Your Problem?" (1964) and "The Engagement Party" (1967), as well as a short nonfiction piece titled "Beat Is a Rhythm, not an Act" (undated), about meeting Jack Kerouac, reprinted from the *Yarmouth Port Register* in Paul Maher Jr.'s *Empty Phantoms: Interviews and Encounters with Jack Kerouac* (2005).

4. The research of Rita J. Simon and Howard Altstein consistently argues that transracial adoptees have adjustment rates comparable to those of inracial adoptees and that the transracial adoption has no major effect on the adoptees' sense of identity. See *Adoption, Race, and Identity.* Other proponents of transracial adoption, such as Elizabeth Bartholet, make similar claims. See *Family Bonds.*

5. Even now, African American transracial adoptees are still finding their voices; two important ethnographic studies involving transracial adoptees include Rita Simon and Rhonda M. Roorda, *In Their Own Voices;* and especially Sandra Patton, *Birth Marks.*

6. See, for example, Goyal; J. Ryan; and Mobley.

CHAPTER 5

1. See Carp, *Family Matters,* chap. 5. Domestic adoption became suspect for reasons that extend beyond the ARM. The perception that white infants were no longer available, coupled with the search movement that suggested to some adopters that their relationship with their children could be disrupted, and several highly publicized disrupted adoptions in the 1980s and 1990s caused adopters to look abroad for children and to view adoptions from overseas in a particularly positive light. See Dorow, chap. 1; and Solinger, *Beggars,* chap. 1.

2. A partial list of Native texts featuring some aspect of adoption includes Linda Hogan's *Solar Storms* (1995); Ella Deloria's *Waterlily* (1988, written ca. 1944); N. Scott Momaday's *The Ancient Child* (1989); Louise Erdrich's *Love Medicine* (1993); and Leslie Marmon Silko's *Ceremony* (1977). Nonfiction representations of American Indian adoption include Greg Sarris's *Mabel McKay* (1994) and Michael Dorris's *The Broken Cord* (1989).

3. Mary Rowlandson wrote *The Sovereignty and Goodness of God* (1682). Eunice Williams's story is told by her father, John Williams, in *The Redeemed Captive* (1707), and Mary Jemison's was published by James E. Seaver in *A Narrative of the Life of Mrs. Mary Jemison* (1823).

4. See Askeland on the Iroquois Confederacy's adoption practices in *Children and Youth*, chap. 1; and Pauline Turner Strong's *Captive Selves*, 80–83 (on the Iroquois) and 56–57 (on the Powhatan).

5. Because both of Kingsolver's novels have been frequent subjects of criticism in regard to their representation of adoption, my analysis is somewhat curtailed to focus on the insight yielded from reading them in the context of captivity and rescue and the responses that they garnered. For discussions of these texts, see also Marianne Novy's *Reading Adoption* and Barbara Melosh's *Strangers and Kin*. See also essays by Strong, "To Forget Their Tongue"; Fagan, "Adoption as Fantasy"; and Homans, "Adoption Narratives."

6. See Marianne Novy's discussion of it as a form of catharsis in *Reading Adoption* (193–95).

7. In contrast to prohibitions on interracial marriage among white Americans and African Americans and some other ethnic groups in certain states, the U.S. government facilitated alliances between tribe members and nontribal members (Jaimes 130). In the late nineteenth century, government policies actively encouraged marriages between white men and Indian women, while early twentieth-century antimiscegenation laws in individual states generally did not prohibit marriages between whites and Indians (Berger 633–35). Jaimes sees the leasing of tribal lands to nontribal members as a policy that "virtually ensured that . . . intermarriage would steadily result" and also notes that the 1950s federal relocation program that moved individuals from reservations to urban areas encouraged "biological hybridization" that, in the context of blood quantum measures, diminished tribal membership (130).

8. The editors of the *Outsiders Within* anthology, for instance, call their book "a corrective action" in response to their perception that white adoptive parents and adoption professionals have defined adoptees' experiences for them (Oparah et al. 1). The volume's contributors represent a diverse range of adoptee points of view.

9. In the late 1880s, Wovoka prophesied that ancestors and animals would return from the dead if Native people practiced the Ghost Dance. The massacre at Wounded Knee in 1890 ended the Ghost Dance for the Lakota, and after a few more years, it died out (Rollings 131). See also Giles, chap. 8, on the Ghost Dance in *Indian Killer*. A performance of the Ghost Dance also figures prominently in Silko's *Gardens in the Dunes*.

10. Barbara Melosh briefly makes a similar point in her discussion of *Indian Killer* in *Strangers and Kin* (188–91).

11. Barbara Melosh takes this point one step further when she says that Alexie "suggest[s] an ironic distance on his own metaphor of transracial adoption as deracination. John's problem may not be adoption after all but rather a deluded fixation on stable identity" (*Strangers and Kin* 190).

12. Alexie's 2007 novel, *Flight*, could also qualify as a corrective to *Indian Killer*, as it, too, deals with adoption, although it differs substantially in the sense that Zits, the main character, is an older child with an established sense of identity when he is adopted, and adoption is the narrative's resolution rather than its more central concern, as is the case in *Indian Killer* and "The Search Engine."

CHAPTER 6

1. On her birth certificate, Sui Sin Far's name is Edith Maude Eaton, but biographer Annette White-Parks has determined that Sui Sin Far was not simply a pseudonym but

the name of address used by her family in her early childhood; furthermore, she used that name publicly to draw attention to her Chinese ancestry (xvi). For these reasons, I have chosen to refer to her by the name under which she published most often.

2. For more detailed discussion of anti-Chinese policies and the status of other Asian American populations at the turn of the century, see Chan.

3. Ronald Takaki outlines some of the dominant stereotypes of the Chinese at the end of the nineteenth century and notes that the characteristics assigned to the Chinese— "morally inferior, savage, childlike, and lustful"—resemble those associated with African Americans and American Indians, calling all three "Calibans of color" (*A Different Mirror* 205). Jacob Riis's account of Chinatown in his exposé of urban poverty, *How the Other Half Lives* (1890), offers an insightful example of negative attitudes toward the Chinese at the time (77–83).

4. White-Parks notes that Far describes Harrison in terms of temptation, as the serpent in the Garden who plies Pat with candy and toys (White-Parks 223).

5. This message is also conveyed in some of Far's other writing, including "A Chinese Boy-Girl" (1904), set in Chinatown, and "The Sugar Cane Baby" (1910), set in the Caribbean.

6. This attitude becomes abundantly clear in the case Linda Gordon calls the Arizona "orphan abduction," in which children from an Irish Catholic orphanage in New York were placed by nuns in Mexican Catholic homes in Arizona, only to meet fierce resistance from white citizens of the town who felt that it was inappropriate for white children to be raised in Mexican families. Highlighting the varying racial and religious frames of the regions (and the period), the children's religion was paramount to the Catholic nuns, while "race" prevailed over religion for the white townspeople. See Jerng's discussion of religion in adoption and the Arizona orphan abduction in *Claiming Others*, chap. 3.

7. David Shih argues that many scholars have claimed Far as a foremother of contemporary Asian American literature, a delineation that "requires her interpellation as a discrete *racial* and *national* subject—a Chinese American—to the neglect of alternate subject positions developed in her autobiography, positions that deliberately work to destabilize race as a dangerous trope of difference" (49).

8. I am grateful to Mark Jerng for suggesting that I explore religion as a connection between the two eras addressed in this chapter.

9. Tyler mentions in an interview that she and her daughter went to the airport to pick up someone and saw an adoptive family waiting for the child's arrival. She references that experience by including a woman and her daughter as onlookers in *Digging to America*'s opening scene (Gray).

10. Such strategies have become the norm for international adopters attempting to address questions of difference for their children. See Cheng, chap. 4; Dorow; and Volkman, "Embodying."

11. This argument is advanced by many of the essays in the *Outsiders Within* anthology (Trenka et al.) and several blogs, including Jae Ran Kim's *Harlow's Monkey* and *Jane's Blog*, written by Jane Jeong Trenka.

12. As anthropologist Signe Howell observes, some adoptive parents develop narratives around the adoption process itself to establish common experiences as a substantive bond in the absence of biological origins shared between parents and child. Howell cites the journey to the child's country of origin—initially to pick up the available child

and later on "roots trips" shared by adoptive parent and child—as a means of developing a sense of common origins through a shared experience of place (214).

13. Although many readers' reviews on bookstore Web sites are positive, several note the problematic representation of transracial adoption in the novel. See, for example, "Digging." Some of the most trenchant critiques of international and transracial adoptions have taken place in cyberspace. See Kim; Trenka, *Jane's Blog;* and Shin.

14. Not only is the term *exotic* problematic in how it racializes Susan, the term also has specific implications in the context of international adoption, as Kim Park Nelson argues. Nelson sees international adoption as an act of (white and/or economic) privilege that commodifies children from developing nations as "authentically exotic" because of their ethnicity and foreignness (93–94). This kind of analysis calls attention to the power dynamics of international adoption, which tend to get masked by the generally positive discourse of "rescue" that surrounds it.

15. Carnegie and Blondie in particular seem to be trying to convince the audience at certain points. For example, Carnegie says, "Lan. Of course we have started the story with Lan, on whose account so much eventually came to pass. But I hereby restart it to begin two years earlier, when my mother was still alive; for in the beginning, believe me, was Mama Wong. Is this not allowed? Never mind" (24). He seems to appeal to an outside authority for permission to alter the narrative conventions.

16. See Dorow for a brief history of the association between international adoption and "rescue" (49–56) and chapter 5 of this study for a more general discussion.

Works Cited

Adamec, Christine, and William L. Pierce. *The Encyclopedia of Adoption.* 2nd ed. New York: Facts on File, 2000. Print.

"Adoption Studies." Adamec and Pierce 19–20.

"African-American Adoptions." *Adoption History Project.* Ed. Ellen Herman. Department of History, University of Oregon. 11 July 2007. Web. 9 Jan. 2009.

Alcoff, Linda Martín. *Visible Identities: Race, Gender, and the Self.* New York: Oxford UP, 2006. Print.

Aldama, Frederick Luis. Rev. of *Gardens in the Dunes,* by Leslie Marmon Silko. *World Literature Today* 74.2 (2000): 457–58. Print.

Alexie, Sherman. *Flight.* New York: Black Cat, 2007. Print.

Alexie, Sherman. *Indian Killer.* New York: Warner Books, 1996. Print.

Alexie, Sherman. "The Search Engine." *Ten Little Indians.* New York: Grove Press, 2003. 1–52. Print.

Allen, Chadwick. *Blood Narrative: Indigenous Identity in American Indian and Maori Literary and Activist Texts.* Durham: Duke UP, 2002. Print.

Allen, Chadwick. Introduction. *Winter Count.* By Dallas Chief Eagle. Lincoln: Bison Books–U of Nebraska P, 2003. vii–xv. Print.

Askeland, Lori, ed. *Children and Youth in Adoption, Orphanages, and Foster Care.* Westport: Greenwood, 2006. Print.

Askeland, Lori. *Dependent Children in American Fiction and Culture, 1850–1860.* Diss. University of Kansas, 1997. Ann Arbor: UMI, 1997.

Askeland, Lori. "Informal Adoption, Apprentices, and Indentured Children in the Colonial Era and the New Republic, 1605–1850." Askeland 3–16.

Banner-Haley, Charles T. *The Fruits of Integration: Black Middle-Class Ideology and Culture, 1960–1990.* Jackson: UP of Mississippi, 1994. Print.

Bartholet, Elizabeth. *Family Bonds: Adoption and the Politics of Parenting.* New York: Houghton Mifflin, 1993. Print.

Berebitsky, Julie. *Like Our Very Own: Adoption and the Changing Culture of Motherhood, 1851–1950.* Lawrence: UP of Kansas, 2000. Print.

Berger, Bethany R. "Red: Racism and the American Indian." *UCLA Law Review* 591 (2009): 591–656. *LexisNexis.* Web. 13 Aug. 2009.

"Beyond Race Cliché." Rev. of *Curling,* by Robert E. Boles. *Christian Science Monitor* 18 Apr. 1968: 11. Print.

Bird, Gloria. "The Exaggeration of Despair in Sherman Alexie's *Reservation Blues*." *Wicazo Sa Review* 11.2 (1995): 47–52. Print.

Blanchard, Evelyn. "The Question of Best Interest." Unger 57–60.

Boles, Robert. "Beat Is a Rhythm, Not an Act." *Empty Phantoms: Interviews and Encounters with Jack Kerouac.* Ed. Paul Maher, Jr. New York: Thunder's Mouth Press, 2005. 260–64. Print.

Boles, Robert. *Curling.* New York: Houghton Mifflin, 1968. Print.

Boles, Robert. "The Engagement Party." *The Best Short Stories by Negro Writers: An Anthology from 1899 to the Present.* Boston: Little, Brown, 1967. 479–89. Print.

Boles, Robert. *The People One Knows.* New York: Houghton Mifflin, 1964. Print.

Boles, Robert. "What's Your Problem?" 1964. *Calling the Wind: Twentieth-Century African American Short Stories.* Ed. Clarence Major. New York: Harper Perennial, 1993. 226–31. Print.

Byler, William. "Indian Child Welfare Program." U.S. Senate Subcommittee on Indian Affairs. Liftingtheveil.org/byler.htm. n. pag. Web. 3 Jan. 2010.

Callahan, Cynthia A. *Birth Writes: Adoptive Identities in American Literature.* Diss. University of Delaware, 2004. Ann Arbor: UMI, 2004.

Callahan, Cynthia A. "'The Confounding Problem of Race': Passing and Adoption in Charles Chesnutt's *The Quarry.*" *Modern Fiction Studies* 48.2 (2002): 312–40. Print.

Campbell, Duncan. "Sherman Alexie: Voice of the New Tribes." *Guardian* 4 Jan. 2003: n. pag. guardian.co.uk. Web. 4 Mar. 2009.

Carp, E. Wayne, ed. *Adoption in America: Historical Perspectives.* Ann Arbor: U of Michigan P, 2002. Print.

Carp, E. Wayne. *Family Matters: Secrecy and Disclosure in the History of Adoption.* Cambridge: Harvard UP, 1998. Print.

Carp, E. Wayne, and Anna Leon-Guerrero. "When in Doubt, Count: World War II as a Watershed in the History of Adoption." Carp, *Adoption* 181–217.

Cassill, R. V. "A Man 'Without.'" Rev. of *Curling,* by Robert E. Boles. *Book World* 1968: 26. Print.

Chan, Sucheng. *Asian Americans: An Interpretive History.* Ed. Thomas J. Archdeacon. Twayne's Immigrant Heritage of America Series. Boston: Twayne, 1991. Print.

Chen, Su-ching. "Disjuncture at Home: Mapping the Domestic Cartographies of Transnationalism in Gish Jen's *The Love Wife.*" *Tamkang Review* 37.2 (2006): 1–32. Print.

Cheng, Vincent J. *Inauthentic: The Anxiety over Culture and Identity.* New Brunswick: Rutgers UP, 2004. Print.

Chesnutt, Charles W. "Her Virginia Mammy." *Charles W. Chesnutt: Selected Writings.* 1899. Ed. SallyAnn H. Ferguson. New York: Houghton Mifflin, 2001. 209–22. Print.

Chesnutt, Charles W. *The House Behind the Cedars.* 1900. Ed. Donald B. Gibson. New York: Penguin, 1993. Print.

Chesnutt, Charles W. *The Marrow of Tradition.* 1901. Ed. Eric J. Sundquist. New York: Penguin, 1993. Print.

Chesnutt, Charles W. *Paul Marchand, FMC.* ca. 1921. Ed. Dean McWilliams. Princeton: Princeton UP, 1999. Print.

Chesnutt, Charles W. *The Quarry.* ca. 1928. Ed. Dean McWilliams. Princeton: Princeton UP, 1999. Print.

Chief Eagle, Dallas. *Winter Count*. 1967. Ed. Chadwick Allen. Lincoln: Bison Books–U of Nebraska P, 2003. Print.

Chopin, Kate. "Désirée's Baby." 1893. *The Complete Works of Kate Chopin*. Ed. Per Seyersted. Baton Rouge: Louisiana State UP, 1969. 240–45. Print.

Coontz, Stephanie. *The Social Origins of Private Life: A History of American Families 1600–1900*. New York: Verso, 1988. Print.

Deans, Jill. *"Divide the Living Child in Two": Adoption and the Rhetoric of Legitimacy in Twentieth-Century American Literature*. Diss. U of Massachusetts, Amherst, 1998. Ann Arbor: UMI, 1998.

Deloria, Ella Cara. *Waterlily*. Lincoln: U of Nebraska P, 1988.

Dempsey, David. "Between Two Worlds." Rev. of *Curling*, by Robert E. Boles. *New York Times Book Review* 3 Mar. 1968: 40. Print.

"Digging to America." Chapters.indigo.ca. N.p. n.d. Web. 31 Dec. 2009.

Dorow, Sara K. *Transnational Adoption: A Cultural Economy of Race, Gender, and Kinship*. New York: New York UP, 2006. Print.

Dorris, Michael. *The Broken Cord*. New York: Harper and Row, 1989.

Doyle, Laura. "The Body Against Itself in Faulkner's Phenomenology of Race." *American Literature* 73.2 (2001): 339–64. *MLA International Bibliography*. Web. 15 Dec. 2008.

Du Bois, W. E. B. *The Souls of Black Folk*. 1903. New York: Penguin, 1989. Print.

Du Bois, W. E. B. "The Talented Tenth." *The Negro Problem: A Series of Articles by Representative American Negroes of Today*. New York: J. Pott and Company, 1903. 33–75. Print.

Durst, Ilene. "Valuing Women Storytellers: What They Talk About When They Talk About Law." *Yale Journal of Law and Feminism* 11 (1999): n. pag. *LexisNexis*. Web. 11 July 2000.

Duvall, John N. "Descent in the 'House of Chloe': Race, Rape, and Identity in Toni Morrison's *Tar Baby*." *Contemporary Literature* 38.2 (1997): 325–49. *MLA International Bibliography*. Web. 14 Aug. 2007.

Dyer, Richard. *White*. New York: Routledge, 1997. Print.

Egan, Timothy. "An Indian Without Reservations." *New York Times* 18 Jan. 1998: n. pag. nytimes.com. Web. 30 May 2001.

Eng, David L. "Transnational Adoption and Queer Diasporas." *Social Text* 21.3 (2003): 1–37. *MLA International Bibliography*. Web. 12 Oct. 2008.

English, Daylanne K. *Unnatural Selections: Eugenics in American Modernism and the Harlem Renaissance*. Chapel Hill: U of North Carolina P, 2004. Print.

Erdrich, Louise. *Love Medicine*. New York: Perennial-HarperCollins, 1993.

Evan B. Donaldson Adoption Institute. adoptioninstitute.org. Web. 2 Apr. 2009.

Fadiman, Regina K. *Faulkner's* Light in August: *A Description and Interpretation of the Revisions*. Charlottesville: UP of Virginia, 1975. Print.

Fagan, Kristina. "Adoption as National Fantasy in Barbara Kingsolver's *Pigs in Heaven* and Margaret Laurence's *The Diviners*." Novy, *Imagining Adoption* 251–66.

Fanshel, David. *Far from the Reservation: The Transracial Adoption of American Indian Children*. Metuchen: Scarecrow Press, 1972. Print.

Far, Sui Sin. "Americanizing not Always Christianizing." Ling and White-Parks 257–58.

Far, Sui Sin. "A Chinese Boy-Girl." Ling and White-Parks 155–59.

Far, Sui Sin. "Leaves from the Mental Portfolio of an Eurasian." Ling and White-Parks 218–30.

Far, Sui Sin. *Mrs. Spring Fragrance, and Other Writings.* Ed. Amy Ling and Annette White-Parks. Urbana: U of Illinois P, 1995. Print.

Far, Sui Sin. "Pat and Pan." 1912. Ling and White-Parks 160–68.

Far, Sui Sin. "The Sugar Cane Baby." Ling and White-Parks 258–62.

Farrell, Betty G. *Family: The Making of an Idea, an Institution, and a Controversy in American Culture.* Boulder: Westview Press, 1999. Print.

Faulkner, William. *Light in August.* 1932. Ed. Noel Polk. New York: Vintage International, 1985. Print.

Faulkner, William. "Session Fourteen." Gwynn and Blotner 107–23.

Faulkner, William. "Session Nine." Gwynn and Blotner 71–81.

Fauset, Jessie Redmon. *Plum Bun: A Novel Without a Moral.* 1928. Boston: Beacon Press, 1990.

Gailey, Christine Ward. "Ideologies of Motherhood and Kinship in U.S. Adoption." *Ideologies and Technologies of Motherhood: Race, Class, Sexuality, Nationalism.* Ed. Helena Ragone and France Winddance Twine. New York: Routledge, 2000. 11–55. Print.

Gates, Henry Louis. Introduction. "Writing 'Race' and the Difference It Makes." *Race, Writing, and Difference.* Ed. Henry Louis Gates. Chicago: U of Chicago P, 1985. 1–20. Print.

Gilbert, Matthew. "The Moral Passions of Barbara Kingsolver." *Boston Globe* 23 June 1993: n. pag. *LexisNexis.* Web. 14 Sept. 2000.

Giles, James R. *The Spaces of Violence.* Tuscaloosa: U of Alabama P, 2006. Print.

Ginsberg, Elaine K. "Introduction: The Politics of Passing." *Passing and the Fictions of Identity.* Ed. Elaine K. Ginsberg. Durham: Duke UP, 1996. Print.

Gordon, Linda. *The Great Arizona Orphan Abduction.* Cambridge: Harvard UP, 1999. Print.

Gossett, Thomas. *Race: The History of an Idea in America.* 2nd ed. New York: Oxford UP, 1997. Print.

Goyal, Yogita. "The Gender of Diaspora in Toni Morrison's *Tar Baby.*" *Modern Fiction Studies* 52.2 (2006): 393–414. *MLA International Bibliography.* Web. 16 Aug. 2007.

Gray, Jennifer Morgan. "Author Interview: A Conversation with Anne Tyler." *Digging to America Written by Anne Tyler.* Random House. n.d. Web. 3 Mar. 2009.

Gwynn, Frederick L., and Joseph L. Blotner. *Faulkner in the University: Class Conferences at the University of Virginia 1957–1958.* Charlottesville: UP of Virginia, 1959. Print.

Herman, Ellen. *Kinship by Design: A History of Adoption in the Modern United States.* Chicago: U of Chicago P, 2008. Print.

"History Behind Enactment of the Indian Child Welfare Act." *Indian Child Welfare Act Law Center.* Icwlc.org. n. pag. Web. 3 Jan. 2010.

Hogan, Linda. *Solar Storms.* New York: Scribner–Simon & Schuster, 1995.

Hogue, W. Lawrence. "An Existential Reading of Charles Wright's *The Messenger;* Critical Essay." *MELUS* 26.4 (2001): n. pag. *LexisNexis.* Web. 18 Aug. 2008.

Hollinger, Joan Heifetz. "Second Parent Adoptions Protect Children with Two Mothers or Two Fathers." *Families by Law: An Adoption Reader.* Ed. Naomi R. Cahn and Joan Heifetz Hollinger. New York: New York UP, 2004. 235–47. Print.

Holt, Marilyn Irvin. *Indian Orphanages.* Lawrence: UP of Kansas, 2001. Print.

Homans, Margaret. "Adoption and Essentialism." *Tulsa Studies in Women's Literature* 21 (2002): 257–74. Print.

Homans, Margaret. "Adoption Narratives, Trauma, and Origins." *Narrative* 14.1 (2006): 4–26. *MLA International Bibliography.* Web. 15 Jan. 2007.

Homans, Margaret. "Origins, Searches, and Identity: Narratives of Adoption from China." *Contemporary Women's Writing* 1.1–2 (2007): 59–79. *MLA International Bibliography.* Web. 2 July 2009.

Hopkins, Pauline. *Of One Blood, or, The Hidden Self.* 1903. Ed. Hazel V. Carby. *The Magazine Novels of Pauline Hopkins.* New York: Oxford UP, 1988. 440–621. Print.

Howell, Signe. "Self-Conscious Kinship: Some Contested Values in Norwegian Transnational Adoption." *Relative Values: Reconfiguring Kinship Studies.* Ed. Sarah Franklin and Susan McKinnon. Durham: Duke UP, 2001. 203–23. Print.

Hughes, Langston. "Passing." 1934. Miller 46–48.

Hughes, Langston. *The Short Stories.* Ed. R. Baxter Miller. Columbia: U of Missouri P, 2002. Print.

Hughes, Langston. "Who's Passing for Who?" 1952. Miller 163–66.

Ibold, Hans. "The Toughest Indian in the World: An Interview with Poet, Novelist, Filmmaker Sherman Alexie." *Idaho Mountain Express and Guide* 21–27 June 2000: n. pag. mtexpress.com. Web. 6 Oct. 2008.

"Indian Child Welfare Act of 1978." Askeland 134–35.

"International Adoption Facts." Evan B. Donaldson Institute.

Jaggi, Maya. "All Rage and Heart." *Guardian* 3 May 2008: n. pag. guardian.co.uk. Web. 6 Oct. 2008.

Jaimes, M. Annette. "Federal Indian Identification Policy: A Usurpation of Indigenous Sovereignty in North America." *The State of Native America.* Ed. M. Annette Jaimes. Boston: South End Press, 1992. 123–38. Print.

Jen, Gish. *The Love Wife.* New York: Vintage Contemporaries, 2004. Print.

Jerng, Mark C. *Claiming Others: Transracial Adoption and the Reproduction of Personhood.* Minneapolis: U of Minnesota P, 2010. Print.

Johnson, James Weldon. *The Autobiography of An Ex-Colored Man.* 1912. New York: Penguin, 1990. Print.

Kakutani, Michiko. "Who's the Outsider? Well, That Depends on Where You Stand." *New York Times* 7 Sept. 2004: n. pag. nytimes.com. Web. 13 Dec. 2007.

Karenga, Maulana (Ron). "Black Art: Mute Matter Given Force and Function." *Black Poets and Prophets.* Ed. Woodie King and Earl Anthony. New York: Mentor Books, 1972. 174–79. Print.

Karpen, Lynn. "The Role of Poverty." *New York Times* 27 June 1993: n. pag. nytimes.com. Web. 31 Dec. 2009.

Kawash, Samira. *Dislocating the Color Line: Identity, Hybridity, and Singularity in African-American Narrative.* Stanford: Stanford UP, 1997. Print.

Keller, Frances Richardson. *An American Crusade: The Life of Charles Waddell Chesnutt.* Provo: Brigham Young UP, 1978. Print.

Kelley, Robin D. G. "Into the Fire: 1970 to Present." *To Make Our World Anew: The History of African Americans from 1800.* Vol. 2. Ed. Robin D. G. Kelley and Earl Lewis. New York: Oxford UP, 2000. 265–342. Print.

Kim, Jae Ran. *Harlow's Monkey.* http://harlowmonkey.typepad.com/. n.d. Web. 11 Mar. 2009.

Kingsolver, Barbara. *The Bean Trees*. New York: Harper Perennial, 1988. Print.

Kingsolver, Barbara. *Pigs in Heaven*. New York: HarperCollins, 1993. Print.

Kubitschek, Missy Dehn. *Toni Morrison: A Critical Companion*. Westport: Greenwood, 1998. Print.

Ladner, Joyce A. *Mixed Families: Adopting Across Racial Boundaries*. New York: Anchor/Doubleday, 1978. Print.

Larsen, Nella. *Passing*. 1929. New York: Penguin, 1997. Print.

Li, Stephanie. "Domestic Resistance: Gardening, Mothering, and Storytelling in Leslie Marmon Silko's *Gardens in the Dunes*." *Studies in American Indian Literature* 21.1 (2009): 18–37. *MLA International Bibliography*. Web. 13 Aug. 2009.

Ling, Amy, and Annette White-Parks. Introduction. Ling and White Parks, *Mrs. Spring Fragrance* 11–16.

Lundie, Catherine. "Doubly Dispossessed: Kate Chopin's Women of Color." *Louisiana Literature* 11.1 (1994): 126–44. *MLA International Bibliography*. Web. 14 Sept. 2007.

Mannes, Marc. "Factors and Events Leading to the Passage of the Indian Child Welfare Act." *Child Welfare* 74.1 (1995): 264–82. Print.

Matheson, Lou. "The Politics of the Indian Child Welfare Act." *Social Work* 41.2 (1996): 232–35. Print.

Melosh, Barbara. "Adoption Stories: Autobiographical Narrative and the Politics of Identity." Carp, *Adoption* 218–45.

Melosh, Barbara. *Strangers and Kin: The American Way of Adoption*. Cambridge: Harvard UP, 2002. Print.

Metteer, Christine. "*Pigs in Heaven*: A Parable of Native American Adoption Under the Indian Child Welfare Act." *Families by Law: An Adoption Reader*. Ed. Naomi R. Cahn and Joan Heifetz Hollinger. New York: New York UP, 2004. 228–31. Print.

Minow, Martha. *Not Only for Myself: Identity, Politics, and the Law*. New York: New Press, 1997. Print.

Miranda, Deborah A. "A Gynostemic Revolution: Some Thoughts About Orchids, *Gardens in the Dunes*, and Indigenous Feminism at Work." *Reading Leslie Marmon Silko: Critical Perspectives Through Gardens in the Dunes*. Ed. Laura Coltelli. Pisa: Edizioni Plus–Pisa University Press, 2007. 133–48. Print.

Mobley, Marilyn E. "Narrative Dilemma: Jadine as Cultural Orphan in Toni Morrison's *Tar Baby*." *Southern Review* 23 (1987): 761–70. *MLA International Bibliography*. Web. 15 Nov. 2007.

Modell, Judith S. *Kinship with Strangers: Adoption and Interpretations of Kinship in American Culture*. Berkeley: U of California P, 1994. Print.

Momaday, N. Scott. *The Ancient Child*. New York: Doubleday, 1989.

Morrison, Toni. *The Bluest Eye*. New York: Penguin, 1970. Print.

Morrison, Toni. "An Interview with Toni Morrison: Conducted by Nellie McKay." *Contemporary Literature* 24.4 (1983): 413–30. *MLA International Bibliography*. Web. 14 Aug. 2007.

Morrison, Toni. "Rootedness: the Ancestor as Foundation." *Black Women Writers 1950–1980: A Critical Evaluation*. Ed. Mari Evans. Garden City: Anchor Press/Doubleday, 1984. 339–45. Print.

Morrison, Toni. *Tar Baby*. New York: Alfred A. Knopf, 1981. Print.

"NABSW Statement." Askeland 131–4.

Nelson, Antonya. "Heaven in Oklahoma." *Los Angeles Times* 4 July 1993: n. pag. *Lexis-Nexis.* Web. 14 Sept. 2000.

Nelson, Claudia. *Little Strangers: Portrayals of Adoption and Foster Care in America, 1850–1929.* Bloomington: Indiana UP, 2003.

Nelson, Kim Park. "Shopping for Children in the International Marketplace." Trenka et al. 89–104.

Novy, Marianne. *Imagining Adoption: Essays on Literature and Culture.* Ann Arbor: U of Michigan P, 2001.

Novy, Marianne. *Reading Adoption: Family and Difference in Fiction and Drama.* Ann Arbor: U of Michigan P, 2005.

"Oglala Sioux." Unger 88.

Oparah, Julia Chinyere, Sun Yung Shin, and Jane Jeong Trenka. Introduction. Trenka et al. 1–18.

Owens, Louis. *MixedBlood Messages: Literature, Film, Family, Place.* Norman: U of Oklahoma P, 1998. Print.

Partridge, Jeffrey F. L. "Review Essay: Adoption, Interracial Marriage, and Mixed-Race Babies: The New America in Recent Asian American Fiction." *MELUS* 30.2 (2005): 242–51. *MLA International Bibliography.* Web. 17 Dec. 2007.

Patton, Sandra. *Birthmarks: Transracial Adoption in Contemporary America.* New York: New York UP, 2000. Print.

Peel, Ellen. "Semiotic Subversion in 'Désirée's Baby.'" *American Literature* 62.2 (1990): 223–37. *MLA International Bibliography.* Web. 20 Aug. 2008.

Perry, Donna. "Barbara Kingsolver." *Backtalk: Women Writers Speak Out.* New Brunswick: Rutgers UP, 1993. 143–69. Print.

"Private Domestic Adoptions." Research: Adoption Facts. n.d. Evan B. Donaldson Adoption Institute. 13 Jan. 2009.

Quiroz, Pamela Anne. *Adoption in a Color-Blind Society.* Lanham: Rowman & Littlefield, 2007. Print.

"Relative Choices." *New York Times* 2 Nov.–4 Dec. 2007. nytimes.com. Web. 7 Mar. 2009.

Riis, Jacob. *How the Other Half Lives.* 1890. New York: Dover, 1971. Print.

Roberts, Dorothy. "Adoption Myths and Racial Realities in the United States." Trenka et al. 49–58.

Robinson, Owen. "'Liable to Be Anything': The Creation of Joe Christmas in Faulkner's *Light in August.*" *Journal of American Studies* 37.1 (2003): 119–33. *MLA International Bibliography.* Web. 20 Nov. 2008.

Rollings, Willard Hughes. "Indians and Christianity." *A Companion to American Indian History.* Ed. Philip J. Deloria and Neal Salisbury. Malden: Blackwell Press, 2002. 121–38. Print.

Rowlandson, Mary White. *The Sovereignty and Goodness of God by Mary Rowlandson, with Related Documents.* 1682. Ed. Neal Salisbury. Boston: Bedford Books, 1997. Print.

Ryan, Judylyn S. "Contested Visions/Double-Vision in *Tar Baby.*" *Modern Fiction Studies* 39.3–4 (1993): 597–621. *MLA International Bibliography.* Web. 16 Aug. 2007.

Ryan, Maureen. "Barbara Kingsolver's Lowfat Fiction." *Journal of American Culture* 18.4 (1995): 77–82. *MLA International Bibliography.* Web. 30 Dec. 2009.

Saks, Eva. "Representing Miscegenation Law." *Interracialism: Black-White Intermarriage in American History, Literature, and Law.* Ed. Werner Sollors. New York: Oxford UP, 2000. 61–80. Print.

Sarris, Greg. *Mabel McKay: Weaving the Dream.* Berkeley: U of California P, 1994.

Satz, Martha, and Lori Askeland. "Civil Rights, Adoption Rights." Askeland, *Children* 45–61.

Savage, Dan. *The Commitment: Love, Sex, Marriage, and My Family.* New York: Dutton-Penguin, 2005. Print.

Savage, Dan. *The Kid: What Happened after My Boyfriend and I Decided to Go Get Pregnant.* New York: Plume, 2000. Print.

Schneider, David. *American Kinship: A Cultural Account.* Englewood Cliffs: Prentice-Hall, 1968. Print.

Seaver, James E. *A Narrative of the Life of Mrs. Mary Jemison.* 1823. Norman: U of Oklahoma P, 1992. *NetLibrary.* Web. 30 Dec. 2009.

Shell, Marc. *Children of the Earth: Literature, Politics, and Nationhood.* New York: Oxford UP, 1993. Print.

Shih, David. "The Seduction of Origins: Sui Sin Far and the Race for Tradition." *Form and Transformation in Asian American Literature.* Ed. Zhou Xiaojing and Samina Najmi. Seattle: U of W Press, 2005. Print.

Shin, Sun Yung. Blog. sunyungshin.com. N.p. n.d. Web. 31 Dec. 2009.

Silko, Leslie Marmon. "Books: Notes on Mixtec and Maya Screenfolds, Picture Books of Preconquest Mexico." *Yellow Woman and a Beauty of the Spirit: Essays on Native American Life Today.* New York: Simon & Schuster, 1996. 155–65. Print.

Silko, Leslie Marmon. *Ceremony.* New York: Penguin, 1977. Print.

Silko, Leslie Marmon. *Gardens in the Dunes.* New York: Scribner–Simon & Schuster, 1999. Print.

Simon, Rita J., and Howard Altstein. *Adoption, Race, and Identity: From Infancy to Young Adulthood.* 2nd ed. New Brunswick: Transaction Publishers, 2002. Print.

Simon, Rita J., and Rhonda M. Roorda. *In Their Own Voices: Transracial Adoptees Tell Their Stories.* New York: Columbia UP, 2000. Print.

Singley, Carol. "Teaching American Literature: The Centrality of Adoption." *Modern Languages Studies* 34.1–2. (2004): 76–83. *MLA International Bibliography.* Web. 13 Aug. 2009.

Solinger, Rickie. *Beggars and Choosers: How the Politics of Choice Shapes Adoption, Abortion, and Welfare in the United States.* New York: Hill and Wang, 2001. Print.

Solinger, Rickie. *Wake Up, Little Susie: Single Pregnancy and Race Before Roe v. Wade.* New York: Routledge, 1992. Print.

Sollors, Werner. *Beyond Ethnicity: Consent and Descent in American Culture.* New York: Oxford UP, 1986. Print.

Sollors, Werner. *Neither Black nor White yet Both: Thematic Explorations of Interracial Literature.* New York: Oxford UP, 1997. Print.

Solomon, Andy. "For the Sake of a Child." *St. Petersburg Times* 20 June 1993: n. pag. *LexisNexis.* Web. 14 Sept. 2000.

Stark, Heidi Kiiwetinepinesiik, and Kekek Jason Todd Stark. "Flying the Coop: ICWA and the Welfare of Indian Children." Trenka et al. 125–38.

Stephens, Robert O. *The Family Saga in the South: Generations and Destinies*. Baton Rouge: Louisiana State UP, 1995. Print.

Strong, Pauline Turner. *Captive Selves, Captivating Others*. Boulder: Westview Press, 1999.

Strong, Pauline Turner. "To Forget Their Tongue, Their Name, and Their Whole Relation: Captivity, Extra-Tribal Adoption, and the Indian Child Welfare Act." *Relative Values: Reconfiguring Kinship Studies*. Ed. Sarah Franklin and Susan McKinnon. Durham: Duke UP, 2001. 468–93. Print.

Sundquist, Eric J. *To Wake the Nations: Race in the Making of American Literature*. Cambridge: Harvard UP, 1993. Print.

Takaki, Ronald. *A Different Mirror: A History of Multicultural America*. Boston: Little, Brown, 1993. Print.

Tompkins, Jane. *Sensational Designs: The Cultural Work of American Fiction 1790–1860*. New York: Oxford UP, 1985. Print.

"Total Adoptions to the United States." *Intercountry Adoption*. United States Department of State. n.d. Web. 2 Jan. 2010.

Toth, Emily. "Kate Chopin and Literary Convention: 'Désirée's Baby.'" *Southern Studies* 20.2 (1981): 201–8. *MLA International Bibliography*. Web. 17 Dec. 2007.

"Transracial Adoption." Adamec and Pierce 272–75.

Trenka, Jane Jeong. *Jane's Blog*. jjtrenka.wordpress.com. n.d. Web. 11 Mar. 2009.

Trenka, Jane Jeong. *The Language of Blood*. Saint Paul: Graywolf Press, 2005. Print.

Trenka, Jane Jeong, Julia Chinyere Oparah, and Sun Yung Shin, eds. *Outsiders Within: Writing on Transracial Adoption*. Cambridge: South End Press, 2006. Print.

Tucker, William H. *The Science and Politics of Racial Research*. Urbana: U of Illinois P, 1994. Print.

Twain, Mark. *The Tragedy of Pudd'nhead Wilson*. 1894. New York: Signet Classic, 1964. Print.

Tyler, Anne. *Digging to America*. New York: Knopf, 2006. Print.

Unger, Steven, ed. *The Destruction of American Indian Families*. New York: Association on American Indian Affairs, 1977. Print.

Volkman, Toby Alice. *Cultures of Transnational Adoption*. Durham: Duke UP, 2005.

Volkman, Toby Alice. "Embodying Chinese Culture: Transnational Adoption in North America." *Cultures of Transnational Adoption*. Ed. Toby Alice Volkman. Durham: Duke UP, 2005. 81–113. Print.

Wald, Gayle. *Crossing the Line: Racial Passing in Twentieth-Century U.S. Literature and Culture*. Durham: Duke UP, 2000. Print.

Watkins, Mel. "Caged Man." Rev. of *Curling*, by Robert E. Boles. *New Leader* 8 Apr. 1968: 25–26. Print.

Watkins, Mel. "Hard Times for Black Writers." *New York Times* 22 Feb. 1981: n. pag. *LexisNexis*. Web. 18 Aug. 2008.

Wegar, Katarina. *Adoption, Identity, and Kinship: The Debate over Sealed Birth Records*. New Haven: Yale UP, 1997. Print.

Westermeyer, Joseph. "The Ravage of Indian Families in Crisis." Unger 47–56.

Wexler, Laura. "The Fair Ensemble: Kate Chopin in St. Louis in 1904." *Haunted by Empire: Geographies of Intimacy in North American History*. Ed. Ann Laura Stoller. Durham: Duke UP, 2006. 271–96. Print.

White-Parks, Annette. *Sui Sin Far/Edith Maude Eaton*. Urbana: U of Illinois P, 1995. Print.

Williams, John. *The Redeemed Captive*. 1707. Ed. Edward W. Clark. Amherst: U of Massachusetts P, 1976. Print.

Wonham, Henry B. Introduction. *Criticism and the Color Line: Desegregating American Literary Studies*. Ed. Henry B. Wonham. New Brunswick: Rutgers UP, 1996. 1–15. Print.

Yngvesson, Barbara, and Maureen A. Mahoney. " 'As One Should, Ought, and Wants to Be': Belonging and Authenticity in Identity Narratives." *Theory, Culture & Society* 17.6 (2000): 77–110. *OhioLink*. Web. 5 Aug. 2009.

Index